CW00823577

# LOTUS ELAN AND +2 SOURCE BOOK

Matthew Vale

**SpeedPro Series**
4-Cylinder Engine Short Block High-Performance Manual – New Updated & Revised Edition (Hammill)
Aerodynamics of Your Road Car, Modifying the (Edgar and Barnard)
Alfa Romeo DOHC High-performance Manual (Kartalamakis)
Alfa Romeo V6 Engine High-performance Manual (Kartalamakis)
BMC 998cc A-series Engine, How to Power Tune (Hammill)
1275cc A-series High-performance Manual (Hammill)
Camshafts – How to Choose & Time Them For Maximum Power (Hammill)
Competition Car Datalogging Manual, The (Templeman)
Custom Air Suspension – How to install air suspension in your road car – on a budget! (Edgar)
Cylinder Heads, How to Build, Modify & Power Tune – Updated & Revised Edition (Burgess & Gollan)
Distributor-type Ignition Systems, How to Build & Power Tune – New 3rd Edition (Hammill)
Fast Road Car, How to Plan and Build – Revised & Updated Colour New Edition (Stapleton)
Ford SOHC 'Pinto' & Sierra Cosworth DOHC Engines, How to Power Tune – Updated & Enlarged Edition (Hammill)
Ford V8, How to Power Tune Small Block Engines (Hammill)
Harley-Davidson Evolution Engines, How to Build & Power Tune (Hammill)
Holley Carburetors, How to Build & Power Tune – Revised & Updated Edition (Hammill)
Honda Civic Type R High-Performance Manual, The (Cowland & Clifford)
Jaguar XK Engines, How to Power Tune – Revised & Updated Colour Edition (Hammill)
Land Rover Discovery, Defender & Range Rover – How to Modify Coil Sprung Models for High Performance & Off-Road Action (Hosier)
MG Midget & Austin-Healey Sprite, How to Power Tune – Enlarged & updated 4th Edition (Stapleton)
MGB 4-cylinder Engine, How to Power Tune (Burgess)
MGB V8 Power, How to Give Your – Third Colour Edition (Williams)
MGB, MGC & MGB V8, How to Improve – New 2nd Edition (Williams)
Mini Engines, How to Power Tune On a Small Budget – Colour Edition (Hammill)
Motorcycle-engined Racing Cars, How to Build (Pashley)
Motorsport, Getting Started in (Collins)
Nissan GT-R High-performance Manual, The (Gorodji)
Nitrous Oxide High-performance Manual, The (Langfield)
Optimising Car Performance Modifications (Edgar)
Race & Trackday Driving Techniques (Hornsey)
Retro or classic car for high performance, How to modify your (Stapleton)
Rover V8 Engines, How to Power Tune (Hammill)
Secrets of Speed – Today's techniques for 4-stroke engine blueprinting & tuning (Swager)
Sportscar & Kitcar Suspension & Brakes, How to Build & Modify – Revised 3rd Edition (Hammill)
SU Carburettor High-performance Manual (Hammill)
Successful Low-Cost Rally Car, How to Build a (Young)
Suzuki 4x4, How to Modify For Serious Off-road Action (Richardson)
Tiger Avon Sportscar, How to Build Your Own – Updated & Revised 2nd Edition (Dudley)
Triumph TR2, 3 & TR4, How to Improve (Williams)
Triumph TR5, 250 & TR6, How to Improve (Williams)
Triumph TR7 & TR8, How to Improve (Williams)
V8 Engine, How to Build a Short Block For High Performance (Hammill)
Volkswagen Beetle Suspension, Brakes & Chassis, How to Modify For High Performance (Hale)
Volkswagen Bus Suspension, Brakes & Chassis for High Performance, How to Modify (Hale)
Weber DCOE, & Dellorto DHLA Carburetors, How to Build & Power Tune – 3rd Edition (Hammill)

**Workshop Pro Series**
Car Electrical and Electronic Systems (Edgar)
Modifying the Electronics of Modern Classic Cars (Edgar)
Setting up a Home Car Workshop (Edgar)

**RAC Handbooks**
Caring for your car – How to maintain & service your car (Fry)
Caring for your car's bodywork and interior (Nixon)
Caring for your bicycle – How to maintain & repair your bicycle (Henshaw)
Caring for your scooter – How to maintain & service your 49cc to 125cc twist & go scooter (Fry)
Efficient Driver's Handbook, The (Moss)
Electric Cars – The Future is Now! (Linde)
First aid for your car – Your expert guide to common problems & how to fix them (Collins)
How your car works (Linde)
How your motorcycle works – Your guide to the components & systems of modern motorcycles (Henshaw)
Motorcycles – A first-time-buyer's guide (Henshaw)
Motorhomes – A first-time-buyer's guide (Fry)
Pass the MoT test! – How to check & prepare your car for the annual MoT test (Paxton)
Selling your car – How to make your car look great and how to sell it fast (Knight)
Simple fixes for your car – How to do small jobs for yourself and save money (Collins)

**Enthusiast's Restoration Manual Series**
Beginner's Guide to Classic Motorcycle Restoration, The (Burns)
Citroën 2CV Restore (Porter)
Classic British Car Electrical Systems (Astley)
Classic Car Bodywork, How to Restore (Thaddeus)
Classic Car Electrics (Thaddeus)
Classic Car Suspension, Steering & Wheels, How to Restore & Improve (Parish – translator)
Classic Large Frame Vespa Scooters, How to Restore (Paxton)
Classic Small Frame Vespa Scooters, How to Restore (Paxton)
Classic Cars, How to Paint (Thaddeus)
Classic Off-road Motorcycles, How to Restore (Burns)
Ducati Bevel Twins 1971 to 1986 (Falloon)
Honda CX500 & CX650, How to restore – YOUR step-by-step colour illustrated guide to complete restoration (Burns)
Honda Fours, How to restore – YOUR step-by-step colour illustrated guide to complete restoration (Burns)
Jaguar E-type (Crespin)
Kawasaki Z1, Z/KZ900 & Z/KZ1000, How to restore (Rooke)
Norton Commando, How to Restore (Rooke)
Reliant Regal, How to Restore (Payne)
Triumph TR2, 3, 3A, 4 & 4A, How to Restore (Williams)
Triumph TR5/250 & 6, How to Restore (Williams)
Triumph TR7/8, How to Restore (Williams)
Triumph Trident T150/T160 & BSA Rocket III, How to Restore (Rooke)
Ultimate Mini Restoration Manual, The (Ayre & Webber)
Volkswagen Beetle, How to Restore (Tyler)
VW Bay Window Bus (Paxton)
Yamaha FS1-E, How to Restore (Watts)

**Expert Guides**
Land Rover Series I-III – Your expert guide to common problems & how to fix them (Thurman)
MG Midget & A-H Sprite – Your expert guide to common problems & how to fix them (Horler)
Triumph TR4 & TR4A – Your expert guide to common problems & how to fix them (Hogan)
Triumph TR6 – Your expert guide to common problems & how to fix them (Hogan)

**Essential Buyer's Guide Series**
Alfa Romeo Alfasud (Metcalfe)
Alfa Romeo Alfetta: all saloon/sedan models 1972 to 1984 & coupé models 1974 to 1987 (Metcalfe)
Alfa Romeo Giulia GT Coupé (Booker)
Alfa Romeo Giulia Spider (Booker)
Audi TT (Davies)
Audi TT Mk2 2006 to 2014 (Durnan)
Austin-Healey Big Healeys (Trummel)
BMW Boxer Twins (Henshaw)
BMW E30 3 Series 1981 to 1994 (Hosier)
BMW GS (Henshaw)
BMW X5 (Saunders)
BMW Z3 Roadster (Fishwick)
BMW Z4: E85 Roadster and E86 Coupé including M and Alpina 2003 to 2009 (Smitheram)
BSA 350, 441 & 500 Singles (Henshaw)
BSA 500 & 650 Twins (Henshaw)
BSA Bantam (Henshaw)
Choosing, Using & Maintaining Your Electric Bicycle (Henshaw)
Citroën 2CV (Paxton)
Citroën DS & ID (Heilig)
Cobra Replicas (Ayre)
Corvette C2 Sting Ray 1963-1967 (Falconer)
Datsun 240Z 1969 to 1973 (Newlyn)
DeLorean DMC-12 1981 to 1983 (Williams)
Ducati Bevel Twins (Falloon)
Ducati Desmodue Twins (Falloon)
Ducati Desmoquattro Twins – 851, 888, 916, 996, 998, ST4 1988 to 2004 (Falloon)
Fiat 500 & 600 (Bobbitt)
Ford Capri (Paxton)
Ford Escort Mk1 & Mk2 (Williamson)
Ford Focus RS/ST 1st Generation (Williamson)
Ford Model A – All Models 1927 to 1931 (Buckley)
Ford Model T – All models 1909 to 1927 (Barker)
Ford Mustang – First Generation 1964 to 1973 (Cook)
Ford Mustang – Fifth Generation (2005-2014) (Cook)
Ford RS Cosworth Sierra & Escort (Williamson)
Harley-Davidson Big Twins (Henshaw)
Hillman Imp (Morgan)
Hinckley Triumph triples & fours 750, 900, 955, 1000, 1050, 1200 – 1991-2009 (Henshaw)
Honda CBR FireBlade (Henshaw)
Honda CBR600 Hurricane (Henshaw)
Honda SOHC Fours 1969-1984 (Henshaw)
Jaguar E-Type 3.8 & 4.2 litre (Crespin)
Jaguar E-type V12 5.3 litre (Crespin)
Jaguar Mark 1 & 2 (All models including Daimler 2.5-litre V8) 1955 to 1969 (Thorley)
Jaguar New XK 2005-2014 (Thorley)
Jaguar S-Type – 1999 to 2007 (Thorley)
Jaguar X-Type – 2001 to 2009 (Thorley)
Jaguar XJ-S (Crespin)
Jaguar XJ6, XJ8 & XJR (Thorley)
Jaguar XK 120, 140 & 150 (Thorley)
Jaguar XK8 & XKR (1996-2005) (Thorley)
Jaguar/Daimler XJ 1994-2003 (Crespin)
Jaguar/Daimler XJ40 (Crespin)
Jaguar/Daimler XJ6, XJ12 & Sovereign (Crespin)
Kawasaki Z1 & Z900 (Orritt)
Land Rover Discovery Series 1 (1989-1998) (Taylor)
Land Rover Discovery Series 2 (1998-2004) (Taylor)
Land Rover Series I, II & IIA (Thurman)
Land Rover Series III (Thurman)
Lotus Elan, S1 to Sprint and Plus 2 to Plus 2S 130/5 1962 to 1974 (Vale)
Lotus Europa, S1, S2, Twin-cam & Special 1966 to 1975 (Vale)
Lotus Seven replicas & Caterham 7: 1973-2013 (Hawkins)
Mazda MX-5 Miata (Mk1 1989-97 & Mk2 98-2001) (Crook)
Mazda RX-8 (Parish)
Mercedes-Benz 190: all 190 models (W201 series) 1982 to 1993 (Parish)
Mercedes-Benz 280-560SL & SLC (Bass)
Mercedes-Benz G-Wagen (Greene)
Mercedes-Benz Pagoda 230SL, 250SL & 280SL roadsters & coupés (Bass)
Mercedes-Benz S-Class W126 Series (Zoporowski)
Mercedes-Benz S-Class Second Generation W116 Series (Parish)
Mercedes-Benz SL R129-series 1989 to 2001 (Parish)
Mercedes-Benz SLK (Bass)
Mercedes-Benz W123 (Parish)
Mercedes-Benz W124 – All models 1984-1997 (Zoporowski)
MG Midget & A-H Sprite (Horler)
MG TD, TF & TF1500 (Jones)
MGA 1955-1962 (Crosier)
MGB & MGB GT (Williams)
MGF & MG TF (Hawkins)
Mini (Paxton)
Morgan Plus 4 (Benfield)
Morris Minor & 1000 (Newell)
Moto Guzzi 2-valve big twins (Falloon)
New Mini (Collins)
Norton Commando (Henshaw)
Peugeot 205 GTI (Blackburn)
Piaggio Scooters – all modern two-stroke & four-stroke automatic models 1991 to 2016 (Willis)
Porsche 356 (Johnson)
Porsche 911 (964) (Streather)
Porsche 911 (991) (Streather)
Porsche 911 (993) (Streather)
Porsche 911 (996) (Streather)
Porsche 911 (997) – Model years 2004 to 2009 (Streather)
Porsche 911 (997) – Second generation models 2009 to 2012 (Streather)
Porsche 911 Carrera 3.2 (Streather)
Porsche 911SC (Streather)
Porsche 924 – All models 1976 to 1988 (Hodgkins)
Porsche 928 (Hemmings)
Porsche 930 Turbo & 911 (930) Turbo (Streather)
Porsche 944 (Higgins)
Porsche 981 Boxster & Cayman (Streather)
Porsche 986 Boxster (Streather)
Porsche 987 Boxster and Cayman 1st generation (2005-2009) (Streather)
Porsche 987 Boxster and Cayman 2nd generation (2009-2012) (Streather)
Range Rover – First Generation models 1970 to 1996 (Taylor)
Range Rover – Second Generation 1994-2001 (Taylor)
Range Rover – Third Generation L322 (2002-2012) (Taylor)
Reliant Scimitar GTE (Payne)
Rolls-Royce Silver Shadow & Bentley T-Series (Bobbitt)
Rover 2000, 2200 & 3500 (Marrocco)
Royal Enfield Bullet (Henshaw)
Subaru Impreza (Hobbs)
Sunbeam Alpine (Barker)
Triumph 350 & 500 Twins (Henshaw)
Triumph Bonneville (Henshaw)
Triumph Herald & Vitesse (Ayre)
Triumph Spitfire and GT6 (Ayre)
Triumph Stag (Mort)
Triumph Thunderbird, Trophy & Tiger (Henshaw)
Triumph TR2 & TR3 - All models (including 3A & 3B) 1953 to 1962 (Conners)
Triumph TR4/4A & TR5/250 - All models 1961 to 1968 (Child & Battyll)
Triumph TR6 (Williams)
Triumph TR7 & TR8 (Williams)
Triumph Trident & BSA Rocket III (Rooke)
TVR Chimaera and Griffith (Kitchen)
TVR S-series (Kitchen)
Velocette 350 & 500 Singles 1946 to 1970 (Henshaw)
Vespa Scooters – Classic 2-stroke models 1960-2008 (Paxton)
Volkswagen Bus (Copping)
Volkswagen Transporter T4 (1990-2003) (Copping/Cservenka)
VW Golf GTI (Copping)
VW Beetle (Copping)

# www.veloce.co.uk

First published in December 2020 by Veloce Publishing Limited, Veloce House, Parkway Farm Business Park, Middle Farm Way, Poundbury, Dorchester DT1 3AR, England.
Tel +44 (0)1305 260068 / Fax 01305 250479 / e-mail info@veloce.co.uk / web www.veloce.co.uk or www.velocebooks.com.
ISBN: 978-1-787114-59-3; UPC: 6-36847-01459-9.

Readers with ideas for automotive books, or books on other transport or related hobby subjects, are invited to write to the editorial director of Veloce Publishing at the above address. British Library Cataloguing in Publication Data – A catalogue record for this book is available from the British Library. Typesetting, design and page make-up all by Veloce Publishing Ltd on Apple Mac. Printed in India by Replika Press.

# LOTUS ELAN AND +2 SOURCE BOOK

A comprehensive purchasing, maintenance, and restoration guide

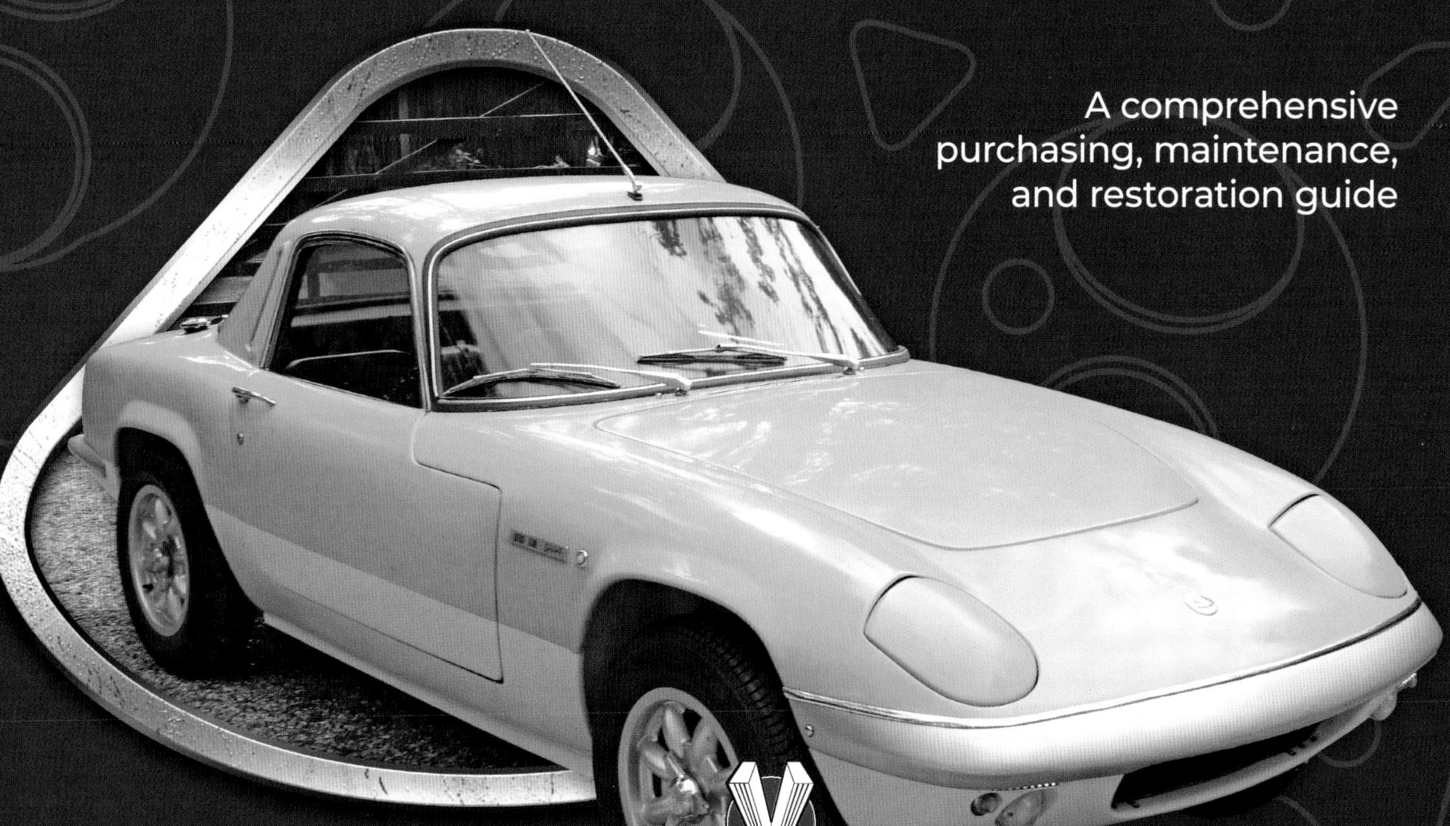

VELOCE PUBLISHING
THE PUBLISHER OF FINE AUTOMOTIVE BOOKS

Matthew Vale

# Contents

# Introduction and Acknowledgements

## AUTHOR'S INTRODUCTION

The Lotus Elan and +2 were the cars that made Lotus a success. The Elan replaced the Elite, and was a relatively affordable small sports car that Lotus could sell at a profit. When it appeared in 1962, it set new standards for performance, roadholding and handling that were never matched by its competitors. The +2 emerged in 1967, and was a widened and lengthened Elan, with room for a pair of small passengers in the back and a very different look to the Elan. Today both of the cars are classics, and this book's aim is to give prospective and actual owners the information they need on the cars' characteristics and foibles to make ownership a pleasurable experience. Taking the author's experiences of owning, restoring and running several +2s, as well as recounting owners' experiences and knowledge, the book aims to provide the reader with the benefit of many years' experience of running the cars. Based on knowledge built up by many owners, the book gives advice on how to look after these undeniably delicate – but incredibly rewarding – cars, and provides advice on originality. The book looks to dispel the many myths around the 'Loads Of Trouble, Usually Serious' reputation of the Elan and +2, and provide a rich source of information that will enable owners to service, modify and restore their cars.

## ACKNOWLEDGEMENTS

Many thanks are due to the Elan and +2 owners who allowed me to interview them and photograph their cars. These included:

Jeff Boughton, John Bradbury, Paddy Byers, Brian Goodison, Dave Groves, Glenn Moule, Melody and Henry Kozlowski.

Thanks also to Mike Ostrov for the early Elan production pictures, and John Underwood and David Beresford for pictures of the John Player Special +2. Finally, I'd like to thank my wife Julia and daughter Elizabeth for their help, encouragement and support while writing this book.

CHAPTER 1

# Introduction to the Elan and +2

## INTRODUCTION

The Elan was Lotus' first really successful road car, eclipsing the Lotus Elite in price and reliability – if not in looks and innovation – and is probably the best small sports car ever. Produced in greater numbers than any previous Lotus, the Elan introduced the combination of a backbone chassis and glass reinforced plastic (GRP) body, which would become the 'trademark' feature of the following generations of Lotus road cars, in the form of the Europa, +2 and the Elite/Éclat/Excel/Esprit series. In addition, the Elan was fitted with Lotus' own engine, the Ford-based 'Twin-cam,' and this – along with the intelligent, race car engineering-based underpinnings – marked it out as something rather better than the many other low-volume sports cars being produced by the likes of TVR, Reliant, Marcos et al.

Production of the Elan started in October 1962. This is Paddy Byers' 1963 Series 1, sporting a racing-style front bumper. ➤

The Elan coupé was launched in 1965 to provide a slightly more civilised car. This Series 4 Sprint is the last of the line, with its Big Valve engine. Note the aftermarket fabric sunroof – these were often fitted by Lotus dealers to the cars when new. ➤

Introduced in 1967 as a longer and wider car, with two extra seats able to accommodate two small passengers behind the front seats, the Elan +2 was aptly named.

The original Elan had an arguably perfect combination of lightness, compliant long travel suspension, a powerful engine, and an excellent appearance, all of which gave the car its unmatched mix of performance, roadholding and style. It was with this combination of virtues that the Elan rewrote the sports car rule book. The car would go on to spawn a closed version, the Elan coupé, and a larger version with room for two small persons in the back, the aptly named Elan +2. With constant development and refinement the Elan sold well through the 1960s and early '70s, while the +2 gave the family man the same mix of performance and handling in a slightly larger package. Even today, both versions offer the discerning customer an exceptional driving experience.

## BRIEF HISTORY OF THE CARS

### INTRODUCTION

Introduced in 1963, the Elan was a small two-seat sports car with a glass fibre body, a lightweight folded steel backbone chassis (or subframe), and was powered by Lotus' own Twin-cam engine. Produced initially in open top form with a fabric hood, later versions of the car were available in open topped or closed coupé form. The Elan's place in the market was as a performance car for the younger, more sporting driver, and – with its good performance and looks – it amply filled that role for a decade.

The +2 was a longer and wider version of the Elan. It retained the Elan's mechanical elements and layout, with its folded steel backbone subframe/chassis and glass fibre bodyshell, but offered room for two small children behind

The Elan Series 4 was introduced in March 1968, and marks the final evolution of the Elan styling. This example has been in the second owner's hands for more than 40 years.

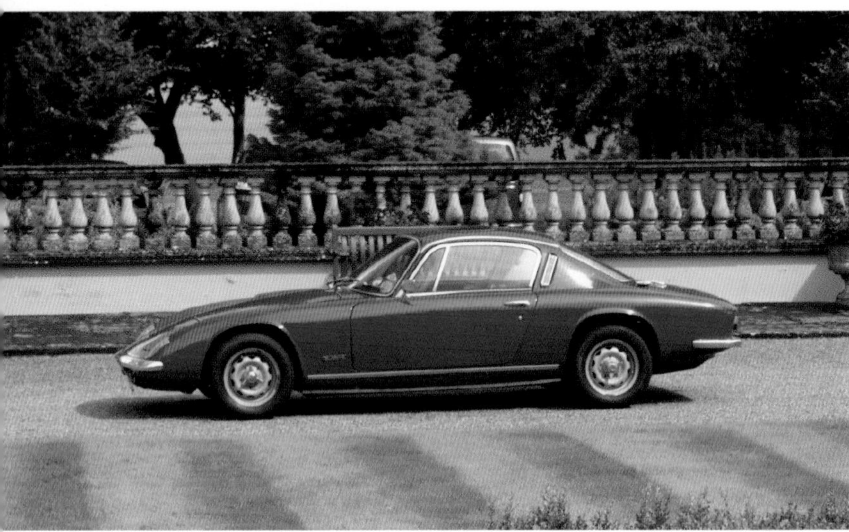

This 1968 +2 is an early car, and helped to move Lotus upmarket. The sleek lines of the car are complemented by the elegant surroundings.

The forerunner of the Elan was the Lotus Elite. First produced in the late 1950s, it was a complex car, with a glass fibre monocoque and a Coventry Climax 'fire pump' engine with racing heritage. Its looks still turn heads today.

the driver and passenger. Its market was the more mature driver, who wanted the Elan's handling and performance but in a more civilised, family-oriented package. Introduced in 1967, the +2 was only offered as a closed two-door coupé, and through its life gained an increasingly luxurious interior, as befitted its status as a businessman's express.

The Elan and +2 were designed by a team headed up by Ron Hickman, a world-class engineer who went on to design – among other projects – the Black and Decker Workmate. Hickman was both talented and practical, and Colin Chapman's brief to him was to produce a road car that could replace the Type 14 Elite, but which would be easier and hence cheaper to produce. While Chapman's main interest was in racing and winning, he knew that Lotus had to be as successful as possible in producing profitable road cars in order to fund its racing programme. He knew the way to finance the company's racing effort would be to produce a road car that could be sold in significant numbers, and racing success was the best marketing tool Chapman knew – the classic 'Win on Sunday, Sell on Monday' scenario. If successful, this would develop into a virtuous circle: the racing would improve the breed, with improvements flowing down into the road cars, which would enhance their performance and reputation, the road cars would then sell more, thereby enabling the race programme to continue to get the finance it needed to be successful ...

All this meant that the new car would have to sell in significant numbers and make Lotus money. Lotus' current 'road' cars in the early 1960s were the Seven and the Type 14 Elite, which were not selling in the sort of numbers needed. The Seven was a development of the original Lotus 6, and was much more of a racer than a road car, with its lack of roof, very basic interior and minimal passenger space, compensated for by its electric performance and trademark Lotus handling.

The Elite was an advanced closed coupé with a glass fibre monocoque bodyshell and a race-derived Coventry Climax engine. It did have some creature comforts – unlike the Seven it came with doors and a roof, as well as a nicely specified and trimmed interior – but suffered from a lack of refinement, mainly due to excessive noise resonating through the shell.

Chapman has been quoted as saying the Elite was "supposed to be 75 per cent road- and 25 per cent race-oriented, but ended up the other way around." Not only that,

⮝ Lotus' other road car of the 1950s and early 1960s was the Seven. While stripped back and basic, the car offered scintillating performance and outstanding handling.

⮝ The Elite used the 1216cc Coventry Climax FWE engine. A single overhead camshaft all-alloy unit, the engine was both light and powerful, and very popular with racers.

but the Elite was expensive to make, as it relied on third parties to supply its major components, the bodyshell and the engine, so the profit margin for Lotus was slim if not non-existent. Despite these flaws, the Elite had generally very favourable reviews in the contemporary press and an excellent record of racing success, and so its replacement had a lot to live up to. Chapman knew what he wanted: a small, reasonably priced two-seat sports car that could be used as a daily driver while also having some club-level competition potential, although Lotus at the time did not anticipate supporting the Elan in such competition. This is where Hickman's practical streak came out; the new car would have to appeal to the reasonably affluent single young man who had an interest in motorsport and knew a good car when they saw one, it would have to cost less than the Elite, and still be civilised enough to be used as a daily driver.

So the Elan was aimed at that specific market, which at the time was dominated by the larger manufacturers such as MG (via BMC) and Triumph, both of which had small- and medium-sized two-seater sports cars. To control costs and avoid paying over the odds to outside suppliers, the decision was taken that Lotus would build as much of the new car as possible in-house.

When the Elan made it into production, the bodyshell was much simpler and easier to make than Elite, the folded steel

The Elan and +2 were powered by the Lotus Twin-cam engine throughout their production lives. The 1558cc double overhead camshaft unit was based on a Ford Kent engine block, and fitted with a Lotus light alloy cylinder head and timing cover to give a state-of-the-art performance engine. ➤

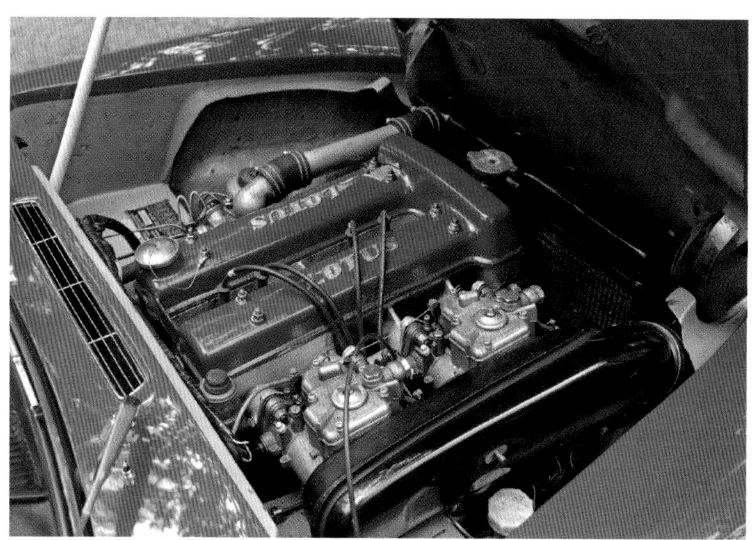

The Elan – fitted here with aftermarket Minilite alloy wheels – was powerful and light, which meant its 1600cc Twin-cam engine gave it an outstanding performance. This is Paddy Byers' Series 1.

sheet chassis / subframe was cheap and light, and the use of Lotus' own Twin-cam engine was a lot cheaper than the Elite's Coventry Climax unit. These factors meant that the production costs to make an Elan were significantly less than those of the Elite, and the new Elan was priced around 40 per cent less than the Elite.

## INTRODUCING THE ELAN

When the Elan burst onto the market proper in 1963 it was unlike any other small sports car, and gave the prospective purchaser an unrivalled combination of performance, roadholding and handling. The Elan had a length of 145in (368.3cm), width of 56in (142.2cm), wheelbase of 84in (213.4cm) and a track of 47in (119.4cm) front and rear, and a weight of 1288lb (584kg). The cockpit could comfortably seat the driver and passenger along with a bit of luggage space behind the seats, and a decent sized lockable boot along with reasonable weather protection from the hood and pull-up windows lent the car a good level of practicality. Its state-of-the-art 1558cc Twin-cam engine produced over 100bhp, and with independent suspension and disc brakes on all four wheels, its specification was closer to that of the racing cars of the day than its road car rivals from the major British manufacturers.

With a UK price of £1499 built (or £1095 in kit form), a top speed of 110mph (177km/h), a 0-60 time of around 8.5 seconds, and weighing a mere 1300lbs (590kg), the lightweight Elan outperformed all its rivals on everything other than price. Dimensionally, the Elan was small and close in size to the Triumph Spitfire and MG Midget, however its performance and price placed it into the next tier up alongside the Triumph TR4 and the MGB. The MGB retailed at £834, and had a top speed of 109mph and a 0-60 time of 9.5 seconds, its performance blunted by the lumbering B-series engine and its 2044lb (927kg) weight. The TR4, meanwhile, retailed at £1032 and had a top speed of 109 mph and a 0-60 time of 10.9 seconds, its performance again blunted by its tractor-derived four-cylinder pushrod engine and its 2184lb (991kg) weight.

## THE ELAN RANGE – SERIES 1 TO THE SPRINT

The original Elan, retrospectively called the Series 1 but badged as the Elan 1600, was initially introduced in October 1962. The very first five Elans produced were fitted with a 1498cc Twin-cam engine and badged as the 'Elan 1500.' These were in effect pre-production models and were not available to the general public, and all were re-engined with

997 NUR is a very early Elan Series 1 that was originally owned by Lotus racing driver Jim Clark. Note the individual round rear lights, and the hardtop, which was an option on the Series 1 and Series 2 cars.

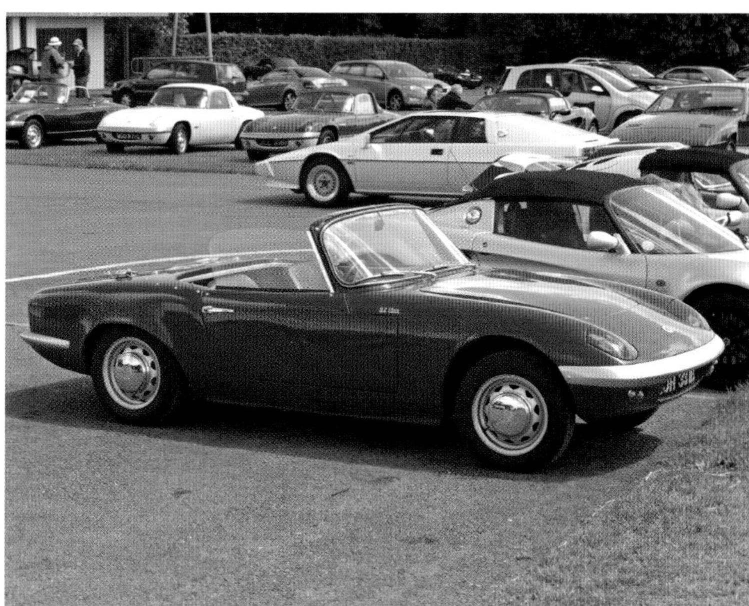

The Elan Series 2 was an incremental improvement on the Series 1, with a number of minor changes. This was pictured alongside some more modern Lotus cars at a Club Lotus track day at the Castle Combe circuit in Wiltshire.

1558cc Twin-cams once the definitive production version of the engine was introduced. The Series 1 recognition points are the boot lid set flush on the top of the rear deck, the rounded wheelarches, pull-up side windows, and the 'do it yourself' roof. This had clip-on cant rails that fitted on top of the door windows, and the whole structure – cant rails, frame and cover – had to be lifted off the bodyshell and stored in the boot when not in use. All true production Elan Series 1s were then badged as Elan 1600s, and produced up to October 1964.

The Series 1 was superseded by the Series 2 in November 1964. The Series 2 featured new one-piece rear lights from Vauxhall, along with minor revisions that included a full-width dashboard, although the change-over period was – like many Lotus specification changes – somewhat 'relaxed,' with the first Series 2 cars still having the Series 1 separate round rear lights. The Series 2 was also made available in SE or S/E (Special Equipment) specification. The SE specification gave the owner a 115bhp engine, knock-on wheels with radial tyres, 3.5:1 differential, indicator repeaters on the front wings, chrome steel strips just below the doors, a leather-covered steering wheel, anti-dazzle rear view mirror, inertial reel seatbelts, and a fully carpeted interior.

The Series 3 emerged in September 1965, and had a number of significant changes to the Series 2, the most significant being the introduction of an all-new bodyshell, recognisable from its revised and slightly flattened wheelarches and the boot lid, which overlapped the rear panel. Initially the Series 3 was introduced as a coupé, and was produced alongside the Series 2 Convertible. The Series 2 Convertible was then replaced by the Series 3 Convertible in June 1966, which used the same body as the coupé but with the roof removed. The Series 3 Convertible had an all-new roof and frame that was bolted to the body and folded down into a well behind the cockpit.

Towards the end of Series 3 production, Lotus introduced the Elan 'Super Safety' badged 'SS,' and aimed at the US or Federal market. It was an interim model with a range of design features to make the Series 3 Elan conform with recently announced US safety standards. These new

The introduction of the coupé in September 1965 resulted in an all-new bodyshell, which eventually was used on the Series 3 drop head. The rear lights used on this Series 3 coupé were also used on later Series 2 cars.

The Series 3 drop head was introduced in June 1966, nine months after the coupé first appeared. The bodyshell was taken from the coupé moulds and featured various revisions, including restyled wheelarches, when compared to the Series 2 cars.

standards were introduced as a result of campaigner Ralf Nader's book *Unsafe at Any Speed*, which documented the many flaws of existing car designs that had resulted in an unacceptable level of personal injury to car drivers and passengers in the USA. For the Elan, this meant changes were needed in the cockpit to eliminate any protruding items that could cause damage to the driver or passenger in the event of a crash. Externally, the main change was to the three-eared spinners for the knock-on wheels. These were initially modified to have the ears angled inwards to avoid pedestrians' legs, and were ultimately superseded by the octagonal 'Nader Nuts' named after the campaigner. While these cars were aimed firmly at the US export market there are several right-hand drive SS models in the UK.

The Series 4 of March 1968 was an evolution of the Series 3, having a revised bodyshell with slightly wider wheelarches and a modified interior with some safety features, such as flush-fitting rocker switches, seen on the SS models. The door locks were also changed to anti-burst units, which used the rectangular flush-fitting

The Elan Super Safety, or SS, was an interim model, based on the Series 3 but with various safety features mandated by the US market. This is Jeff Boughton's example, which never made it to the US and has lived in the UK all its life.

The Elan coupé was introduced with no grilles in its B pillar. However, a through-flow ventilation system was quickly developed, resulting in air extractor grilles being sited on the pillar. The Series 4 car has the later type of grille, shared with the +2.

The last iteration of the Elan was the Sprint. This Sprint is unusually finished in a metallic green.

The Series 4 Elan drop head had small indicator repeaters on the front wings. John Humfryes' 1969 car still sports its factory-fitted Lotus 'Quality Reliability' QR sticker.

The Sprint was more commonly painted in a two-tone finish, with a white lower half. This is Dave Groves' 1972 Sprint coupé in its striking Pistachio over white colours.

interior handles from the British Leyland parts bin. The main exterior change was to the rear lights, where the Vauxhall units were replaced with rectangular Lucas units first seen on the +2. These units were similar to those used on the Series 2 and 3 E-type Jaguars, but the Jaguar units did not have the integrated reversing lights seen on the Lotus units.

The final iteration of the Elan was the Sprint, which went on sale in February 1971 and started life as a rehash of unsold Series 4 cars. The Sprint's main change from the S4 was a tuned engine, with larger inlet valves, a raised compression ratio, a ported head and new 'Sprint' camshafts that pushed out a healthy 126bhp – a significant increase over the standard Twin-cam's 105bhp, but maybe not such a boost over the SE's 118bhp. The Sprint only needed a differential brace and revised stronger and stiffer rubber Rotoflexes on the driveshafts to take the power boost, and the car was introduced at the October 1970 London Motor show. The production cars were distinguished by a two tone paint finish – usually a standard Lotus colour on top and white under the waist line, with a gold decal separating the two. This was the 'standard' finish from the factory – if a customer wanted a single colour they were charged extra! The Sprint also featured gold painted bumpers. The final Sprints, both DHC and FHC, were produced in February 1973.

## THE +2 RANGE

Planning for the +2 started in 1963, not long after the Elan had gone into production, showing that Chapman was still looking ahead. The thinking behind the +2 was simple – if Lotus was going to continue expanding, a second car was needed to complement the Elan, and to target those original Elan customers who were getting older, settling down and starting families – just as Chapman was in the mid 1960s. So, rather than another pure sports car, a larger, more comfortable car was needed – in fact, a GT car. Lotus did briefly consider upping the engine capacity of the new car and looked at engines from various outside plants, including the Daimler V8, several Ford units (including the 1600 Crossflow and the then-new V4 and V6), Triumph's straight-six, and the Buick-derived Rover V8 (which only made it into production cars during 1966, but Rover had decided to use it in 1963). Chapman eventually vetoed the idea of using an outside supplier's engine as it wouldn't be "... in keeping with the Lotus image ..." and so the +2 retained the famous Twin-cam engine. The Elan had demonstrated that having your own engine in your car meant a lot to customers, even if the bottom end was all Ford (and, of course, in the Elan and +2's engine bay the customer could only see the top end of the motor, with the Twin-cam head and prominent 'Lotus' badging on the cam cover, which happily concealed the humble Ford underpinnings). As a concession to the greater weight of the new car, the +2's Twin-cam was supplied in 'SE' specification as standard, which gave the car a healthy 115bhp.

The +2 was launched in September 1967, and was a closed coupé with a pair of small seats behind the driver and passenger seats that were really only suitable for children, but could take a small adult at a pinch. The car was 24in (61cm) longer and 10in (25cm) wider than the Elan. At 169in (429cm) long and 66in (167cm) wide the +2 was a relatively large car, with a lot of the increased length coming from extra bodywork in the nose and tail. The wheelbase – at 96in (243cm) – was only 12in (30.5cm) longer than the Elan, giving just enough room for the two rear seats. The weight of the +2 was 2083lb (944kg), some 523lb (237kg) more than the Elan Series 3 coupé's 1560lb (707kg). The +2 had its all-new bodyshell mounted on a lengthened Elan chassis, and while the rear crossmember was extended to increase the rear track by 8in (20.32cm) to 55in (139.7cm), the front crossmember of the chassis was the same as the Elan's, and longer wishbones were employed to extend the front track by 7in (17.8cm) to 54in (137.2cm).

Melody and Henry Kozlowski's 1968 +2 is an early car and features the Italian-sourced Carello rear light clusters, boot opening handle, and combined door handle and locks. ➤

The author's +2 has been tricked out to look like a late S 130. Spotlights in the nose, contrasting roof, and Lotus alloy wheels are all later additions.

The first 177 +2s were fitted with Italian Carello rear light units, which were superseded with larger Lucas versions that incorporated reversing lights in the cluster.

The first major change to the +2 range was the introduction of the +2S in late 1968: this had the distinction of being the first Lotus road car not available in kit form. The +2 bodyshell was updated at this time to incorporate various changes, such as remote boot opening, as well as fog- and spotlights. With a more luxurious interior than the +2, the 'S' had an extra pair of minor instruments in the walnut-veneered dash. In the name of safety, the original toggle switches were replaced with flush-fitting rocker switches, and the instruments were fitted with flat bezels. All the instruments were unique to the +2S, and had revised graphics (although retaining the white lettering on black backgrounds), and were fitted with red needles. The next model was the +2S 130 that was announced in October 1970 and went on sale in February 1971. This was basically the +2S fitted with the Sprint specification motor. The final iteration of the +2 was introduced in October 1972 as the +2S 130/5, and had the optional Lotus five-speed gearbox fitted. +2 production ended in December 1974.

From the rear the muscular stance of the +2 is apparent. Contrast the later Lucas rear light clusters with the Carello examples on the earlier +2s.

## LAYOUT AND MAJOR DESIGN FEATURES OF THE ELAN AND +2

### CHASSIS OR SUBFRAME

Originally, the design of the Elan was envisaged as a glass fibre monocoque, similar to that of the Elite but with a much simplified construction to reduce the costs of the unit, when compared to the complex and difficult-to-produce structure that was the Elite. As it struggled to engineer enough strength into an open-roofed glass fibre monocoque body, Hickman's design team adopted a cheap and lightweight folded steel backbone chassis (or subframe) to act as a slave unit to prove and test the suspension, engine and transmission.

Legend has it that the design of the slave unit was originally sketched out by Chapman on the back of a napkin whilst brainstorming a solution with Hickman. Once fabricated, the slave chassis was clothed with a proprietary glass fibre bodyshell from Falcon, which allowed the mechanical components to be thoroughly tested on the road. When the team realised that building a sufficiently strong and rigid open bodyshell in glass fibre was not going to be achievable within the project's time scale,

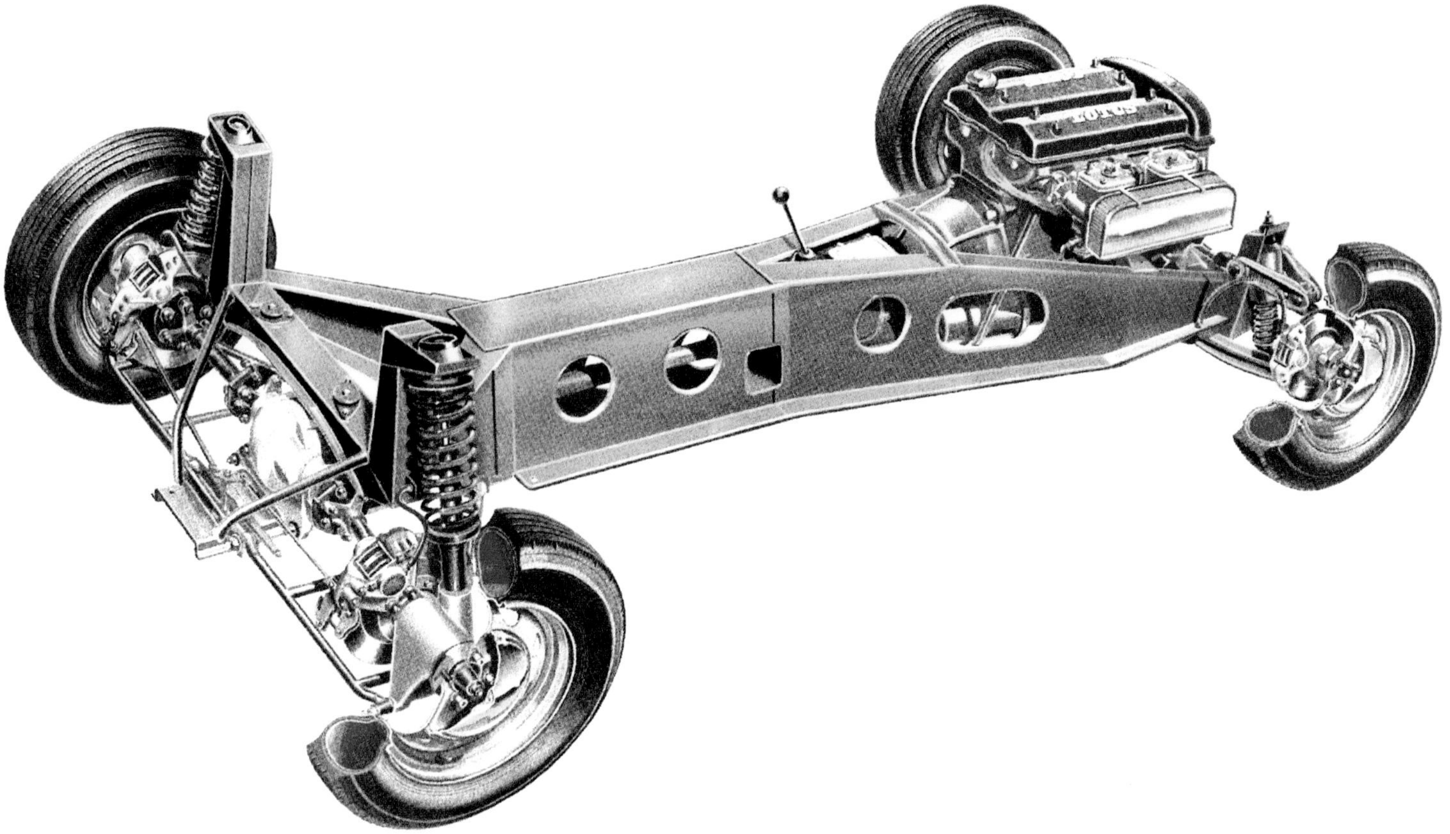

## CHASSIS SPECIFICATION

**Chassis** Welded steel backbone type, fully rust proofed.

**Front Suspension** Unequal length wishbones, independent, coil spring telescopic shock absorbers.

**Rear Suspension** Fully independent, by wide based wishbones, coil springs and telescopic shock absorbers.

**Brakes** Hydraulically operated calipers on 9½ inch diameter discs on front wheels. 10 inch diameter discs on rear. Hand brake operating on rear wheels only.

**Gearbox** Four forward speeds and reverse. Synchromesh on all forward ratios. Oil capacity 1¾ imp. pints (2·1 U.S. pints, 0·99 litres).

**Final Drive** Chassis mounted hypoid unit, sound insulated. Oil capacity 2 imp. pints (2·4 U.S. pints, 1·13 litres).

**Steering** Rack and pinion, with telescopic and collapsible steering column. Optional right or left hand drive, 15 inch diameter dished wood-rimmed steering wheel, 2½ turns lock to lock.

**Wheels** 13 inch diameter special Lotus high speed pressed steel. Four stud fixing. Bright metal hub caps.

**Tyres** 520 x 13.

▲ Taken from the first Lotus Elan brochure, the folded steel chassis picks up all the mechanical elements of the car. (Courtesy Lotus Cars)

it adopted the slave chassis and redesigned the Lotus bodyshell to fit. When the body and chassis/subframe were bolted together they formed a rigid structure which would accept the engine, transmission and suspension, with the subframe providing all the mechanical attachment points for the engine, transmission and suspension, relieving the bodyshell of those duties.

Dave Groves' Elan Sprint has been recently refreshed and is looking lovely. The knock-on Minilite wheels are a popular upgrade in Elan circles. ➤

## CHASSIS DESIGN AND CONSTRUCTION

The Elan and +2 chassis are virtually identical in construction, with only minor changes to accommodate the +2's increased length and width. The chassis on both models comprised a fabricated box section front crossmember, which has a welded-on platform on its front face to carry the steering rack. There is a steel spindle welded into each end of the crossmember, on which are mounted the lower wishbones. A pair of vertical box section turrets are welded to each end of the crossmember, and these carry the upper wishbone spindle, shock absorber top fixing, and a body fixing plate. Running back from each turret is a Z-shaped pressed-steel plate, and these converge at the front of a central box section tunnel, forming a Y-shaped structure for the engine and gearbox to nestle in. The engine mounts are positioned about a third of the way back from the front crossmember on the Y plates, and each side section has large flanged access holes punched through them – two on the right-hand side and one on the left. On the lower flange, just before the tunnel starts, there are a pair of captive nuts which locate the gearbox mount. There is a U section crossmember, or brace, positioned about halfway down the lower face of the Y section. One of the differences between the Elan and +2 chassis is that on the Elan this cross brace is welded in place, while on the +2 it is bolted on. The central tunnel is a rectangular box section, again made from 16-gauge folded steel sheet. Approximately halfway along on the lower part of the side is a welded-in transverse-threaded tube that provides the seatbelt mounting. At the rear of the tunnel the sides and top of the tunnel branch out and up to form a short Y section that carries a rear crossmember. The floor of the tunnel extends backwards, with the far end of the floor supported by a pair of tubes running from the outer edges of the crossmember down and inwards. The crossmember carries the top differential mount points, and at each end is a short vertical turret with a square top section to carry the 'Lotocones' that locate the top of the rear 'Chapman struts.' The floor of the tunnel (and its rear extension) carries the lower wishbone mounts, and the front ends of the differential torque rods are bolted into the lower flange of the tunnel floor. The original chassis was painted in red oxide primer, and usually had a blowover of black bitumen-based paint on top of the primer as a slightly futile gesture towards rust proofing.

On the +2's chassis, the length of the central tunnel was increased to provide the +2's extra length. The wider track of the +2 was achieved by increasing the width of the rear crossmember above the differential which spaced the location of the rear Lotocone carriers wider apart, while at the front the chassis dimensions remained the same as the Elan, but the length of the +2's wishbones was increased.

## BODY

Having seen how glass fibre experts Maximar, and then Bristol, struggled to produce the Elite's complex, multi-part bodyshell, Lotus recognised that in order to make a cheap, high quality unit, much more thought had to be put into the design of the Elan's body so it could be produced quickly and easily. Production of the Elite also taught

Taken in the Bourne factory, this picture shows the construction of the Elan's glass fibre bodyshell. This picture shows the mould used to make the top half of the bodyshell, with its steel frame that maintained rigidity and allowed the mould to be rotated, providing access to lay up the shell. (Courtesy Mike Ostrov)

Lotus the valuable lesson that the more of the production of the Elan that was kept in-house, then the higher the potential profit was to be made on the car. This resulted in a lot of work on both the body design and the production techniques. Design-wise, the body was simplified so that it would need the minimum amount of separate parts and use the minimum amount of materials. From a production point of view, the 'Unimould' process was adopted, where a complete mould was created from a number of individual sub-moulds that were bolted together.

This meant that the complex shapes incorporated in the Elan and +2's outer shell – especially the tumblehome, where the lower sides of the body curved inwards – could be accommodated in the Unimould made up from a number of bolt-together sub-moulds, and the resulting moulding could be released from the mould by unbolting the sub-moulds. In contrast to the Elite's six major body mouldings, which had to be bonded together to form a single shell, the Elan and +2 body was made from two mouldings. These comprised a top moulding, incorporating all of the visible body, and a smaller inner or bottom moulding which formed the floor with transmission tunnel, inner wheelarches, inner engine bay and the boot floor.

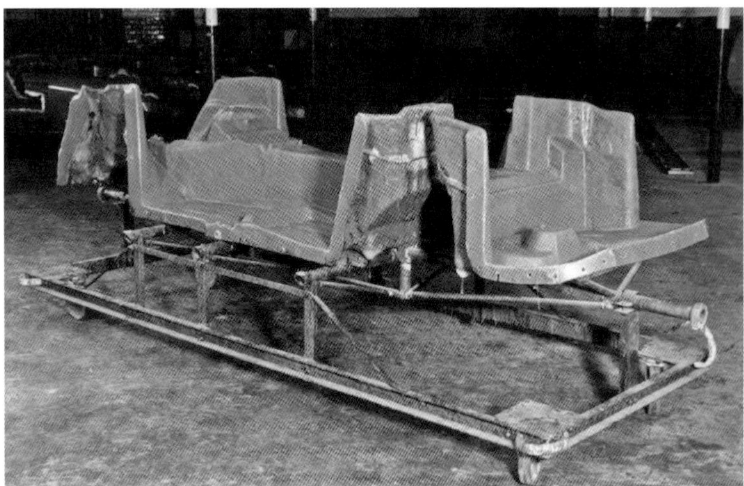

The inner shell was produced on this mould. It just shows the ribbing used in the floorpan; a feature of the Bourne-produced shells, which was not carried through when body production was moved in-house. (Courtesy Mike Ostrov)

These two mouldings were relatively easy to bond together outside of the moulds as they cured, and thus created the complete Elan shell, which was light, strong and rigid in its own right, and made a significant contribution to the car's overall stiffness when bolted to the folded steel chassis/subframe. The simplified design meant that the Elan body was much easier to make and was significantly cheaper than the Elite body.

The same production process was applied to produce the +2 bodyshell, which again was moulded in two halves that were then bonded together as the individual mouldings were curing.

Initially, the Elan's bodyshell was made by Bourne Mouldings, but after the first few hundred were made, production was taken in-house, and the +2 body was made by Lotus from the start of production. The production of the chassis was always outsourced, as the unit cost was so low – some reports at the time put the cost at under £20 – that it made no sense to bring production in house.

While glass fibre was the main constituent of the shell, both the Elan and the +2 had some steel reinforcement

Here, the top bodyshell moulding is being laid up. The mould has been rotated to give the person tasked with laying up access to the nose through the bonnet opening. (Courtesy Mike Ostrov)

The complete shell, with the top and bottom halves bonded together and ready for finishing. Note the latticework reinforcement around the door openings, and the characteristic Series 1 and 2 boot lid set into the rear deck.

incorporated in their body shells. The Elan's shell was reinforced around each door aperture with a U-shaped latticework structure made from solid steel rod, which was bonded into the bodyshell and ran from the top of the aperture, around its base, and then back up to the waistline of the shell.

Each side comprised a pair of rods bent into a 'U' shape, which were joined together by welding a number of shorter angled rods between the two outers in a zig-zag pattern. Steel was also used around the windscreen aperture. When the coupé was introduced, towards the end of Series 2 production, its body had a new subtly-altered design (notwithstanding the addition of the roof), most noticeably the flattened and wider wheelarches. The fixed-head coupé moulds were adopted for production of the Series 3 and Series 4 open DHC bodies, so there was a single design of mould used to produce both open and closed cars. When the author approached Mike Kimberly, he described how the open car bodies were laid up as normal up to the roof line, then the resin and mat applied was tapered, with a thin skin only across the majority of the roof. This was to maintain the body shape when it was taken out of the Unimould – without the roof moulding the body was very floppy, according to Mike. Mike joined Lotus in 1969 as an engineer and eventually rose to become CEO. When he first joined Lotus, Chapman made Mike work on the manufacturing line to show him how Lotus did things, and how different it was from Jaguar!

In the +2, the main body steel reinforcement was in the sills. A fabricated steel box section girder was housed inside each sill, and these were through-bolted to three rectangular plates fitted on the inside edge of the sill. The forward plate was in the front footwell, the central plate was level with the front seat, and the rearward plate was in the rear footwell. The girder also provided front and rear jacking points. As well as strengthening the bodyshell, in both cases the reinforcement also gave some protection to the cabin from side impacts.

On the Elan and +2, the inner seatbelt mounts were both bolted through reinforced points on the chassis backbone. Upper mounts were attached to steel brackets that were bolted to the top of the rear turrets. The +2's lower outboard

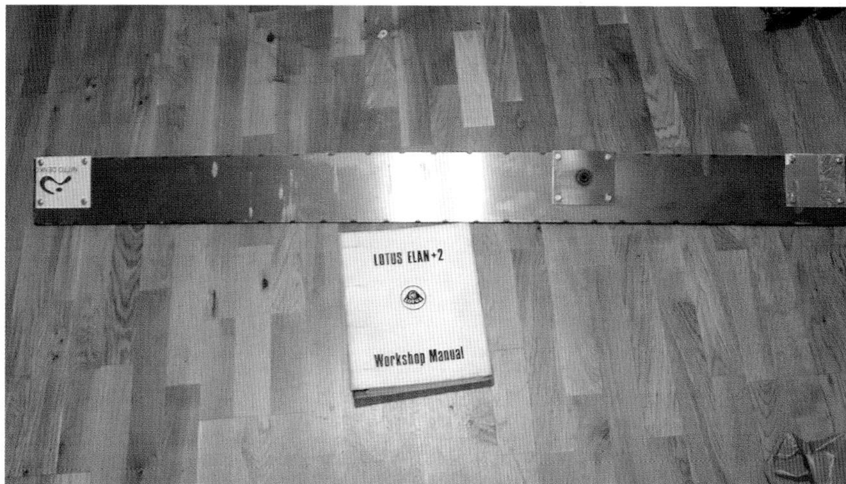


Each sill of the Plus 2 should have a fabricated steel box section sill. From new these were poorly protected and rusted – galvanised or stainless steel replacements are available. They bolt through the inner sill to three plates mounted on the inner sill in the cabin, with the centre plate carrying seat belt mount, and have a jacking point at each end.

The +2's rear bumper was made for Lotus, and used the end pressings of a Riley Elf or Wolseley Hornet rear bumper with a new mid section welded on. Here is the author's +2 and Dave Groves' Riley Elf.

seatbelt mounts were bolted through plates incorporated in the sill reinforcing girder, while on the Elan they are bolted into a threaded hole incorporated into the base of the rear of the reinforcing lattice. Depending on the type of seatbelt fitted to the Elan, this can have screwed into it either a hoop that the seatbelt was hooked onto, or a simple bolt.

Protection for the body from minor parking knocks was provided by foam-filled glass fibre wrap-round bumpers in the Elan, usually painted silver but also offered in gold on some Sprints. The +2 had more substantial chromed steel units on the front and rear. The front was a Ford Anglia 105E item, while the rear was unique to the +2, but used the end pieces from the Austin Mini-based Riley Elf and Wolseley Hornet's rear bumper joined together with a new central section.

## INTERIOR

The Series 1 Elan's cabin was actually well appointed for a British sports car interior, with a well-instrumented wooden dashboard, comfortable, supportive seats, and a sports steering wheel. The plywood dashboard was veneered with oiled teak, and was 'r' shaped, covering the area in front of the driver and then sweeping down to cover the centre of the dash, from the dash top down to the transmission tunnel.

It carried the speedometer and tachometer – two large 4in dials directly in front of the driver – and these were flanked by a smaller combined water temperature/oil pressure gauge and a fuel level gauge. Various toggle and push and pull switches were also scattered around the dash in a slightly random pattern. The top centre of the dash

◄ While the Elan's interior was basic, it was by no means badly equipped or uncomfortable. This is the Series 1 Elan's dash, in which the structural wooden dashboard only extended to the centre console. A separate glove box faced the passenger.

◄ From the Series 2 Elan on, the dashboard was extended to fit the full width of the cabin. This is Brian Goodison's Series 2, which has a walnut-veneered dash for the look of some extra luxury. Note the pull-up windows with no frame.

was firmly bolted to the body, and its lower centre edge was bolted to a bracket that was, in turn, bolted through the body to the chassis, helping to stiffen the shell. On top there was a vinyl-covered pad that filled the space between the dash and the windscreen, and carried the grille that directed heater air onto the screen for demisting. In front of the passenger seat was an open cubby hole or glove box. The floor was covered in a rubber matting material, generally referred to as rhino or elephant hide, the seats were trimmed in vinyl, and the hood was a build-it-yourself affair, with side rails that clipped onto the rear deck and windscreen. The side windows were frameless glass and were designed to be manually pushed up or down, and a small chromed tab on the top edge of the window gave the driver or passenger the purchase needed to operate them. Further trim panels, covered in vinyl, were used to cover any remaining exposed glass fibre. All in all, the interior was a nice place to be and a credit to the Lotus designers, who managed to provide a well-styled cabin that was functional, stylish and contemporary. Over the years the Elan's cabin did not change much. During the life of the Series 1 the dash was extended over the passengers side (making it into a 'T' shape and allowing for the fitment of a lid over the glove box), carpets replaced the rubber mats, but the seats remained the same and vinyl continued to be used on the seats and door cards.

▲ John Humfryes' Series 4 Elan interior shows the last type of dash, with recessed rocker switches for safety, extra switches for electric windows, and chromed surrounds for the side windows. Note also the eyeball air vents in the corners of the dash.

The Series 3 saw the introduction of electric windows, which meant the doors had a chromed frame formed around the window, and the convertible had a new hood which had its frame bolted to the car and no longer had to be dismantled and stored in the boot when taken down.

The main changes in appearance came with the Series 4 (and the Super Safety cars), and its elimination of protuberances into the cabin which could injure the driver or passenger. This meant the toggle switches were replaced with rocker switches that were recessed into the dash, as were the instruments. Oblong-shaped flush-fitting interior door latches from the British Leyland parts bin replaced the pull levers used previously, and the door latches were anti-burst types. Sprints carried on the Series 4 interior with no significant changes.

The +2 was always intended to be more upmarket than the Elan, and its interior reflected this. The first +2 retained the Elan's slim and comfortable front seats, and the two rear seats were formed by placing upholstered panels over the interior of the bodyshell to from two reasonably comfortable passenger seats separated by the transmission tunnel. Entry to the back seat meant the entire seat pivoted forward on its front mounts.

Vinyl was used throughout as the trim material – covering the front seats, rear panels and seats, and door cards – and a light-coloured perforated cloth was used for the headlining. The dash was more ornate than the Elans, with a highly polished walnut veneer finish, and was fitted with the speedometer and tachometer in front of the driver, as well as four minor instruments sited in the centre of the dash above the tunnel.

These were fuel level, engine temperature, oil pressure, and charging in the form of an ammeter. Between these two pairs was a radio slot, and beneath that the slider controls

➤ Early +2 interiors were quite luxurious. This is Melody and Henry Kozlowski's early car, and shows the original style door handles placed low down in front of the arm rest.

➤ The +2 dashboard was walnut veneered from the word go, and was equipped with four minor gauges in the centre console, with the larger speedometer and rev counter in front of the driver.

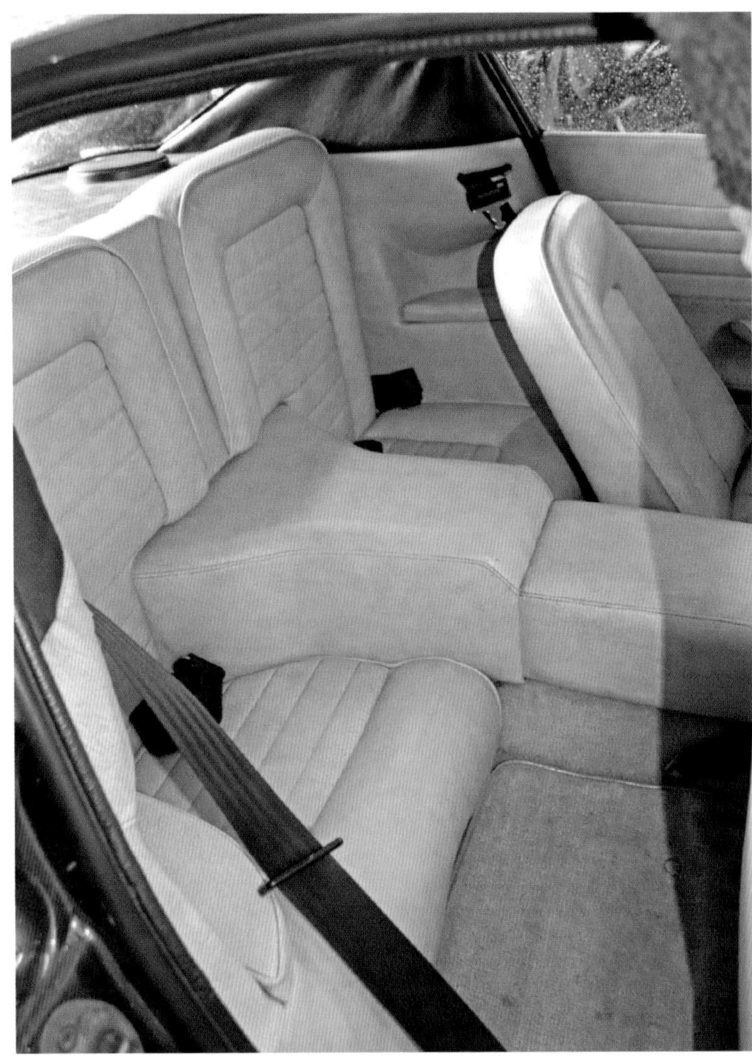

The final +2S cars had plush and well-padded seats to make an inviting but somewhat cramped rear seating area. Oatmeal was a popular colour for the interior trim on the later cars.

The last +2S had a plush interior. The walnut veneer dash was fully equipped with six minor instruments, along with many recessed rocker switches.

for the heater. As in the Elan toggle switches were scattered over the dash to operate the electrical ancillaries, and a pair of chromed recessed rocker switches operated the standard electric windows. A quirk of the +2 meant that there were two light switches – a toggle switch to power the side lights and headlights, and a pull switch to lift the headlamps. Between these switches was a flush-fitting pull-out ashtray. The first +2s were fitted with small chromed lever-type door handles, mounted just ahead of the door armrests, but with the introduction of the +2S these were then changed to the flush-fitted ones as seen on the Elan S4.

When it was introduced, the +2S took the interior up a level. New plush front seats with adjustable backrests replaced the Elan-derived originals, and the dashboard received an additional two minor instruments: an ambient temperature gauge, and a clock. The toggle switches seen on the original dash were also replaced with recessed rectangular rockers. To the rear, the backrest of the rear seats could be folded down over the squabs to form a flat load area. As time went on the interior trim was offered in oatmeal as well as the original black, and the front seats had cloth centre panels fitted.

## UNDERPINNINGS

The suspension design at the front of the Elan and +2 was based on that used on the Triumph Herald family, which included the Spitfire and GT6. The Elan used the Triumph uprights combined with Lotus' own wishbones, and initially also used the standard hubs with bolt-on steel disc wheels.

⮝ The Elan and +2 shared the same front and rear suspension, though the +2 has longer wishbones. At the front, twin wishbones support Triumph Herald-derived uprights and Spitfire disc brakes.

At the rear, the suspension is pure Lotus. The lower A-frame locates the wheel and is longer in the +2, and the top of the Chapman strut is rubber mounted to allow for the side-to-side movement of the shock absorber. Disc brakes are mounted on the inside of the hub carrier, and this car still has Rotoflex couplings. ➤

Later on, the unique Lotus design of peg-driven knock-on wheels meant the substitution of the Triumph four-stud hub with one of Lotus' design. The uprights and stub axle assembly were manufactured by Alford and Adler. Triumph also supplied the steering rack, and the brakes were Girling discs and callipers from the Spitfire.

This resulted in what was, at the time, a state-of-the-art front end, constructed from readily available and cheap – but high quality and well-engineered – components that proved ideal for the Elan. At the rear, Lotus ploughed its own path, with a wide-based lower wishbone, or A-frame, linked to a Lotus-designed hub carrier which had a 'Chapman strut' incorporated to provide springing and damping. The top of the strut was fixed to the top of the rear turrets on the chassis using a resilient rubber mount, called a 'Lotocone.' This mount allowed the top of the strut to flex, taking up the transverse movement of the strut as the suspension moved. Each driveshaft was fitted with a pair of rubber donut-shaped couplings, one at each end. These were generally know as 'Rotoflexes,' or donuts, and fulfilled the role that is now performed by constant-velocity joints and sliding joints; they allowed the driveshaft to move up and down, and took up the changes in distance between the hub carrier and

the differential output shafts as the suspension moved. Also used on the Hillman Imp (but with only one on each shaft), these were an intelligent and elegant engineering solution, offering a simple, practical and economical way of allowing for the movement of the driveshafts. The original Elan prototype had the rear discs mounted inboard, next to the differential as seen on the original Elite. However, this meant that if the car was braked to a halt and then the handbrake applied, then the car would be rolled back by as much as half a wheel's circumference, due to the Rotoflexes being in compression – a state usually referred to as 'wind-up.' This effect led to the discs in the production cars being mounted on the hub carrier outboard of the donuts, so the car was not affected by the wind-up when the handbrake was applied.

When the Sprint and S 130 were introduced they were fitted with heavy-duty Rotoflexes with steel reinforcement, as the original types could not handle the extra power. The final cars also had pins and tubes mounted on each end of the driveshaft and spiders to keep the driveshaft in position should a Rotoflex break. Over the years the Rotoflex system has come in for a lot of criticism, some deserved, some not. Their being replaced with solid driveshafts on the Type 26R indicates that even early on they were not strong enough for racing, and the introduction of strengthened units with the Sprint supports the view that they were only just adequate for road use. While the wind-up of the drive system that the Rotoflexes introduced was commented on at the time, the smoothness of the transmission was also praised.

The result was a neat, simple independent rear suspension system that gave long, well-damped wheel travel with properly controlled and predictable wheel movement. The system successfully achieved virtually no changes of wheel camber or toe in – side effects that bedevilled many other independent rear suspension systems of the time – and was largely responsible for giving the Elan and +2 their superlative handing and roadholding.

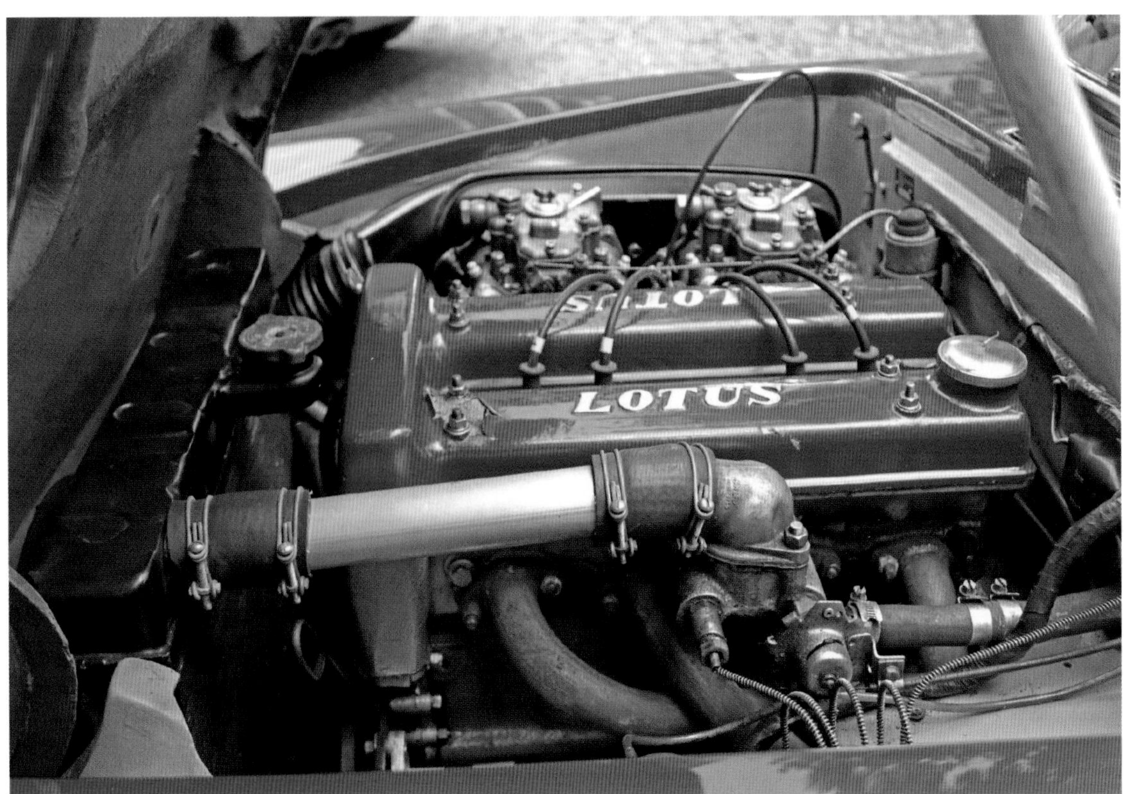


All the Elans and +2s were powered by the Lotus Twin-cam engine. The first cars were fitted with this style of cam cover, and the oil filler cap was round. ➤

## THE LOTUS TWIN-CAM ENGINE

### HISTORY

Open the bonnet of an Elan or a +2, and the engine bay is dominated by the handsome Twin-cam engine. With a pair of carburettors on the right-hand side, the Lotus name boldly cast into the cam cover, and the cast alloy timing cover encasing the front, it is almost impossible to see any sign of the humble Ford-based bottom end of the unit.

This was all intentional – Chapman wanted Lotus to be accepted as a car manufacturer in its own right, and having its own engine was a vital part of achieving this aim. With their rivals using standard or tuned Ford, Triumph and BMC/MG pushrod engines, the Elan's double overhead camshafts gave the Twin-cam an aura of advanced sophistication, which was more than backed up by the engine's performance. Lotus' use of the engine in competition also enhanced the engine's and Lotus' reputation for performance, which again rubbed off on the Elan and +2. The Twin-cam is truly the heart of the Elan and +2, and it a major factor in giving the cars their performance and character.

The Twin-cam engine was also used in the Lotus Europa Twin-cam from 1971, the Mark 1 and 2 Lotus Cortinas produced between 1963 and 1968, as well as the Ford Escort Twin-cam of 1968. It also powered various Lotus racing cars, and found its way into many other makes and models, thanks mainly to the efforts of adventurous owners.

### LAYOUT AND ENGINEERING

The Twin-cam engine was a mixture of standard Ford parts and special Lotus-designed components. Essentially, the bottom end of the standard Twin-cam is all Ford, while the pistons, cylinder head and timing cover are Lotus. It is a very clever example of how to produce a unique high-performance engine using the maximum proportion of relatively mundane components possible, and a sprinkling of exotica. At the time it was state-of-the-art, using Ford's latest thin wall cast iron technology, combined with Ford's forward thinking short-stroke wide-bore configuration and the latest thoughts on combustion chamber design, with the valves sitting in a semi-hemispherical combustion chamber

▲ By the late 1960s, a new style cam cover was fitted with 'LOTUS' written on the bridge between the camshafts. The oil filler cap now has three ears to make it easier to open.

▲ The Sprint engine, with its larger inlet valves, was introduced in February 1971. The cam cover was changed to incorporate 'LOTUS BIG VALVE' lettering, and the areas above the camshafts were ribbed.

operated by a pair of overhead camshafts. The Ford base for the Twin-cam was the four-cylinder in-line Kent engine, which originally powered the Cortina 1500. The engine had three properties which facilitated its modification into the Twin-cam: it had five main bearings, which gave its crankshaft excellent support; its cast iron block utilised Ford's expertise in thin wall casting techniques, so it was strong and light; and it was an oversquare design with a short stroke and wide bore. This final attribute meant that engine's bores were wide enough to accommodate big valves, and its piston speed was kept relatively low even at high revs, resulting in good reliability, and the engine was able to rev higher. The only downside of the oversquare engine was that it produced less torque than an undersquare unit, but this not a problem in a sports-oriented engine such as the Twin-cam.

The heart of the Twin-cam engine was its cylinder head. The unit was designed by ex-Coventry Climax engineer Harry Mundy, and refined by Steve Saville, who prepared the unit for production. The head was produced in cast alloy and had two valves per cylinder operated by twin overhead camshafts. The valves were operated directly from the camshafts through bucket tappets, and were both angled at 27 degrees from the vertical to give a state-of-the-art – for the day – semi hemispherical combustion chamber.

## STANDARD, SE SPECIFICATION AND BIG VALVE SPRINT ENGINE

The Twin-cam used in the Elan came in a number of states of tune. The original engine specification had a 9:1 compression ratio, B-type camshafts, and was complemented by the SE (or S/E) unit from 1963. This unit was fitted as standard to the +2, and had revised camshafts known as C-type. These camshafts were identified by a single shallow groove machined around the circumference of the boss that accepted the cam chain sprocket.

There was also a 'Super SE' specification released during 1968, which had standard valves but a higher compression ratio and Weber carburettors, along with a camshaft based on the Coventry Climax FWA 3060 cam; the engine gave a power output not far off that of the Sprint. A few of these engines were fitted to some road-going Elans and +2s, and

The Twin-cam's cylinder head had two valves per cylinder, operated directly from the camshafts via bucket tappets. The inlet manifold was cast with the head; this head is a Stromberg-carburettored version. The protrusion in the front of the picture is the thermostat housing. ➤

there is a suspicion that some road test cars were also fitted with them.

The final state of tune was the Sprint or Big Valve unit. This had new 'Super SE or Sprint' specification camshafts, identified by having two rings machined on the cam chain sprocket boss, and also had a higher compression ratio of 10.5:1, achieved by machining 40 thou off the standard head. The diameter of the inlet valves was increased by about 1mm, the cylinder head ports were enlarged, and the carburettors were re-jetted to suit the better breathing.

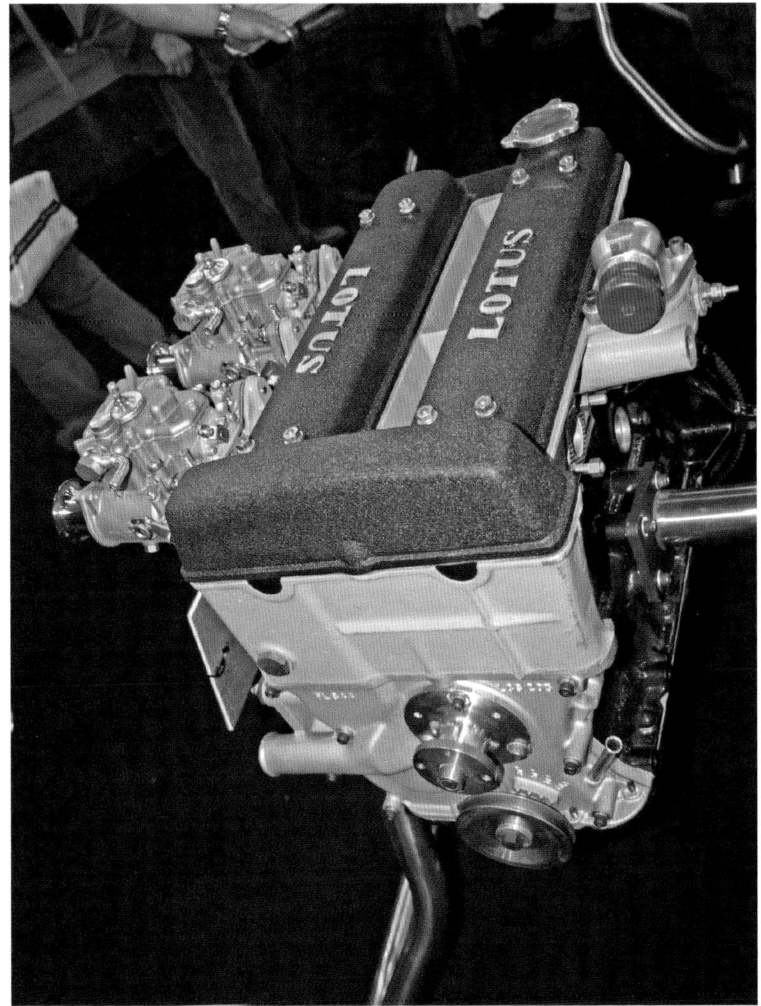


▲ The timing case of the Twin-cam housed the timing chain, along with the water pump. The case was cast in light alloy like the head, and bolted directly onto the front of the cylinder block.

Other outside firms also produced their own takes on tuning the Twin-cam – most notably BRM, whose engineering chief, Tony Rudd, moved to Lotus and was responsible for the development of the Sprint specification for Lotus.

The Lotus Elan workshop manual supposedly gives 'net' power outputs – ie output at the wheels, and subject to transmission losses. It states that the original version produced 90bhp at 5500rpm, along with 108lb/ft of torque. The SE variant was fitted with lumpier cams and gave 93bhp at 6000rpm and 108lb/ft of torque. These values fly in the face of all other published information on the Twin-cam, and it is generally accepted that these figures are wrong and were a misprint. The manual is correct for the Sprint engine, which gave 126bhp at 6500rpm and 113lb/ft of torque. These figures relate to Domestic market Weber- or Dellorto-equipped engines and the workshop manual. Sprint 'Emission' units, equipped with Stromberg carbs, gave 113bhp at 6500rpm and 113lb/ft of torque.

Miles Wilkins' Lotus Twin-cam Engine book (see Bibliography) states that the standard Weber- or Stromberg-equipped engines gave between 103 and 105bhp at 5500rpm, while the SE Weber version gave between 112-115bhp at 6000rpm, and the SE Stromberg units gave between 115-118bhp at 6000rpm. Both standard and SE units gave 108lb/ft of torque at 4500rpm. Big Valve Sprint specification engines with Weber or Dellorto carburettors gave between 125-126bhp at 6500rpm and 113lb/ft at 5500rpm of torque.

Engines for the Federal Market (ie, US market emissions equipped units) were fitted with twin Strombergs and the cross over pipes for charge warming, and gave 108bhp at 6500rpm and 108lb/ft of torque at 4000rpm in SE form, and 110bhp at 6500rpm and 104lb/ft of torque at 5000rpm in Sprint form.

## WEBER, DELLORTO AND STROMBERG CARBURETTORS

The Twin-cam engine came with fitted with a pair of one of three different types of carburettor – twin-choke Webers, twin-choke Dellortos, or constant-velocity Strombergs. A

▲ The most common carburettors fitted to the Twin-cam, certainly in the home market, were a pair of twin-choke Webers. Always popular with the racing fraternity, the Weber was very good at high revs and looked fantastic, but can be tricky to set up.

▲ From November 1968, Lotus fitted a pair of constant-velocity Stromberg carburettors. It reverted back to Webers for the home market after a year or so, but continued to fit Strombergs to Federal models, as the carbs could meet the stringent US emissions regulations.

Final Elans and +2s were fitted with twin-choke Dellorto carburettors. Seen as a slightly cheaper option than the Webers, the Dellortos gave similar performance and looks, and fit directly onto a Weber head. ➤

From the front the Elan shows its streamlined looks and iconic pop up headlights. The car is the epitome of the 1960s British sports car. ➤

quirk of the Twin-cam is that its inlet manifold is cast into the head casting, so while the Weber and Dellorto heads are identical, there is a second type to which the Strombergs are fitted. Weber heads have four separate inlet tracts, while Stromberg units had a pair of siamesed inlets.

Elans and +2s were initially all fitted with Weber carburettors, but in 1968 the change was made to Strombergs. The change was made for two reasons: cost cutting, and meeting US emissions regulations. The cost of using Strombergs was less than that of Webers, even when taking into account the cost of redesigning and retooling the head as well as adding a power bulge to the bonnet to clear the taller units. The second reason to fit the Strombergs was that they could be set up to pass the ever more stringent US emissions legislation. All Elans and +2s built to Federal specification were fitted with a pair of Strombergs and charge warming inlet manifolds. However, as the price of Webers dipped these were reintroduced to non-Federal models during 1970, and remained the standard fitment on home and non-Federal export models until the cheaper Dellortos were introduced during 1972, towards the end of production.

## SUMMARY

The Lotus Elan is a thoroughbred car, which can trace its ancestry back to the cars that started Lotus' success story; its racers of the 1960s and into the '70s. With its iconic Twin-cam engine, good looks and superlative handling and roadholding, the Elan was a car that promised much and delivered more. Alongside the Elan, the +2 capitalised on the Elan's mechanicals to deliver an incredibly competent grand tourer, which, thanks to its wider track and longer wheelbase, possessed even better handling and roadholding. The cars were much more advanced technically than their rivals, and offered the lucky owner a combination of performance and practicality that was unbeatable.

With the prices of some classics – such as the E-Type Jaguar or any Ferrari – climbing out of the reach of the average enthusiast, it is somewhat bizarre that the Elan and +2, with their good looks and race-bred pedigree, are not better thought of by the classic market. One can only assume that this is down to the residual 'kit-car' image that still hangs around Lotus, and a degree of snobbishness over the use of the glass fibre rather than rust-prone steel to produce the body. However, the relatively affordable prices of the Elan and the very affordable prices of the +2 mean that today ownership of these desirable classics are within the means of the average enthusiast.

The +2 looks like – and is – a sophisticated grand tourer, with plenty of room for two and their luggage.

## PADDY BYERS

Paddy Byers has owned his Series 1 Elan since 2007, and in that time he has used it both as a daily commuter and a high days and holidays car. The car is an early one, number 71, and came with its original Bourne bodyshell and engine. Its paint and body had also been restored before he bought it. The interior was in good shape too, but he had to do a fair amount of mechanical work to bring it up to the standard he wanted – a mechanically reliable and good-looking but usable early Elan.

As bought, the car had some practical modifications that increased the reliability and usability of the car, and which Paddy has retained. The car has an alternator fitted and was converted to negative earth, and had an electric fuel pump fitted. The body had been nicely painted and the car had been fitted with wider 26R-style wheelarches. The interior trim was in good condition and mostly standard, but the car was fitted with a non-standard full-width dash that was covered in vinyl, and the instruments were not to original specification.

Paddy Byers stands by his Series 1 Elan. The Elan's small size is apparent.

Paddy's Series 1 Elan sports a Type 26R modified front end, resulting in a shorter front bumper. Period-style Minilite alloy wheels are a neat touch.

Engine-wise, the car needed a top end overhaul, which included fitting a new cam chain and valve springs and a few other parts. The gearbox also needed some attention, and was stripped down, checked, cleaned, and all worn parts were replaced. The differential received the same treatment. Cooling was addressed with a new radiator, and Paddy fitted a modern electric fan, operated automatically from an Otter switch in the radiator. The fan was fitted to the front and left-hand side of the radiator (looking forwards) under the top inlet, so it had maximum effect on the water entering the radiator. The front and rear suspension was completely reworked. Paddy replaced the rear A-frame to chassis bushes and the nylon front lower trunnion bushes with polybushes, and the other bushes in the suspension were replaced with standard metalastic items. The rear drive-train received Elantrickbits constant-velocity joint driveshafts from Australia (which have had good reports on their quality on lotuselan.net), and the outer driveshafts were replaced with stronger Tony Thompson Racing (TTR) items. Paddy had found that the original hubs were not straight, which made fitting the special offset bolt-on Minilite alloys problematical – the hubs were so far out of true that the wheels would hit the outer A-frame bolts, so were replaced with TTR's steel machined items. The full-width dash was removed, and – Paddy was delighted to see – the original dash was still in place behind it. This was restored with new veneer to give the original oiled teak look. The instruments were refurbished with the correct matt black bezels, and the incorrect fuel gauge was replaced. Where necessary the switches were replaced with original-style items to make the dash look very authentic. The steering wheel was with the car when Paddy got it, and is believed to be the original, although

From the front the Series 1 Elan is purposeful, small and sleek. Pop-up headlights are a major styling cue.

From the side the clean lines of the Elan Series 1 can be appreciated. Paddy's car is a fine example, and is used extensively.

there is (as is the way with any early Lotus) some debate as to its authenticity.

The electrics came in for some modification, with Paddy fitting a new loom from Autosparks, as well as relays for the headlamps to cut down power running behind the dash. The headlamps were still vacuum operated, but Paddy fitted a solenoid-operated vacuum switch in the engine bay. This avoids having to run piping to the headlamp switch in the dash, reduces the potential for vacuum leaks, and is a sensible and practical solution given that finding the original switches in good condition is hard today.

One aspect of the car Paddy didn't have to change was the bodyshell and the paint. The 15-year-old cellulose paint, applied by the previous owner, is still in great condition. There are a few minor stress cracks, but in general the body is in excellent condition as well and really is a credit to the previous owner's work. Paddy believes that some of the condition is down to the Bourne-supplied bodyshell – these seem to be a bit heavier and very well made compared to the lighter and possibly more flimsy Lotus shells.

Paddy has used the car extensively since he bought it, and even pressed it into service as his regular commuter for a few years, covering the 10 or so miles between Woking and Guildford. A couple of memorable longer trips have stayed with him. Firstly, he had a wonderful 140 mile drive from Woking down to Wiscombe Park in Southleigh, Devon – the site of the famous hillclimb. There, he was filmed taking runs up and down the hillclimb course – actually the drive to big house – to take part in a BBC documentary on great British sports cars. Unfortunately, the programme never made it to the screen, but Paddy still remembers wondering if he had made a mistake as he sped past a

Paddy's Series 1 Elan interior is pretty original and in great condition. The thin rimmed steering wheel with alloy slotted spokes is lovely.

Under the bonnet, Paddy's Series 1 is as immaculate as the exterior. Note the grey paint; Bourne bodies Elans were finished in a grey gel coat.

From the rear, Paddy's Series 1 displays its separate round rear and indicator lights, and the boot lid which sits in a well on the rear deck.

gritting lorry with his roof down as he started the journey. Luckily, the decent heater in the Elan was working well and he made it down to the venue without having to erect the roof! The second was a brisk 125 mile run up to Droitwich, to take part in an *Absolute Lotus* magazine photoshoot. Again this was a lovely run in decent weather, and the 200-or-so mile round trip gave him plenty of time to savour to delights of driving such a pure example of the genius of Colin Chapman and Ron Hickman.

On the road, Paddy's Elan is a revelation. It is mechanically quiet, virtually vibration-free, and drives smoothly. Its ride is excellent, even over Surrey's somewhat dodgy roads, and the handling is spot on – just how a well set up and well maintained Elan should be. There are no bangs or clunks, and not even any rattles. With the roof down, the lack of window frames on the Series 1 and 2 cars help to give that great British sports car feel of open air motoring with nothing (apart from the windscreen) getting in the way of the views, smells, and noises of the British countryside. All in all, the car gives a great impression of what a revelation the Elan must had been to the public brought up on the rather less refined sports cars that the rest of the British motor industry was producing at the time.

Based on his restoration and driving experiences, Paddy's best tip for Elan owners is to drive the car often. This helps to keep the car in fine fettle and running properly. Remember that back in the day the Elan would have been a daily driver, and like all classic cars benefits from regular use.

# Originality Guide

## INTRODUCTION

The Elan and +2 were the product of a relatively small company, handling volumes that were orders of magnitude smaller than a mass manufacturer of the time. Hence specification changes could, and did, occur at apparently random times during the production run. This is not a surprise, or uncommon for the time. Large manufacturers had well-defined processes for introducing changes, along with tightly controlled ordering and production schedules, and well-designed, highly-automated production lines. In the UK, most car and motorcycle manufacturers operated on a yearly cycle for production. The production schedule would usually start during August, after the workers' one- or two-week summer holiday, and there would be a tightly controlled schedule of parts and components to be delivered to the operational production line over the following 50 weeks. This would continue until the next holiday period, when the factory lines would be shut down, maintenance carried out on the line itself, and the line could be rejigged for the next year's production. This was usually the time that changes were introduced to the product to create the 'next year's model.' This meant that the major manufacturers would have to have a compelling reason for introducing a change to the models scheduled to be built, as it would disrupt the carefully laid-out production plans, and these changes were rare. By contrast, Lotus was not producing anywhere near so many cars, was buying in components probably on a weekly or monthly cycle, and

➤ Paddy Byers' Series 1 Elan is a fine example of an early Bourne-bodied car. While not completely original – with its 26R style front bumper and wings that give room for slightly wider tyres – the car is a fine example of the early Elan.

had a relatively simple, mainly manual production line. This meant it could, and did, introduce changes to production models relatively easily and frequently. Changes could come as a result of an upgrade to a component, or to replace one component with a different one – if, for example, the manufacturer of the original component ceased production, or had none in stock when Lotus needed it.

This means that identifying specific change points to Elans and +2s can be problematic. While the literature – in the form of parts manuals and press releases – will give details of changes, dates and numbers relating to when they were introduced, Lotus' historical records are far from complete, and the only certainty is that if you identify a change point, there will be cars either side of it which have the 'wrong' parts fitted! When new components were introduced, any existing stock of old components would have tended to be used up before the new parts were actually fitted to a production car. As an example, early Series 2 Elans retained the Series 1's separate round rear light clusters, and early coupés used the Series 1- and 2-style boot lid hinges.

Additional problems arise with cars that were produced for one market, not shipped, and then converted in the factory for an alternative market – there are a number of left-hand drive +2s that were originally produced for the US market, but which were not shipped and instead converted later to right-hand drive and UK specification, before being released back onto the UK market as new cars, sometimes with new VIN numbers issued.

The Elan Sprint also had the same sort of thing done to it. When the Sprint was introduced, the first models on the market were revamped Series 4 Elans which – as demand had waned for the model – had been unsold and stockpiled at the factory. So, cars built as Series 4 Elans were reintroduced into the production line, had their undersides painted white, Sprint decals applied, and a Sprint-specification head fitted, along with a few other parts, to make them into Sprints.

So the one definitive thing that can be said about Elan and +2 originality is that no matter how much research is done, as soon as you come up with a 'definitive' statement, someone will pop up with a car which disproves it. As a result, treat the rest of this chapter a guide; there is no definitive source for Elan and +2 originality, but hopefully the following is as close as any!

The last of the Elan family was the +2S 130/5. This is Jon Bradbury's example, resplendent in its Roman Purple paintwork with contrasting silver metal flake roof.

The last Elan was the Sprint with its Big Valve engine. Typically these cars were finished in two-tone, with a white bottom half separated from the coloured top by a gold stripe. The factory charged extra for single colour paintwork.

## ELAN AND +2 PRODUCTION HISTORY OVERVIEW

### ELAN PRODUCTION

The Elan was in production from January 1963 through to March 1973, when the final Sprint was produced. +2 production started in September 1967 and continued through to December 1974, when the final S 130 rolled off the line. The Elan was produced in five versions by Lotus: the first simply named the Elan 1600 (retrospectively named the Series 1), then the Series 2, 3, and 4, with the final version called the Sprint. Three separate Lotus model, or type, numbers were assigned to the Elan. The Series 1 and Series 2 cars were the Type 26, and were both soft tops, but could be fitted with an optional bolt-on hard top. The Elan fixed head coupé was the Type 36, and the Series 3, 4, and Sprint convertibles were Type 45.

The prototype Type 26 Series 1 appeared in October 1962, and was originally named the Elan 1500 due to the first Twin-cam engines having a capacity of 1498cc. The capacity of the Twin-cam engine was quickly raised to the 1558cc found in production versions, and the first production models were on sale in January 1963 with the larger engine, badged as the Elan 1600. The five pre-production Elans equipped with the original engine had their engines replaced with the larger version by the factory. Production of the retrospectively-named Series 1 continued through to November 1964, at which point the Type 26 Elan Series 2 was introduced – though the changes from the Series 1 to 'full' Series 2 specification were introduced piecemeal during December 1964 and January 1965. The most obvious change – the switch from individual round rear lights and indicators to oval-shaped Vauxhall Victor integrated light clusters – did not occur for a couple of months. The first car fitted with them, according to the Type 26 Registry, was 26/4127. The last Series 2 was produced in June 1966.

The Type 36 Series 3 fixed head coupé was introduced in September 1965 with a completely new bodyshell. The replacement for the Series 2 soft top was the Type 45 Series 3 drop head coupé (DHC), which was introduced in June 1966 and shared the FHC moulds less the roof

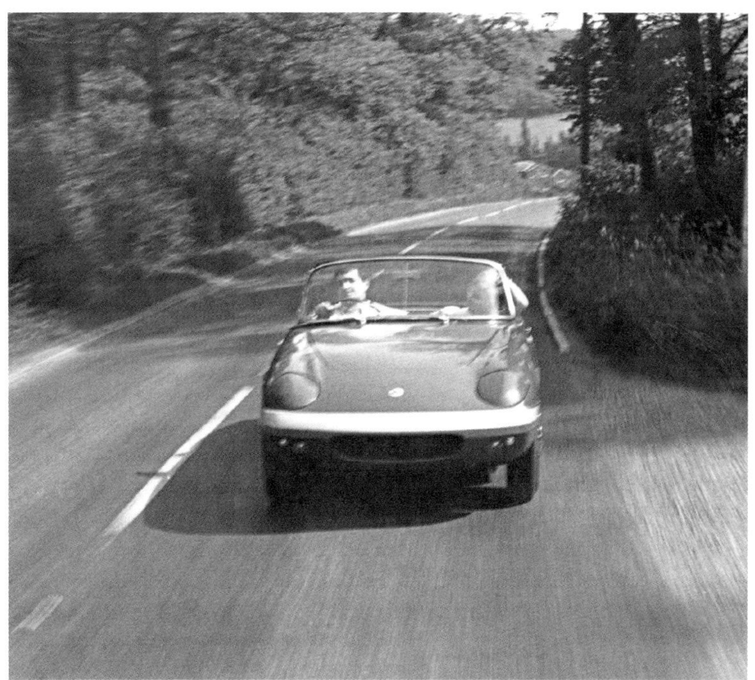

▲ Contemporary picture of an early Elan 1600 (aka the Series 1) on the road.

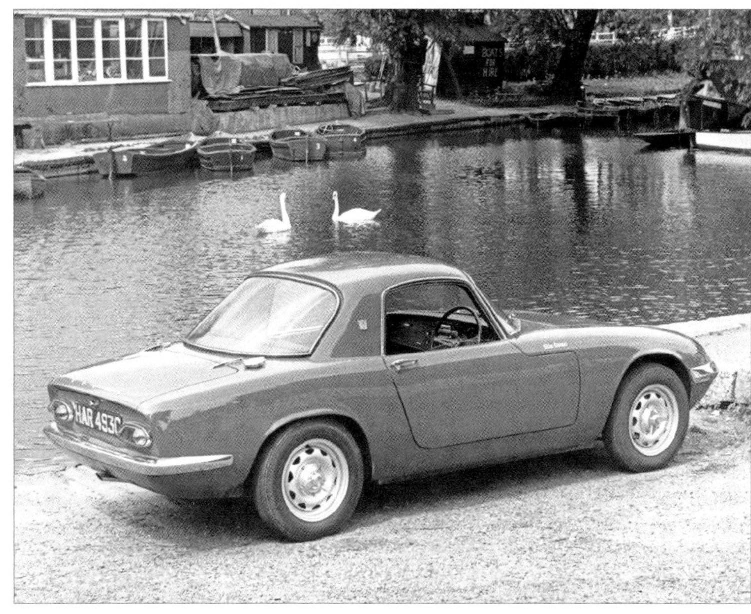


▲ Factory shot of the first of the Elan coupés. This particular model was the press car, and was fitted with experimental chromed plastic bumpers that were not a success, and never actually offered to the public. (Courtesy Lotus Cars)

moulding to produce the DHC. The Series 4 coupé (Type 36) and DHC (Type 45) were introduced in March 1968, with mainly cosmetic changes, including larger oblong rear light clusters shared with the +2. The final iteration of the Type 36 FHC and Type 45 DHC was the Sprint, with production starting in January 1971 and first deliveries during February 1971. Note that there were a significant number of Series 4 cars converted to Sprint specification by the factory to shift stocks of unsold Series 4s held in stock. The final version of the Elan, the Elan Sprint/5, which was fitted with the Lotus 5 speed gearbox was announced in the Lotus press release for the October 1972 Earls Court motor show, but only a handful were produced by the factory.

Research by Tim Wilkes and documented on the Elan Sprint website (see Chapter 6) indicates that the last Elan, a Sprint, was made in March 1973.

| | SERIES 1 & 2 | SERIES 3 & 4 | SPRINT |
|---|---|---|---|
| **ENGINE** | | | |
| *Type* | Lotus Twin-cam | | |
| *Block material* | Cast iron | | |
| *Head material* | Die-cast alloy | | |
| *Cylinders* | 4 in-line | | |
| *Cooling* | Centrifugal pump with water/antifreeze mix | | |
| *Bore and stroke* | 82.5x72.8mm | | |
| *Capacity* | 1558cc | | |
| *Valves* | 2 valves per cylinder, operated by bucket tappets from twin chain-driven overhead camshafts | | |
| *Compression ratio* | 9.5:1 | | 10.5:1 |
| *Carburettor* | Twin Weber 40 DCOE Twin-Choke | 1969/70: Twin Stromberg CD 175 | 1973: Twin Dellorto DHLA 40 Twin-Choke |
| *Max power* | Standard: 105bhp @ 6000rpm<br>SE: 115bhp @ 6000rpm | | 126bhp @ 6500rpm |
| *Max torque* | 108lb/ft @ 4500rpm (Standard and SE) | | 113lb/ft @ 5500rpm |
| **TRANSMISSION** | | | |
| *Gearbox* | Ford four-speed | | |
| *Clutch* | Single dry plate | | |
| *Ratios: 1st* | 2.97:1 | | |
| *2nd* | 2.01:1 | | |
| *3rd* | 1.40:1 | | |
| *4th* | 1.00:1 | | |
| *Reverse* | 2.79:1 | | |
| *Final drive* | 3.77:1<br>3.5:1 (Optional) | | |
| **SUSPENSION AND STEERING** | | | |
| *Front* | Independent by upper and lower wishbones, coil springs, anti-roll bar | | |
| *Rear* | Independent by wide-spaced lower wishbone and strut | | |
| *Steering* | Rack and pinion | | |

| | SERIES 1 & 2 | SERIES 3 & 4 | SPRINT |
|---|---|---|---|
| *Tyres* | 145x13 | 155x13 | |
| *Wheels* | Pressed steel, bolt-on<br>Steel, knock-on (Optional) | | Steel, knock-on |
| *Rim width* | 6in | | |
| BRAKES | | | |
| *Front* | 9.5in (241mm) diameter disc | | |
| *Rear* | 10in (254mm) diameter disc | | |
| DIMENSIONS | | | |
| *Track: Front* | 47.5in (1206mm) | | |
| *Track: Rear* | 47.5in (1206mm) | | |
| *Wheelbase* | 84in (2133mm) | | |
| *Overall length* | 145in (3683mm) | | |
| *Overall width* | 56in (1422mm) | | |
| *Overall height* | 41in (1041mm) | | |
| *Kerb weight* | 1516lb (687kg) | 1560lb (707kg) | |
| *Fuel capacity* | 10gal (45.4L) | | |
| APPROX PERFORMANCE | | | |
| *Top speed* | 112mph (180.2km/h) | SE: 117mph (188.3km/h) | 121mph (195.7km/h) |
| *0-60mph* | 10.0s | SE: 8.1s | 6.7s |

## +2 PRODUCTION

There were four +2 models produced by the factory, and all shared the same model or type number of 50. However, the change-over dates between the four models were not as clean as those for the Elan, with significant overlaps in production dates occurring. The first model produced was simply named the +2, although some early adverts promoted it as the '+2 SE' – this simply reflected the fact that all early +2s were fitted with the SE spec Twin-cam engine.

In March 1968 the company adopted a modified bodyshell, generally known as the 'Federal' body, with various changes needed to meet US market safety

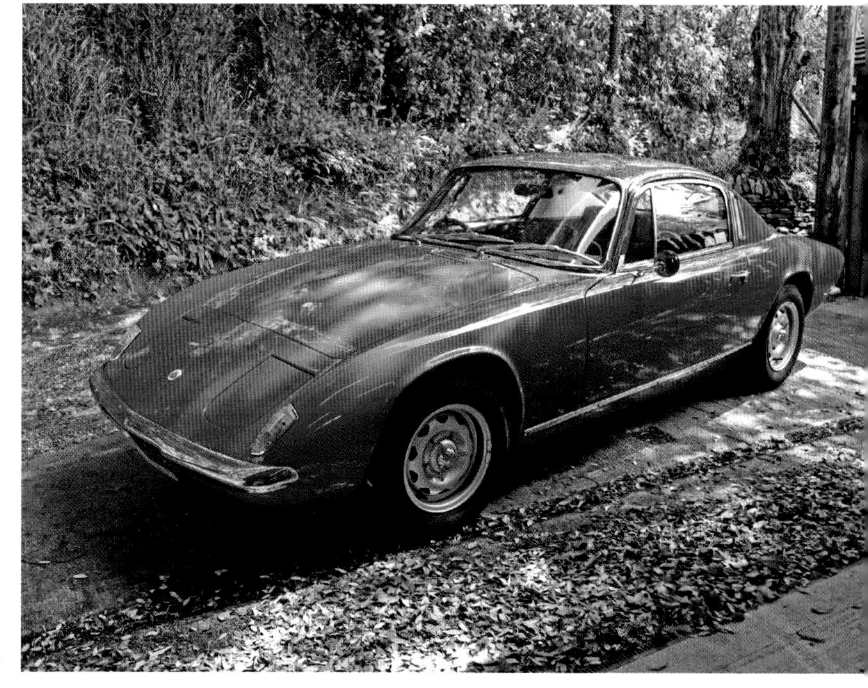

Melody and Henry Kozlowski's +2 was the 60th off the production line, first registered in October 1967, and is a very original car. Note the lack of front fog and spotlights, and the combined door handle and lock. ➤

The +2S 130/5 was fitted with a Lotus five-speed gearbox and the Big Valve Sprint-specification engine. This is Jon Bradbury's fine example on a rainy day on the West Sussex downs.

standards. However, this did not result in any name changes. In March 1969 Lotus introduced the +2S, with its much more luxurious interior and new badging. The original +2 continued in production for some time alongside the S, and was eventually discontinued in December 1969. At the time, Lotus was trying to move away from its kit car past, and the +2S was publicised as being the first Lotus not available in kit form. The impending changes to the UK tax regime would also have had some effect, as the introduction of Value Added Tax in January 1973 removed the tax exempt status of the kit car – effectively killing the kit car market stone dead. The introduction of the Big Valve engine, with a corresponding performance boost, came in January 1971, and gave rise to the ungainly +2S 130 moniker. This was followed in October 1972 with the optional five-speed gearbox, giving the model designation +2S 130/5. Production of the +2 ended in December 1974.

| | +2 | +2S | +2S 130 |
|---|---|---|---|
| **ENGINE** | | | |
| *Type* | Lotus Twin-cam | | |
| *Block material* | Cast iron | | |
| *Head material* | Die cast alloy | | |
| *Cylinders* | 4 in-line | | |
| *Cooling* | Centrifugal pump with water/antifreeze mix | | |
| *Bore and stroke* | 82.55x72.75mm | | |
| *Capacity* | 1558cc | | |
| *Valves* | 2 valves per cylinder, operated by bucket tappets from twin chain-driven overhead camshafts | | |
| *Compression ratio* | 9.5:1 | | 10.3:1 |
| *Carburettor* | Twin Weber 40 DCOE Twin-Choke | 1969/70: Twin Stromberg CD 175 | 1973-on: Twin Dellorto DHLA 40 Twin-Choke |
| *Max power* | 115bhp @ 6000rpm | | 126bhp @ 6500rpm |
| *Max torque* | 108lb/ft @ 4000rpm | | 113lb/ft @ 5500rpm |
| **TRANSMISSION** | | | |
| *Gearbox* | Ford four-speed | | |
| *Clutch* | Single dry plate | | |
| *Ratios: 1st* | 2.97:1 | | |
| *2nd* | 2.01:1 | | |

| | +2 | +2S | +2S 130 |
|---|---|---|---|
| *3rd* | 1.40:1 | | |
| *4th* | 1.00:1 | | |
| *Reverse* | 2.79:1 | | |
| *Final drive* | 3.77:1<br>3.5:1 (Optional) | | |
| **OPTIONAL LOTUS FIVE-SPEED GEARBOX** | | | |
| *Ratios: 1st* | N/A | | 3.20:1 |
| *2nd* | N/A | | 2.01:1 |
| *3rd* | N/A | | 1.37:1 |
| *4th* | N/A | | 1.00:1 |
| *5th* | N/A | | 0.80:1 |
| *Reverse* | N/A | | 3.46:1 |
| *Final drive* | N/A | | 3.77:1<br>3.55:1 (Optional) |
| **SUSPENSION AND STEERING** | | | |
| *Front* | Independent by upper and lower wishbones, coil springs, anti-roll bar | | |
| *Rear* | Independent by wide-spaced lower wishbone and strut | | |
| *Steering* | Rack and pinion | | |
| *Tyres* | 165x13 | | |
| *Wheels* | Steel, knock-on | Steel, knock-on<br>Alloy, knock-on (Optional) | |
| *Rim width* | 6in | | |
| **BRAKES** | | | |
| *Front* | 9.5in (241mm) diameter disc | | |
| *Rear* | 10in (254mm) diameter disc | | |
| **DIMENSIONS** | | | |
| *Track: Front* | 54in | | |
| *Track: Rear* | 55in | | |
| *Wheelbase* | 96in | | |
| *Overall length* | 168.75in (3200mm) | | |
| *Overall width* | 66.25in (1682mm) | | |
| *Overall height* | 47in (1194mm) | | |
| *Kerb weight* | 2086lb (946kg) | | |
| **APPROX PERFORMANCE** | | | |
| *Top speed* | 123mph (197km/h) | | |
| *0-60mph* | 9.4s | | |

## APPROXIMATE PRODUCTION NUMBERS

The actual number of Elans and +2s made is a matter for much conjecture and debate. However, research into the known Elan and +2 VINs, and the incomplete factory records by Tim Wilkes and published in the January 2015 *Club Lotus* magazine, shows that approximately 9205 Elans were built between 1963 and 1973. This was split into:

| | |
|---|---|
| Series 1: | 899 |
| Series 2: | 1911 |
| Series 3: | 2084 |
| Series 4 and Sprint: | 4311 |

The figures also indicate that about 5244 +2s of all types were produced between 1968 and the end of production in 1974. This gives an estimated 14,449 Elans and +2s produced in total. A further issue was the reworking of cars by the factory – both Elans and +2s – whereby cars stockpiled at the factory were modified. This was done either by converting them from left- to right-hand drive, or updating them to the then-current specification – for example, from Series 4 to Sprint specification – and then assigning a new VIN number to the car. It is possible that around 202 such cars were produced, which reduces the overall Elan and +2 production from 14,449 to 14,247.

Tim Wilkes' research also shows that 438 Bourne bodies were produced for Lotus during 1962 and 1963, and the contract with Bourne was terminated in the autumn of 1963, when Lotus took body production in-house. After that date, Elans were produced using either Borne- or Lotus-produced bodies until the stock of Bourne bodies was used up.

## ELAN AND +2 VEHICLE IDENTIFICATION NUMBERS

### INTRODUCTION

All Elans and +2s were identified by their chassis or vehicle identification number (VIN). In compiling this guide to originality the author has relied on a number of sources of information, including original Lotus parts lists and the members of the lotuselan.net forums. As mentioned previously, the only certainty of Lotus 'change points' for components is that as soon as you define a point, someone will surface with proof that it is wrong! This is a reflection of

⮝ This contemporary view of a Series 1 Elan shows the profile of the wheelarches, as well as the bolt-on wheels with their Lotus-embossed chromed hub caps.

⮜ Taken in-period, this picture shows a pair of Series 3 Elans – a coupé and a drop head – in the Cheshunt factory grounds. SAR 120D was the press coupé; note the lack of grilles on its B-pillar, indicating it is a pre-airflow car, and the window surrounds on the drop head that indicate it is a Series 3 car.

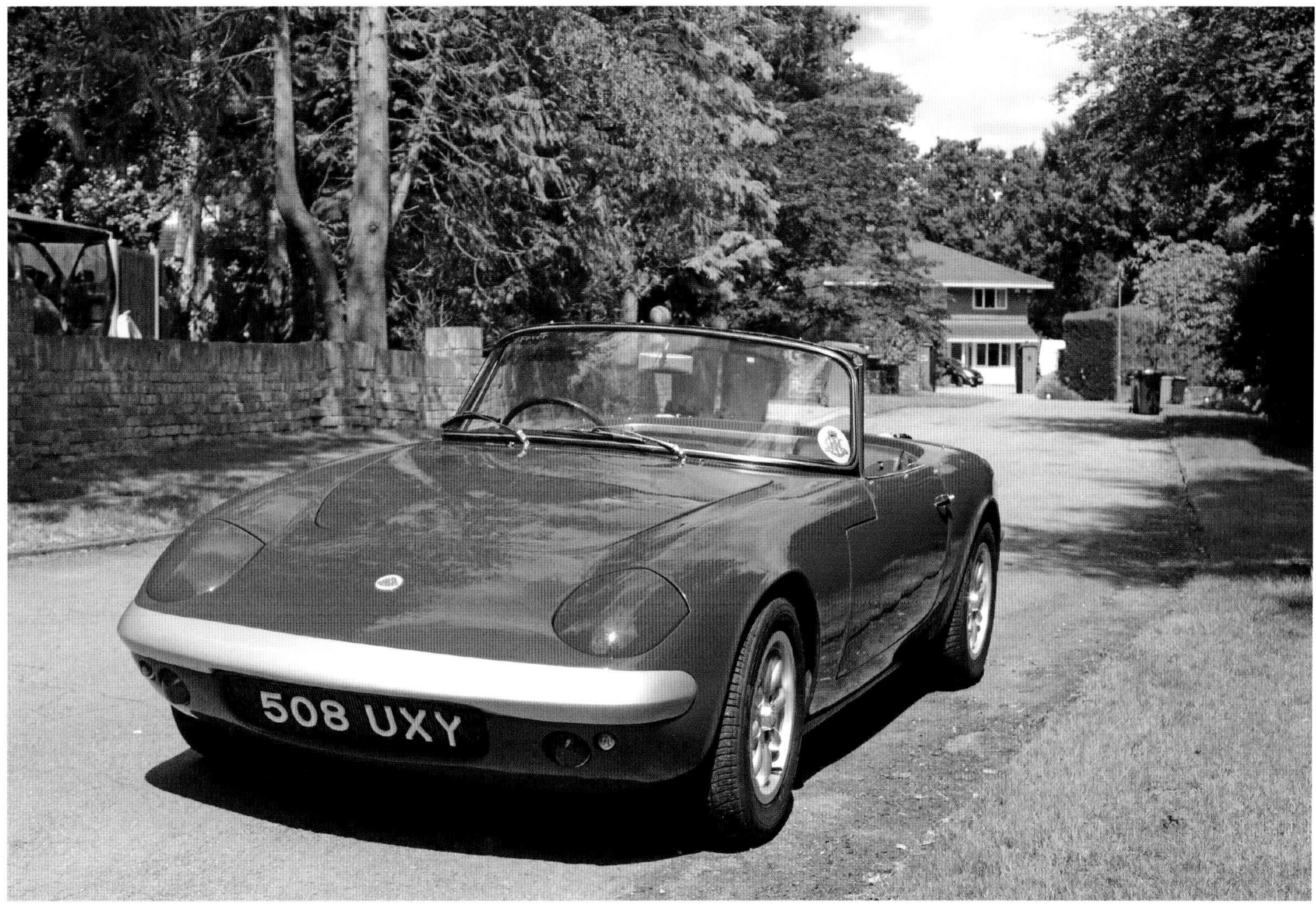


In contrast, Paddy Byers' Series 1 Elan shows its slightly widened wheelarches and shortened 26R front bumper – both common modifications back in the 1960s, especially on race cars.

Lotus' evolution; when the Elan was introduced they were already approaching capacity in the Cheshunt works, and with the move to Hethel in late 1966, the need to maintain production will have resulted in anomalies.

This, combined with the need to keep the production line going when supplies of a component were getting low; the release of cars in kit form resulting in them being registered much later than the factory build date, and the various wheezes indulged by Lotus to shift stocks of unsold cars when the market was flat, resulted in all sorts of anomalies.

The history of the cars is also confused by Lotus changing the format of the VIN number to conform to international standards in 1970. So, while the information in this book is as accurate as the author could achieve at the time of writing, do not regard it as gospel!

## LOTUS VEHICLE TYPE NUMBERING

All Lotus models were assigned a 'type' number from the start of the company. Numbers were assigned in chronological order, according to when development of the model started, and in the early days the type number was often used as the model name. So, for example, the first 'mass' production Lotus was the Type 6, also known as the Lotus 6, and was eventually superseded by the Type 7, or Lotus Seven. Conversely, the original Lotus Elite was Type 14, breaking from this pattern and setting the theme for Lotus road cars having names beginning with 'E.' The Elan Series 1 and Series 2 were both assigned 26 as their type number. The design changes that resulted in the Series 3 fixed head coupé merited a new type number, and as the next number in line was '36,' all subsequent fixed head coupés, whether Series 3, 4, or Sprint, were assigned that number. The Series 3 drop head coupé appeared a year or so after the coupé, and, along with the Series 4 and Sprint DHC, was assigned Type 45. Finally, the +2 was assigned Type 50, which applied to all of the various models under that banner.

## VEHICLE IDENTIFICATION NUMBERING

The original format for the Lotus vehicle identification number was simple – the type code was followed by a four digit number that increased with each vehicle produced. So, as the original Elan was Type 26, the first car's VIN number was 26/0001. The first major change was introduced after 49 of the cars had been produced, at which point Lotus changed the format of the four digit number, replacing the first '0' with a '3' but otherwise continuing the sequence, to give the format '3050.' However, this change was introduced piecemeal, with some cars coming out of the factory numbered '0nnn' and others as '3nnn' (with 'n' representing a digit). The Series 2 continued the sequence, starting at 26/3901. The first Elan coupé, Type 36, had the VIN format 36/4510, indicating that the sequence of numbers was shared between the two models, and the Series 3 drop head coupé, Type 45, started at 45/5704. The Series 4 cars retained the numbers from the Series 3 Type 36 FHC and Type 45, and the sequence continued from 7895.

The +2 was the Type 50, and when it was introduced in 1968 it followed the same format as the original Elan, with 50/0001. When the +2S was introduced in October 1969,

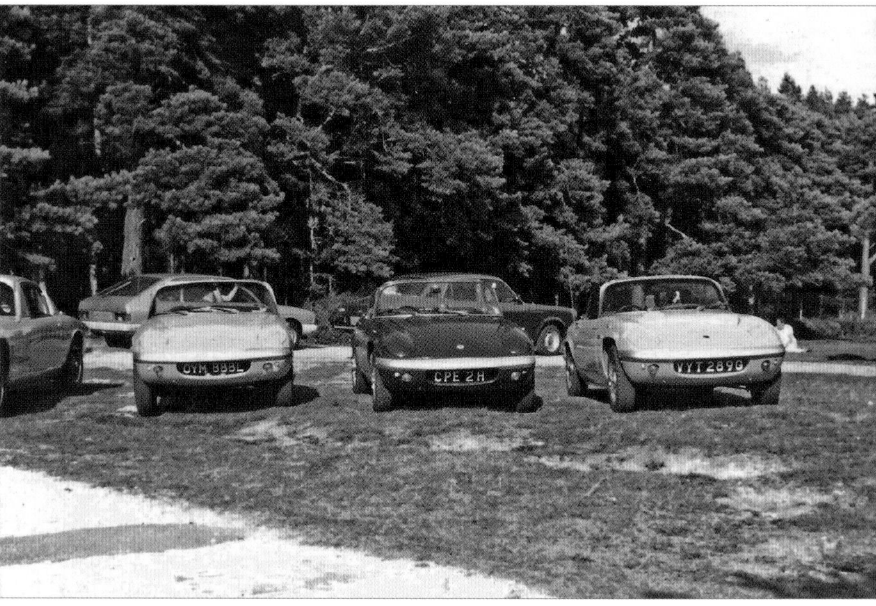


John Humfryes' Elan Series 4 (on the right) is parked up in the New Forest with his mates' Series 4 Elans, in the 1970s. The +2 on the far left is in the rare Lotus colour Colorado Orange.

Jon Bradbury's +2S 130/5 is a nice example of a late +2. The Roman Purple is a Lotus colour; though not original to the car, it really sums up the spirit of the 1970s.

the number sequence was shared between the two models. This continued until the final +2, 50/2407, was produced in December 1969, at which point the sequence continued with the +2S exclusively.

From 1970 onwards the vehicle identification code was redefined, with the resulting VIN looking something like '70.01.010001A.' This format can be broken down like so:

| | |
|---|---|
| 70 | Year of manufacture – ie 1970 |
| . | |
| 01 | Month of manufacture – ie January |
| . | |
| 01 | Production batch |
| 0001 | Unit or chassis number |
| A | Model identification code |

For the Elan and +2, the model identification code comprised A to N, but missing out 'I' to avoid confusion with the number '1.' See following table for a definition of each model.

| MODEL CODE | MODEL | FHC OR DHC | MARKET |
|---|---|---|---|
| A | Elan Standard | FHC | UK |
| B | Elan Standard | FHC | Export |
| C | Elan Standard | DHC | UK |
| D | Elan Standard | DHC | Export |
| E | Elan Special Equipment | FHC | UK |
| F | Elan Special Equipment | FHC | Export |
| G | Elan Special Equipment | DHC | UK |
| H | Elan Special Equipment | DHC | Export |
| J | Elan Federal | FHC | Export (USA) |
| K | Elan Federal | DHC | Export (USA) |
| L | Elan +2S | n/a | UK |
| M | Elan +2S Federal | n/a | Export |
| N | Elan +2S Federal | n/a | Export (USA) |

The code changed again in late 1972, when the two digit production batch number was dropped. This was done in two 'phases': cars produced from the introduction of the change through to an unspecified point early in 1973 had a single '0' between the date code and the unit number (to give a format of '73.01.09999X'). The single '0' was then also dropped, leaving the code in the format '73.01.9999X,' with the year and month taking the first four digits, the unit number the second set of four, and the model identification code as the last letter.

## RACING ELANS

During 1964 and 1965 Lotus produced around 100 racing Elans, and they were called the Type 26R. Approximately the first 50 were based on the Series 1 Elan, with the remaining 50 based on Series 2 cars. The numbering applied to the these cars was in the form '26/R/nnn' for Series 1-based cars, or '26R/S2/nnn' for the Series 2. The VIN plate was a Lotus Components item. All the racing Elans were given numbers from the standard Lotus production – there were no duplications of the number across the two types of car.

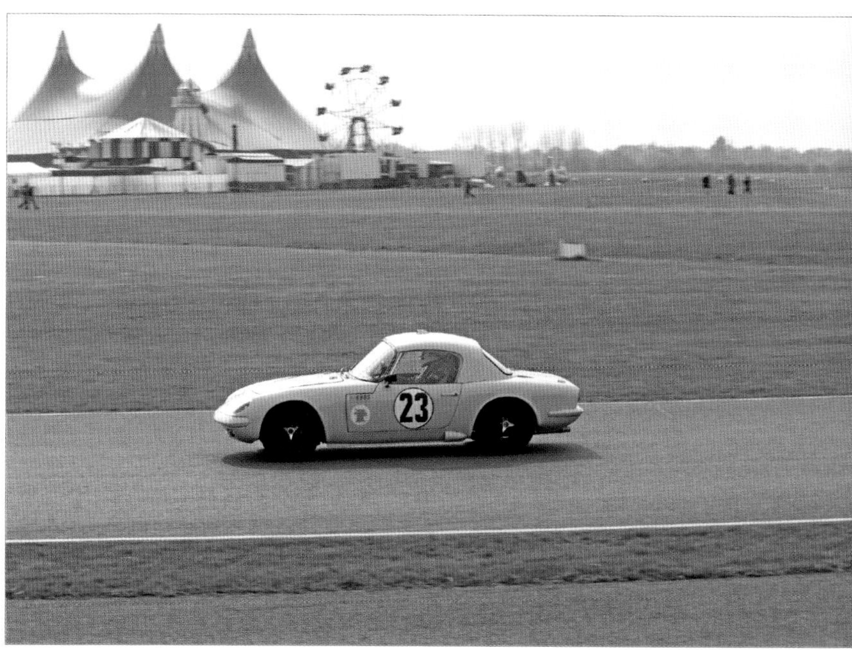


Elans are still raced today. This is Antony Hopkins on the track in a 26R at Goodwood's 77th Members' Meeting.

The late Peter Shaw's Elan GTS. This was used in historic racing, and is a modern evocation of the 26R.

## ENGINE NUMBERING

The engine numbering system was slightly clearer than the unit number. First off, in some cases the engine number was included on the car's data plate. This usually occurred if the car was delivered complete from the factory; kits would have the engine number space on the VIN plate left blank. As a result, all +2S and +2S 130 cars would have the engine number on the data plate, as would most (if not all) export cars. Home-model Elans – from the S1 to the Sprint and the +2 – could be purchased either complete or as kits, so may or may not have the original engine number inscribed on the plate.

## PARTS NUMBERING

All Lotus parts were assigned a part number by Lotus, even if they were re-using other manufacturers' parts. Many parts were shared between the Elan and the +2, and some were also shared with the Europa. The part number allocated by Lotus reflects the first model that used the part, and this part number remained the same across the range. All Lotus part numbers commenced with the model number of the car they were first used on, so a prefix of '026,' '036' or '045' indicates that the part was first used on the Elan: '026' for the Series 1 or Series 2; '036' for the Series 3, Series 4 and Sprint coupé; and '045' for the S3, S4 and Sprint DHC. The +2 in all its guises was only allocated the '050' code. So, as an example, the part number '026 E 0014' was given to the engine's cam chain guide. This was first used on the Elan S1, and the same part number remained the same when it was used on models from the Elan S2 to the Sprint, and all the +2 variants. Conversely, part number '050 B 6138' relates to the ambient temperature gauge, which was only fitted to the +2S and S 130, so gains the +2 '050' model designation.

The only parts not numbered by model type are non-specialist fixtures and fittings, such as nuts, bolts, washers and screws. For these, Lotus devised a system – the Standard Hardware Part Number Coding – that would identify the specification of the particular part. The code comprised eight letters and figures, and were applied to all off-the-shelf fasteners that had standard shank lengths, material specifications and finish. So specialist items – such as head bolts and suspension fixing bolts, which could be high tensile items or have unique dimensions (or both) – were assigned specific Lotus part numbers.

The code for standard fasteners has the format 'ABCD 1234,' and breaks down as follows:

The first letter ('A' in the example above) specifies what type of fastener it is:

| TYPE | DESCRIPTION |
|---|---|
| X | Hexagon-head bolt |
| R | Round-head bolt |
| M | Mushroom-head bolt |
| C | Cheese-head bolt |
| P | Plain screw |
| K | Flat-head countersunk screw |
| D | Raised-head countersunk screw |
| S | Stud |
| L (Nut) | Self-Locking nut |
| A (Nut) | Plain nut |
| Y (Nut) | Nyloc nut |
| L (Washer) | Shake-proof washer |
| A (Washer) | Plain washer |

The second and third letters or digits ('BC' in the example) specify the thread form/type:

| THREAD FORM | DESCRIPTION |
|---|---|
| UF | UNF bolt, screw or nut |
| UC | UNC bolt, screw or nut |
| MM | Metric bolt, screw or nut |
| WD | Wood screw |
| ST | Self-tapping screw |
| Two digits | Internal diameter, in 1⁄16in or mm |

The fourth letter ('D' in the example) identifies the type of fastener:

| IDENTIFIER | DESCRIPTION |
|---|---|
| B | Bolt |
| S | Screw |
| N | Nut |
| W | Washer |
| T | Stud |

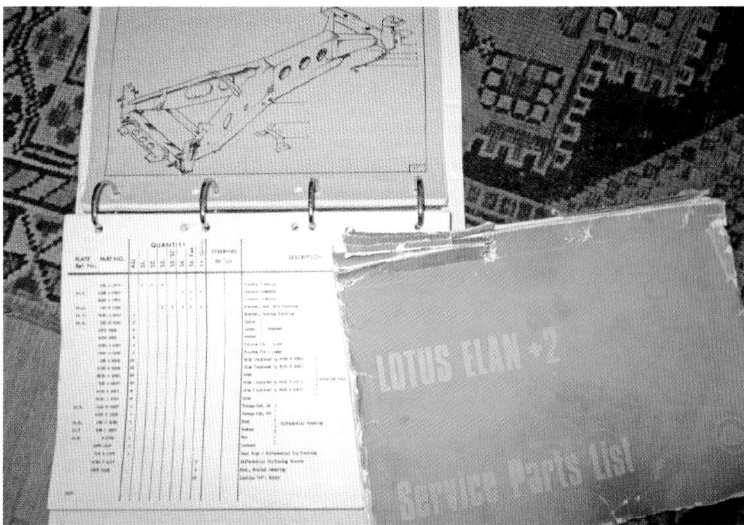


A vital resource to any Elan and +2 owner is the Service Parts List for the car. It provides exploded diagrams of all the car's sub assemblies, which not only identify parts but also how the parts fit together.

The next two digits ('12' in the example) identify various sizes:

| IDENTIFIER | DESCRIPTION |
|---|---|
| Two digits (bolt, screw, nut or stud) | Diameter in 1⁄16in or mm |
| Two digits (plain washer) | Outside diameter, in 1⁄16in or mm |
| 00 | Shake proof washer (all sizes) |
| Two digits (self-tapping and wood screws) | Size |

The last two digits ('34' in the example) identify length, thickness, or type of fastener:

| IDENTIFIER | DESCRIPTION |
|---|---|
| Two digits (bolt or screw) | Length in 1⁄16in or mm |
| 0F or 0H (nuts) | Full or half nut |
| Two digits (plain washer) | Thickness in 0.01in gradients |
| 00 | Shake-proof washer (all sizes) |

For studs only, the last four digits ('1234' in the example) are used to identify thread types:

| IDENTIFIER | DESCRIPTION |
|---|---|
| SUCC | UNC threads each end |
| SUFF | UNF threads both ends |
| SUFC | UNF threads one end, UNC on the other |
| SMMM | Metric threads |

So, a part with the number 'XUFB 0420' can be identified as:
X Hexagon-head bolt
UF UNF thread
B Bolt
04 4⁄16in diameter (ie 1⁄4in)
20 20⁄16in long (ie 1 1⁄4in)

The part is, in fact, the infamous +2 bonnet fixing bolt, voted the most frustrating fixture on the +2 (see Hints and tips in Chapter 3).

## ORIGINALITY: ELAN S1 TO SPRINT
### ELAN FACTORY SPECIFICATIONS

Production of the Elan S1 bodyshell was originally outsourced by Lotus to Bourne Plastics, of Netherfield in Nottingham, some 120 miles north of Cheshunt. Bodyshell production was moved from Bourne Plastics to Cheshunt between October 1963 and January 1964, after between 200 and 300 body shells were produced. Bourne shells have a small badge positioned on the bulkhead in the engine bay, and used a medium grey-coloured gel coat, plus strengthening channels in the floor. The number stamped on a Bourne plate is usually three or so numbers lower than the Lotus VIN number.

Today a certain amount of kudos can be had with Bourne shells, as they are the earliest incarnation of the Elan. However, learning the lesson of the Elite, Chapman always intended that the majority of the Elan would be produced in-house. As the body was the largest and probably the most expensive single component, it was inevitable that production was moved as quickly as possible to Cheshunt, and then Hethel for the remaining life of the Elan – as it was for the other major component, the Twin-cam engine. The +2 body was always produced in-house, and production was scheduled so that it started after the move to Hethel.

A contemporary view of a pair of Elan Series 1 cars in a typically picturesque setting. Note the car on the right has no registration number, and appears to be missing its windscreen!

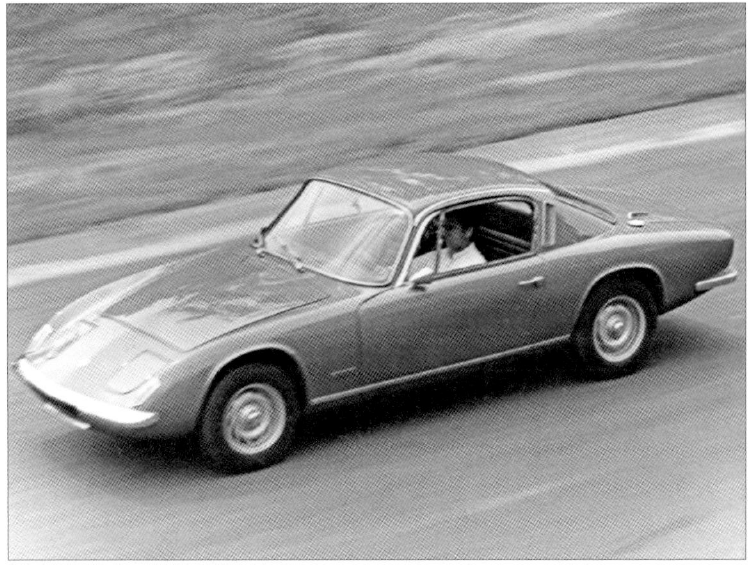

An early +2, identified as such by the lack of spot and fog lights and the one-piece door handle and lock.

## ORIGINAL FINISHES

The main 'finish' of the Elan and the +2 is the paint. However, even here there can be doubt as to the original finish, as some Elans were supplied in primer to dealers. Initially Elan S1s were painted by the factory in the following shades:

| PAINT COLOUR | CODE | ORIGINAL MANUFACTURER |
|---|---|---|
| Medici Blue | ICI P0303192 | Triumph |
| Carmen Red | ICI P0303484 | Jaguar |
| Fiesta Yellow | ICI P0303484 | Austin |
| Ford Sunburst Yellow | Not known | Ford |
| Spruce Green | Not known | BMC |
| Conifer Green | Not known | Triumph |
| Jaguar Racing Green | ICI P0302539 | Jaguar (note this paint is not the same as LO.1 British Racing Green) |

None of the above shades were given actual Lotus paint reference numbers. However, paint codes were fairly quickly introduced after production really got going, and by October 1962 Lotus had its own records for paint used. These are listed below:

| PAINT COLOUR | LOTUS PAINT CODE | OTHER CODES (ICI AND PINCHIN, JOHNSON) | YEAR(S)/ NOTES |
|---|---|---|---|
| British Racing Green | LO.1 | ICI P030 2854 PJ6170 Y2790 | Oct 1962 to Oct 1970 |
| French Blue | LO.2 | ICI P030 7210 PJ 6170 Z1280 | Mid 1967 to Oct 1970 |
| Wedgewood Blue | LO.3 | PJ 6170 Z1290 | Mid 1967 to Oct 1968 |
| Cirrus White | LO.4 | ICI P030 9049 PJ 6170 X0540 | 1962 to Oct 1973 |
| Carnival Red | LO.5 | ICI P030 8385 PJ 6170 X5350 | From 1967 |
| Burnt Sand | LO.6 | ICI P030 8385 PJ 6170 X4570 | 1967 to Oct 1970 |
| Lotus Yellow | LO.7 | ICI P030 9547 PJ 617 X3940 | From 1967 |
| Matt Black | LO.8 | ICI 4523 PJ 0235 X9050RZ | Used in Engine Bay and boot |
| Royal Blue | LO.9 | ICI P030 7557 PJ 6170 Z1920 | Oct 1968 to Oct 1970 |
| Bahama Yellow | LO.10 | ICI P030 6854 PJ 6170 Y3140 | Oct 1968 to Oct 1970 |
| Regency Red (Maroon) | LO.11 | ICI P030 9053 PJ 6170 A1130 | From 1970 |
| Lagoon Blue (Metallic) | LO.12 | ICI P031 4339 PJ 6170 A1130 | From 1970 |
| Pistachio Lime Green | LO.13 | ICI P030 9052 PJ 6170 W2230R1 | From 1970 |
| Colorado Orange | LO.14 | ICI 030 9055 PJ 6170 Z5980RJ | Oct 1970 to Oct 1972 |
| Gloss Black | LO.15 | ICI P030 122 | Sep 1972 to Dec 1973 |
| Ford Tawny (Metallic) | LO.16 | ICI P031 3626 PJ 6170 A4330 | From late 1972 |
| Lotus Renault Mid Green | LO.17 | PJ 6170 A2580 | Not known |
| Glacier Blue | LO.18 | ICI P079 4403 | Not known |
| Sable | LO.19 | ICI P030 7604 | Not known |
| Indigo Blue | LO.20 | Not known | From 1973 |
| Roman Purple | LO.21 | ICI P031 4963 | From 1973 |

Other paint finishes were as follows. The chassis was painted in red oxide, and (in some cases) had a black bituminous coating applied. The radiator shell and core were satin black, as was the inside of the engine bay, although Bourne-bodied cars had grey engine bays. Front suspension wishbones and rear A-frames were stove-enamelled black. The alloy casting of the rear hub was left in its natural alloy, and the steel damper tube which was

⮝ Factory shot of an early Series 1 Elan. Note the 'Elan 1600' badge on the front wing, and the bolt-on wheels and chrome hub caps. (Courtesy Lotus Cars)

fitted into the top of the casting was black. The alloy casting of the differential housing was also in natural alloy, while the nose iron casting was painted black. The engine block head and timing cover was painted a light grey, while the gearbox was usually in a Ford green.

## ELAN: MAJOR CHANGE POINTS

The Series 1 Elan 1600 was produced from early 1962 through to November 1964, when the Series 2 was introduced. The main change and distinguishing feature between the Series 1 and 2 was the new oval one-piece rear light cluster sourced from Vauxhall, which replaced the separate round lights and reflectors fitted to the Series 1. However, the new light was not introduced until chassis number 4127, after a number of Series 2 cars had been built using the Series 1 round rear lights. Knock-on wheels, with their distinctive three-eared spinners, were introduced as an option with the Series 2. Later Federal knock-on

Early Elans had green-painted rocker covers with the Lotus name cast in raised letters, in a script font. Access to the engine and ancillaries in any Elan is tight. ➤

wheels were fitted with an octagonal bolt-on 'spinner' for safety purposes. Some early SS models had three-eared spinners with the ears turned inwards to satisfy the safety requirements.

The Elan coupé, introduced in September 1965, had a new bodyshell that would eventually be passed on to the Series 3 convertible, which was introduced in June 1966, when the Series 2 was discontinued. The Series 3's new bodyshell featured re-profiled wheelarches that were flat-topped and slightly flared to allow for wider tyres. The most obvious change, however, was the redesigned boot lid, which extended over the rear panel and allowed water to drain around the lid and down the back panel, thus eliminating the need for the drain holes and tubes through the boot floor as seen in the Series 1 and 2.

There is some debate as to whether early Series 1 Elans were fitted with separate vacuum tanks for the headlight mechanism. Early cutaway diagrams of the cars show a separate tank mounted in the nose, and some owners report the presence of such tanks. However, some cars had tanks fitted after suffering damage to the front crossmember. Graham Arnold, in his 1981 buyers guide for Club Lotus, says: "... On Elans after 1963 S1 type, check that a vacuum tank has not been fitted due to the failure of the front crossmember vacuum tank through rust penetration," which implies that the Series 1 prior to 1963 *did* have a separate tank. However, on balance, it seems that while the prototype and some pre-production cars were fitted with separate tanks, the production cars were not, and instead used the chassis front crossmember.

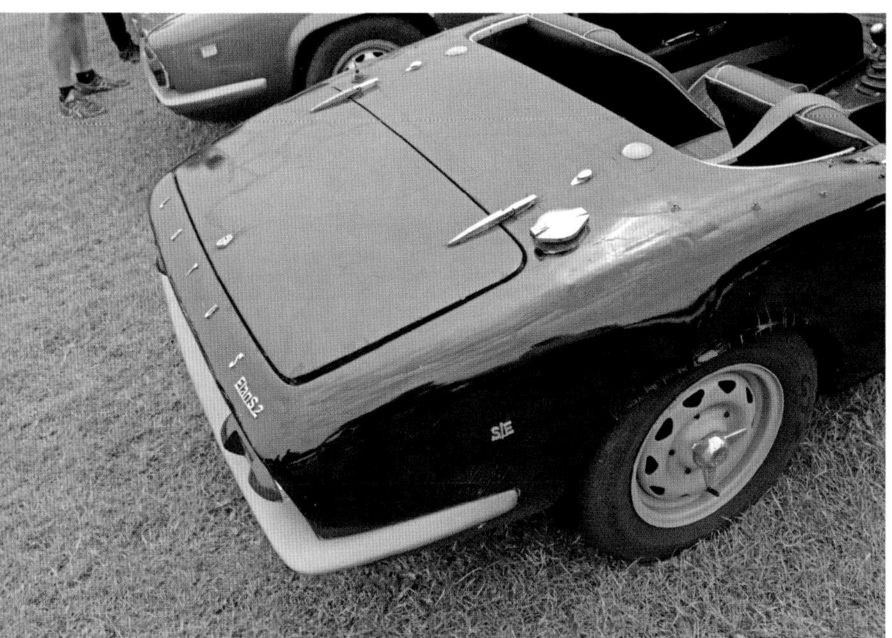


The Series 1 and 2 bodyshell had the boot lid fitted into the rear deck. This necessitated the fitment of a pair of drain pipes in the rear of the well, but the boot was still prone to leaks.

Series 1 and 2 Elans were often fitted with bolt-on wheels. The holes cut into the periphery of the wheel were designed to mirror the shape of the Lotus logo, and this design feature was carried forwards to the knock-on wheels fitted later.

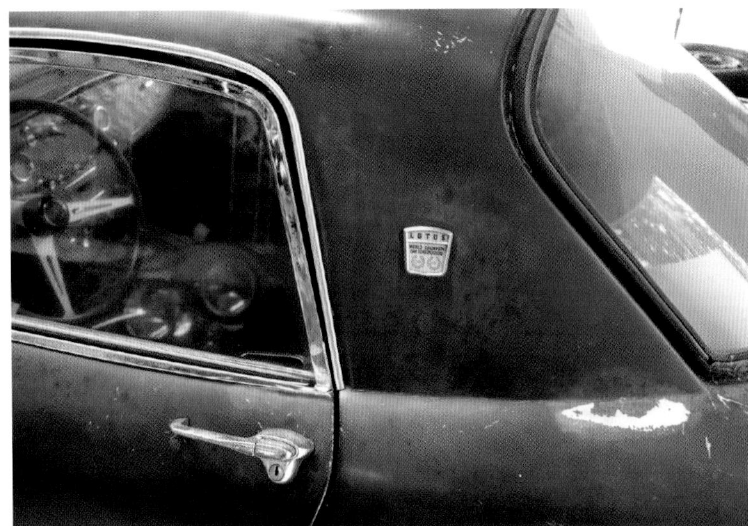

The first of the Elan coupés were not fitted with any extra ventilation other than the standard electric windows. This meant the B-pillar had the space to fit a Lotus 'Shield' badge, which detailed the company's racing successes.

When first introduced, the Elan coupé had no through-flow ventilation system and the B-pillar was plain, with just a shield-shaped badge proclaiming Lotus' Grand Prix wins mounted on it.

From around June 1966, at chassis 36/5811, a through-flow ventilation system was introduced on the coupé, which necessitated the fitment of air extractor grille in each B-pillar.

These were originally flush-fitting chromed items, but were replaced at some stage after the Series 4 was introduced with +2-style recessed cast alloy units. The pillar moulding was modified to feature a small lip in front of the grille to create a low pressure area over the grille, as seen on the +2.

A feature called the 'Hickman Flange' was introduced on the Sprint during production. Originally used on the +2, the Hickman Flange was used to ease production by connecting the boot floor to the rear valance using a flange that could be clamped together, and then taped over quickly and easily during production to provide accurate positioning and a strong bond between the upper and lower mouldings of the bodyshell.

## FEDERAL AND NON-FEDERAL DIFFERENCES

As the US took the lead in vehicle regulation – both for safety and emissions – the Lotus cars destined for the US market had various specification changes made to them. The first specification deviation for cars destined for the US market was the fitment of a pair of extra round red reflectors, which were fitted on the rear of the Series 1, inboard of the rear light and indicator lights. This change

With the introduction of the 'Airflow' through-flow ventilation system, the Elan coupé gained these flush-fitting grilles on the B-pillar that allowed stale air to flow out of the cabin.

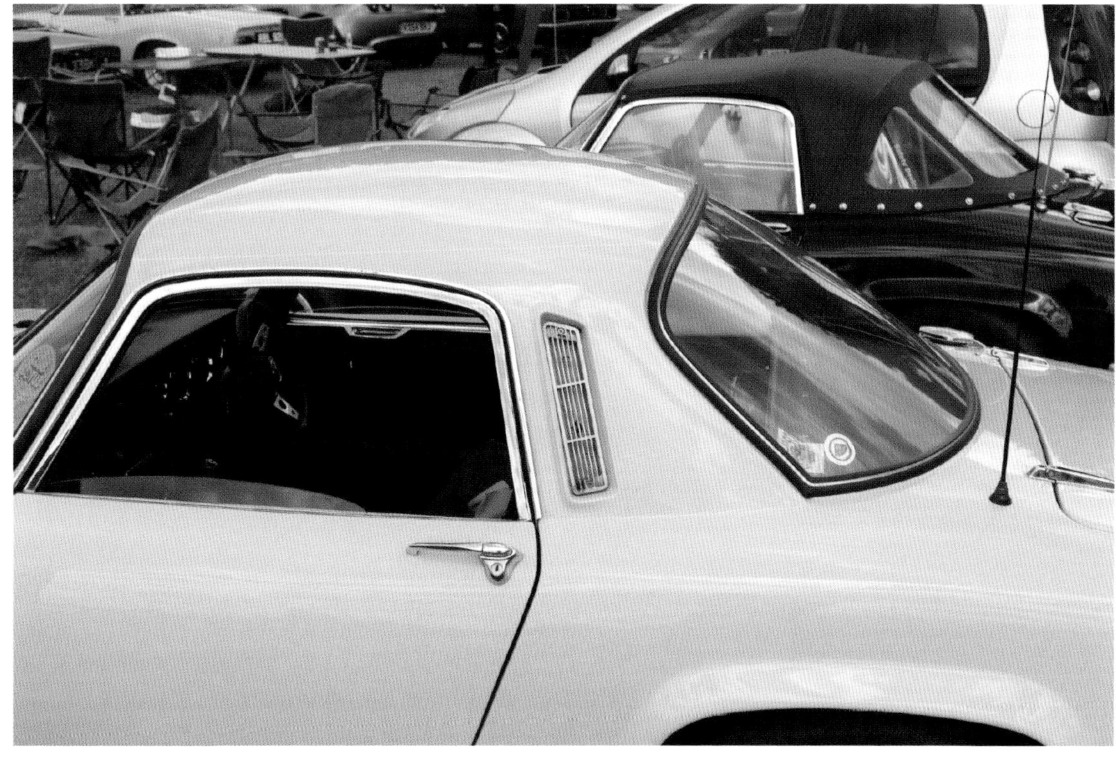

Flush-fitting grilles were replaced with this type, and were also used on the +2. Note the lip in front of the grille, which forced the airflow outwards over the grille, creating a low pressure area and pulling stale air out of the car.

was carried over to the Series 2 prior to fitment of the Vauxhall oval light clusters, which met the requirements. Safety regulations resulted in the 'Super Safety' or 'SS' Elans, which were fitted with flush-fitting switches in the cockpit along with repositioned door handles, and the instruments were recessed into the dash – all measures to protect the driver and passenger from injury on protrusions in the cabin. The main external change was to the wheels; most SS cars appeared to have been supplied with bolt-on wheels, but the few fitted with knock-on wheels had the ears on the spinners reversed, so that they pointed inwards, to avoid injuring passers-by. The interior changes were carried forwards into the Series 4 cars, while the spinners were replaced with octagonal nuts. All the Series 4 cars – for home, export and the US Federal market – also featured anti-burst locks and the infamous British Leyland rectangular flush-fitting interior door handles, while US versions also had hazard warning lights, brake fluid level warning lights, as well as a dual-circuit braking system. The US cars were also the first to get a fail-safe headlamp mechanism, whereby the default position of the headlamp pods was up rather than down. This meant that a vacuum failure did not plunge the driver into darkness at night!

Emissions controls prohibited the escape of petrol fumes into the atmosphere, so the Elan had a closed-circuit system fitted to the fuel tank, which vented into the sealed inlet air box. A charcoal canister captured any fuel vapour while connecting the system to the outside. The emissions control standard necessitated the use of Stromberg carburettors along with a charge warming mechanism. This was basically a pair of pipes which directed the change over the top of the engine to the hot exhaust manifold, where it was warmed up and then returned to the inlet manifold.

## SUMMARY OF ELAN CHANGE POINTS

The following table is the result of analysis of the Elan parts list, and shows at what point significant changes to the Elan's specification were introduced.

| | CHANGE POINT | DETAILS |
|---|---|---|
| **MODEL CHANGES** | | |
| | Chassis no 0001 | First Elan (January 1963) |
| | Chassis no 0049 | Chassis number format changed to 3***, so 0049 becomes 3049 |
| | Chassis no 3901 | Series 2 Elan introduced (November 1964) |
| | Chassis no 4510 | Series 3 fixed head coupé introduced (September 1965) |
| | Chassis no 5702 | Series 3 convertible introduced (June 1966) |
| | Chassis no 5811 | First airflow coupé introduced (June 1966) |
| | Chassis no 7895 | Series 4 fixed head coupé and convertible introduced (March 1968) |
| | Chassis no 71.01 ... | Sprint fixed head coupé and convertible introduced (February 1971) |
| | Chassis no 73.03.0102 | Final Sprint produced (March 1973) |
| **CHASSIS** | | |
| | From chassis no 7000 | Brackets for seatbelt mountings fitted |
| | From chassis no 7895 | Revised chassis upon change to the S4 model . Chassis stiffened by extra welding around the sharp corner on each side where the backbone abuts the closing plate |
| **BODY** | | |
| *Body shell* | Up to chassis no 5810 | Series 1 and Series 2 bodyshell (chassis no 5798 for SE) |
| | From chassis no 5811 | Series 3 coupé and convertible bodyshell |
| | Chassis no 5702 | Series 3 drop head coupé introduced |
| | Chassis no 7895 | Series 4 coupé and convertible bodyshell |
| *Hood* | From chassis no 5811 | Revised hood for Series 3 |
| | From chassis no 7895 | Revised hood for Series 4 |
| *Boot lid* | From chassis no 5811 | New boot lid for S3/S4 bodyshell, along with lock, seal, etc |
| *Bonnet lid* | From chassis no 7894 | Series 4 bonnet with power bulge |
| *Trim* | From chassis no 5811 | Major revisions to interior trim for Series 3 |
| | From chassis no 7894 | Major revisions to interior trim for Series 4 |
| *Air extractor grille* | From chassis no 5811 | Air extractor grille fitted in B-pillar as part of 'airflow' ventilation system. This flush-fitting grille replaced with +2 item at some point on the Series 4. |
| *Dash* | From chassis no 5811 | Series 3 revised dash top crash pad |
| | From chassis no 7400 | Series 3 revised dash top crash pad carried through to Series 4 |
| | From chassis no 6600 | Small 'eye' vents introduced at each side of dash |
| *Door assembly* | From chassis no 5811 | All-new door assembly, including electric windows for Series 3 and Series 4 |
| | Chassis no 7400-7894 | SS door trim and fittings, including flush-mounted interior door handle |
| | From chassis no 7895 | Series 4 door trim and fittings |
| *Vent grille* | From chassis no 8768 | New vent grille ahead of windscreen |

| | CHANGE POINT | DETAILS |
|---|---|---|
| **FRONT SUSPENSION** | | |
| | Front hubs | The front hubs for bolt-on wheels were suplemented by optional knock-on hubs during production of the Series 2 |
| | Front wishbones | At some point in production, lower wishbones were modified to incorporate reinforcing washers to strengthen the hole for the trunnion bolt. Also later top and bottom wishbones were reinforced around the ferrel at the chassis end |
| | From chassis no 9297 | Alternative spring and damper units specified |
| **REAR SUSPENSION AND DRIVESHAFT** | | |
| | From chassis no 7762 | New rear hub assembly, including housing, hub, bearings and outer driveshafts; these later carriers have 'Issue 18' cast into them on the front face below the hub, and utilised improved inner hub bearing. Previous Issue 16 castings had no identifying marks |
| **ENGINE** | | |
| | From engine no LP7799 | Six-bolt crank and flywheel supersedes four-bolt type. New lipped-type crank oil seal replaces rope type |
| | From 1968 | Weber 40 DOCE 18 carburettors replaced with Weber 40 DOCE 31 |
| | From engine no G16000 / chassis no 8600 | Stromberg carburettors replace Webers |
| | Chassis no 9524 | Weber carbs re-introduced on non-Federal cars |
| | Sprint spec | Ported head with larger inlet valves |
| **TRANSMISSION** | | |
| | From Series 3 (chassis no 5811) | Spherical gearlever knob introduced |
| **WHEELS** | | |
| | From S2 SE and S3 coupé | Optional 'knock-on' peg drive steel wheels introduced. New hubs needed to accommodate the wheels |
| | From Sprint | Wheels painted black |
| **STEERING** | | |
| | No significant changes | |
| **BRAKING SYSTEM** | | |
| | From chassis no 4109 | New front callipers fitted |
| | From chassis no 4109 | New 0.7in diameter master cylinder replaced ¾in diameter |
| | Chassis no 7400-7894 | Series 3 SS – dual ¾in master cylinder |
| **COOLING SYSTEM** | | |
| | Chassis no 5811-7894 | Full-width two-core radiator replaced 'narrow' width three-core version, as fitted to S1 and S2 |
| | From chassis no 7895 | Narrow two-core radiator with sheet steel side mounting plates, recuperator bottle and electric fan system |
| **FUEL SYSTEM** | | |
| | From 1971 | Federal cars were equipped with an evaporative loss system, which had a small catch tank mounted in the boot |

| | CHANGE POINT | DETAILS |
|---|---|---|
| ELECTRICAL SYSTEM | | |
| | General | The wiring looms were progressively modified as the levels of electrical equipment increased. |
| | From chassis no 7895 | System went over to negative earth |
| | From chassis no 9076 | New Lucas control box fitted |
| | From chassis no 4127 (after start of Series 2 production) | New Vauxhall Victor oval one piece rear light fittings replaced individual round lights. |
| | From chassis no 7895 | New Lucas rectangular rear lights for S4 and Sprint |
| | Chassis no 7400-7894 | New wiper motor and ancillaries |
| | From chassis no 7895 | New wiper motor and ancillaries |
| | From chassis no 7895 | Series 4 has electric pump-powered windscreen washers |
| | Chassis no 7400-7894 | SS fitted with toggle switches in dash; fitting carried over into Series 4 |
| HEATING AND VENTILATION | | |
| | From chassis no 6640 | Fresh air eyeball vents in corner of dash |
| CLUTCH | | |
| | From engine no LP7799 | Change in size of spigot bearing when six-bolt crank introduced |
| FINAL DRIVE AND PROPSHAFT | | |
| | From chassis no 4180 | Inner driveshafts with reduced spaced holes than before. Different Rotoflexes |
| | Very late S4/Sprint | Stronger inner driveshafts, stronger Rotoflexes |
| | Very late S4/Sprint | Differential brace introduced with Sprint |
| | Late Sprints | Driveshafts fitted with fail-safe pins |
| EXHAUST SYSTEM | | |
| | From chassis no 8850 | Original cast manifold replaced with S4 tubular type |
| | To chassis no 6693 | First type transverse silencer replaced with second type at 6694 |
| | From chassis no 7895 | In-line central twin silencers system introduced, then replaced with in-line single silencer at indeterminate point |

## ORIGINALITY: +2 TO +2S 130/5

### +2 FACTORY CHANGE POINTS

### INITIAL CHANGES

The first couple of hundred +2s exhibited a number of features that would be changed as production continued, but which pre-dated the introduction of the +2S. Up to chassis number 50/0177, +2s were fitted with Italian Carello rear light units, as fitted to contemporary Alfa Romeo Giulietta coupés. These were similar in appearance to the Lucas units fitted from chassis number 50/0177, but were slightly narrower, and did not have provision for reversing lights. The replacement Lucas lights were the same as those fitted to the Series 4 and Sprint Elan, but reversed – those on the Elan are mounted with the long edge topmost, while on the +2 the long edge is on the bottom. So the Elan's right-hand side cluster is the +2's left-hand unit, and vice versa. The early cars had a boot-reinforcing brace fabricated from circular section tubing, which was replaced at an undetermined point by a square section brace.

The first 177 +2s were fitted with Carello rear light clusters, replaced with the Lucas units seen on the Series 4 Elans from chassis number 175. While similar in shape, the Carello units were smaller and did not have the built-in reversing lights.

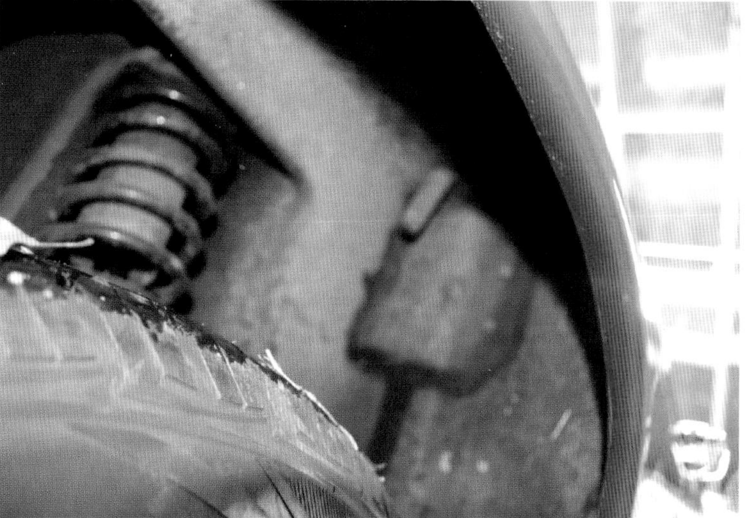

Another feature of the early +2 was the positioning of the fuel tank vent in the upper half of the rear wheelarch. This can lead to a noticeable smell of fuel inside the car, so was changed on later models.

All UK and non-Federal +2s had the fuel tank mounted between the rear Chapman struts, and sitting high above the differential. The fuel filler was on the left-hand side, and entered the tank about halfway down the side. This meant there had to be a vent system to allow the tank to fill above the level of the fuel inlet, so Lotus installed a pair of tubes at the top of each side of the tank, each of which was connected to a ¾in (1.9cm) diameter hose. The hoses ran upwards from the tank, along the B-pillar, looped over the top of the rear screen, and then descended on the opposite side they had started from, before venting into the atmosphere. Initially, these tubes vented into the top front of the rear wheelarches, but on later cars the exit was repositioned to the inside bottom-rear face of the sill, just in front of the rear wheel. The change was probably made at the same time that the Carello lights were changed for Lucas units.

On early +2s the heated rear window was an option, and the window itself was unconventional, with the heating element running vertically rather than the more conventional horizontal elements. The window was changed to a conventional type with horizontal elements some time before introduction of the +2S.

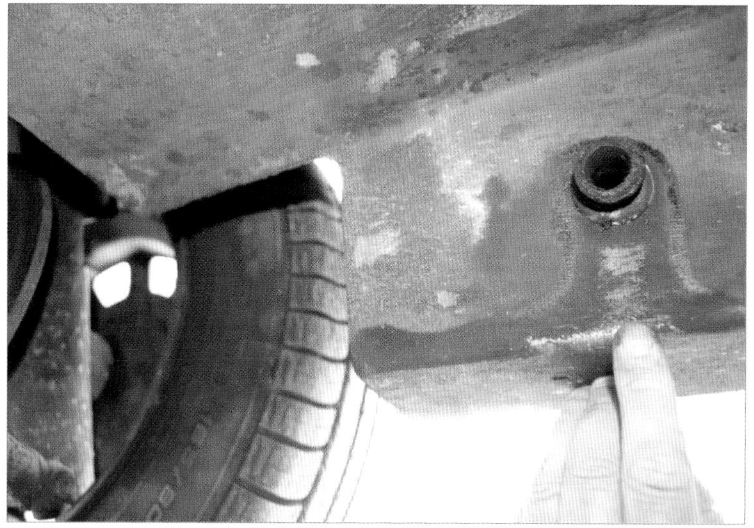

On later cars, the position was changed to vent under the car at the base of the sill. This meant longer vent pipes that helped to reduce the smell of fuel.

Some early cars were fitted with original-style cam covers with the 'Lotus' script over each camshaft, although many also appear to have been fitted with the later cover with 'LOTUS' cast on the front, above the cam chain.

Very early +2s were fitted with optional heated rear windows, which had the heating elements running vertically rather than the more common horizontal type fitted to later cars.

Early +2s had a handle and lock to open and close the boot.

Melody and Henry Kozlowski's very original +2 shows what an early engine bay should look like.

## FIRST BODY MODIFICATIONS

At chassis number 50/928 a plethora of minor changes were made to the car, resulting in significant alterations to the bodyshell, as well as many changes to the subsystems that made up the car.

The early cars' external boot lock was replaced with a flexible cable-operated opening mechanism, with a pull handle in a moulded recess, in the rear of the door jamb

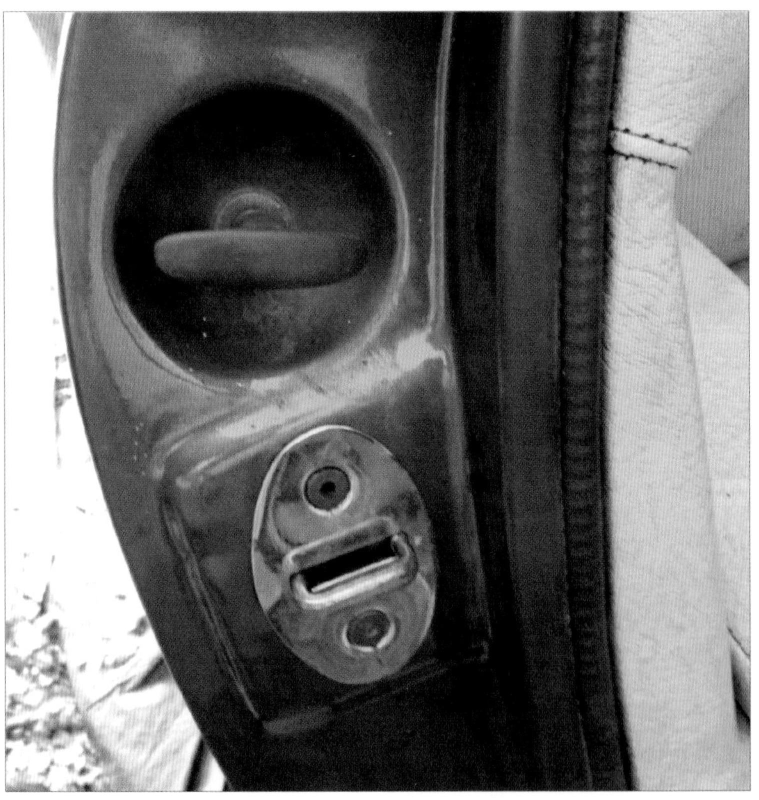

With the introduction of the +2S, the cars gained a remote boot opener with the handle placed in a recess in the door jamb. The door lock was also changed for a 'burst-proof' safety type with secure latches.

⅄ Early +2s had a door handle with an integrated lock.

⅄ The early +2's interior door handle was positioned ahead of the arm rest.

⅄ Early +2 door locks were this type, which could burst open in a crash. This is door jamb fixing.

⅄ This is the early door mechanism, fitted into the rear edge of the door.

above the striker mechanism. On these later remote-opening cars, the recess for the boot opening knob was moulded into both sides, to allow for left- or right-hand drive cars. Earlier cars did not have the recesses moulded-in – their door jambs were smooth. This also resulted in some changes to the boot lid.

The external door handles had the locks incorporated into them up to chassis 928, and internally the lock mechanism was operated by a chromed lever in the front of the door. Post chassis number 928, a new door lock mechanism was fitted, sourced from the British Leyland parts bin. Separate locks were positioned under the door handles, and anti-burst latches were fitted into the doors, which connected to U-shaped striker plates on the B-post to hold the door shut. In the interior, these cars were fitted with flush-fitting rectangular 'safety' latches in black plastic.

From the introduction of the +2S, the door locks were changed to anti-bust types from the British Leyland parts bin. These incorporated flush-fitting interior latches.

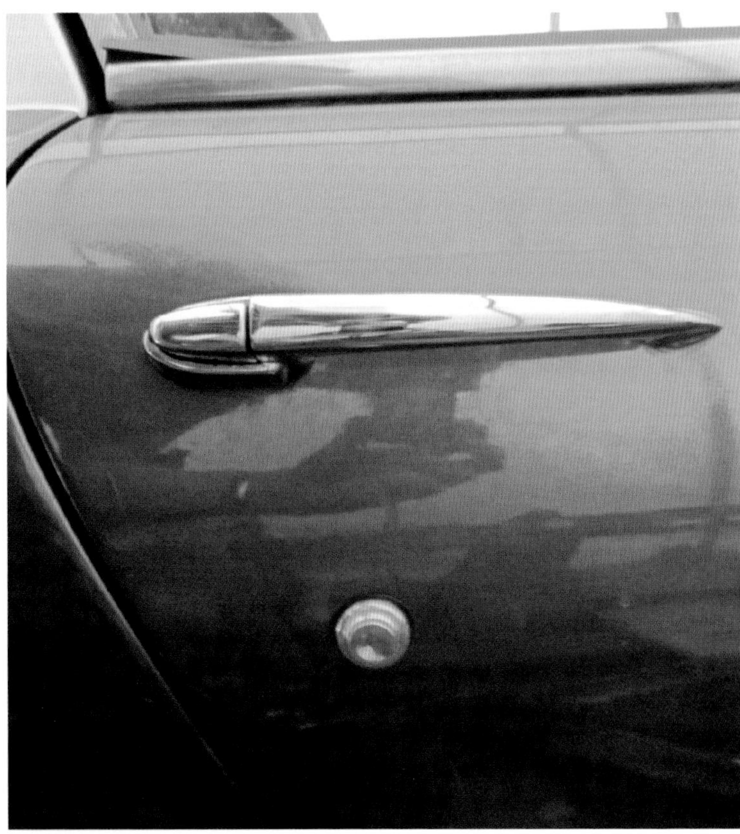

The later BL door locks had chromed handles and a separate lock.

In January 1971, with the introduction of the +2S, Lotus introduced the optional metal flake-finished roof. The finish was produced in the moulding process as the bodyshell was produced, not sprayed on afterwards, with the metal flakes embedded in a layer of clear resin under the gel coat, then having a layer of silver-coloured resin added before the glass fibre mat layers were added. The production process could be a bit patchy, and if the roof did not meet the quality standard it would be sprayed along with the rest of the car and sold as single colour car. It is fairly certain that not all cars were produced with the metal flake roof; it was an expensive process, in terms of both labour and materials, and as mono-coloured cars were still offered it would have been very wasteful to produce all body shells with the metallic finish.

## FEDERAL +2

In order to comply with US regulations, the Federal cars had a number of changes compared to the UK market vehicles. The main exterior change was the fitment of side reflectors at the front, and combined reflectors and position lights on the rear quarter.

Federal +2s had the later type of door locks and side repeater lights as standard.

Federal +2s had a closed-circuit fuel system with a cylindrical catch tank mounted behind the fuel tank, which was fed from a breather on the top of the main fuel tank to collect fuel vapour and prevent it from exiting into the atmosphere, in accordance with US emissions regulations. Vapour collected in the catch tank would then condense and drain back into the main tank. The fuel filler neck had a vent that connected to the top of the fuel tank to allow for rapid fuel filling.

The cars were also fitted with dual-circuit brakes, split front and rear. This meant a tandem or dual-circuit master cylinder was fitted. Dual-brake servos were fitted to provide power assistance to both circuits. There was also provision for a brake fluid level test light mechanism.

For 1971, the Federal cars' fuel system was further modified with an Evaporative Loss Control system designed to meet US legislation. An activated charcoal canister was fitted to the system to catch any fuel vapour from the fuel tank, and a separate cylindrical catch tank was mounted at the top rear of the existing main fuel tank. This acted to catch fuel vapour before it was passed into the canister, preventing the canister being contaminated by neat fuel. There was a small diameter vent from the top of the main tank into the catch tank, and a second vent in the top of the catch tank that led to the top of the charcoal canister. The canister was connected to the carburettors by a pipe that connected to drillings on the inlet, whereby clean air could be injected to purge the fuel vapour from the charcoal, which was fed into the air box. The pair of vent pipes that ran over the rear window were removed, and a single vent ran from the left-hand top of the main tank into the filler neck to allow the tank to be brimmed. The new system meant that the fuel system was no longer open to the atmosphere, and so no fuel vapour would escape.

## MISCELLANEOUS CHANGES

When introduced, the nose of the +2 under the bumper was plain. With the introduction of the +2S, a pair of rectangular lights – fog and spot – were fitted under the bumper on each side of the grille aperture. These were fitted into black plastic inserts, which in turn were riveted into holes cut into the nose moulding on each side of the air inlet. These inserts were replaced with a modified moulding fairly late in production, which had the indents for the spot and fog lights moulded in. If an early car has been given a new front end, this later type was often fitted, as the early one was not readily available and it 'updated' the look of the car.

The front driving and fog lights were first fitted to the +2S upon its introduction in 1968. The parts list shows the two separate nose mouldings (050B1613 and 050B1614) as being fitted up to 0335L for UK cars, 0085M for left-hand drive export cars, and 0066N for Federal cars, after which the nose had the recesses moulded into the panel.

The brochure for the first of the +2S models states that it's the car with 'NO EXTRAS LIST,' and lists twin quartz halogen fog lights as standard (not fog and spot). The pictures show them mounted in the abs pods, which were left black. The car in the brochure is white, so it's pretty obvious. However, checking the various wiring looms for the +2 shows the following combinations:

- +2S (non-Federal) Fog and Spot
- +2S (non-Federal) Alternator Fog and Spot
- +2S (non-Federal) RHD Alternator Spot and Fog
- +2S 130 (non-Federal) Twin Fog Lamps
- +2S (Federal) Fog and Spot
- +2S (Federal) Alternator Spot and Fog
- +2S 130 (Federal) Twin Fog Lamps

The tell-tale sign would be the switches in the dash; there should be one for fog and one for spot, so if there is only a fog switch then you should have twin fogs. So the brochure was probably wrong, and all +2S models apart from the +2S 130 Federal car were fitted with a fog light and a spotlight.

Up to and including chassis number 50/1279, the +2's bonnet was flat. After this point a power bulge was introduced in order to clear the Stromberg carburettors, which were introduced in early 1969. The bonnet retained the power bulge even when UK cars reverted to Weber or Dellorto carburettors.

Under the bonnet there were a few changes. Early cars, up to chassis number 0927, had a full-width radiator from the Triumph Herald, which had two rows of cooling gills. After 0927 the radiator was narrower, but had three rows of cooling gills as well as a pair of side plates bolted to it, so

Prior to the introduction of Stromberg carburettors, +2s and Elans had flat bonnets. This early +2 also has a smooth body under the front bumper with no recesses for fog and spotlights.

With the lights on, the +2's headlights pop up, giving the front of the car a very different look.

Spotlights can be mounted on brackets under the bumper without cutting into the bodyshell, as seen on this +2.

+2 cylinder heads have vacuum take-offs on the front and rear of the manifold – the front one operated the headlamps, the rear the servo. These are arrowed on the picture.

that it would fit in the same gap in the body as the previous one. These side plates were also used as a convenient mounting point to bolt on various ancillaries as production continued.

The +2 was fitted with the SE-specification Twin-cam engine from the start. The only major engine change came with the introduction of the +2S 130, in February 1971, when the Sprint-specification engine, with its revised porting and larger inlet valves, was fitted.

The +2 cylinder head had two vacuum take-offs: one on the front inlet port for the headlamps, and one on the rear inlet port for the servo. The Elan had a single take-off on the front inlet port that fed a T-piece to provide vacuum to the headlamps and servo.

The exhaust system for the +2 originally (up to chassis number 50/0928) had a silencer that was positioned transversely on the right-hand side under the boot, with the tailpipe exiting under the right-hand side rear light. The replacement system's single silencer box was fitted longitudinally to the rear right-hand side of the car, and necessitated a revised boot floor moulding to accommodate it. This revised floor meant a much narrower platform for the battery location.

Early cars had a transversely-mounted exhaust silencer box under the boot, with the tailpipe exiting on the right-hand side.

The only official 'Limited Edition' +2 was the John Player Special. Introduced in May 1973, this had black paint, gold metal flake sills and roof, and special badges. (Courtesy Jon Underwood)

Early +2s were fitted with a positive earth electrical system. From chassis number 50/0856 for Federal (US) models, and 50/1086 for Domestic market models, this was changed to a negative earth system. Safety driveshafts were introduced sometime after 1970. Lotus had become concerned with Rotoflex failures resulting in flailing driveshafts entering the cabin, and so devised a pin and tube system to locate the driveshaft should a Rotoflex fail catastrophically. This comprised of a welded-on tube at each end of the driveshaft, which fitted loosely over a pin welded onto the inboard differential driveshaft and the outboard driveshaft.

The only special edition +2 made by Lotus was the +2 JPS (for John Player Special), which was introduced in May 1973 to celebrate Lotus winning the Formula 1 World Championship the previous year. The cars were based on the +2S 130, and there is some debate as to whether they were all fitted with the five-speed gearbox – the Lotus records are unclear. The body was finished in gloss black with a gold metal flake roof (rather than the standard silver), gold sill trims, and the interior trim was oatmeal with cloth inserts. There were supposed to be a limited edition of 50, but the factory actually produced around 85.

## +2 PARTS LIST ANALYSIS SHOWING MAJOR CHANGE POINTS

The following analysis of the +2 parts List shows where major changes to the +2's specification were introduced.

The JPS badges commemorated Lotus' first 50 Grand Prix wins. The black and gold colour scheme reflected the JPS colours of the Lotus Formula One cars. (Courtesy Jon Underwood)

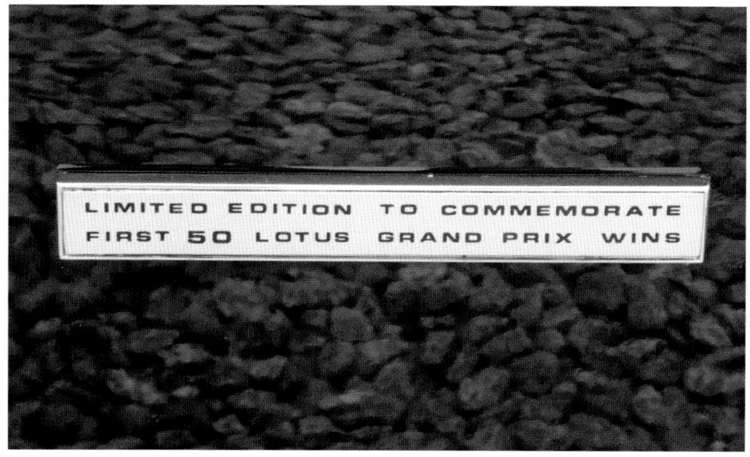

| | CHANGE POINT | DETAILS |
|---|---|---|
| **MODEL CHANGES** | | |
| | Chassis no 50/0001 | +2 introduced (June 1967) |
| | Chassis no 50/1554 | +2S introduced (March 1969) |
| | Chassis no 71.01 ... | +2S 130 introduced (February 1972) |
| | Chassis no 72.10 ... | +2S 130/5 – five-speed gearbox option – introduced (October 1972) |
| | Chassis no 74.12.1990L | Last +2S produced (December 1974) |
| **CHASSIS** | | |
| | No changes indicated | |
| **BODY** | | |
| | From chassis no 0929 | New bodyshell introduced. Includes remote boot opening, new door shells with revised locks and revised interior, new seats, etc |
| | Chassis no 2407 | Final +2 produced |
| | From chassis no 0335L and 0085M | Revised bodyshell |
| | From chassis no 1280 | Bonnet lid with power bulge to clear Stromberg carburettors |
| | From chassis no 0928 | New boot lid to allow for revised opening mechanism |
| | From chassis no 70.01.020001N | Bonded-in windscreen introduced |
| | From Feb 1970 | Revised drip gutter mouldings fitted |
| | From chassis no 1174 | Fail-safe headlamp system on Federal cars |
| | Up to chassis no 0335L, 0085M, and 0066N | Separate bowls for fog and spotlights fitted; replaced with new nose moulding. |
| | From chassis no 0366 | Single wide pedal box and mounting bracket replaced with new box and two separate brackets |
| | From chassis no 0929 | New pedal box introduced with no side flanges and bolt-in stop light switch mounted on front face |
| | From chassis no 72.05.0717L, 72.05.0235M and 72.05.0272N | Folding rear seat back replaced with fixed version |
| **FRONT SUSPENSION** | | |
| | No significant changes | |
| **REAR SUSPENSION** | | |
| | From chassis no 0250 | New rear hub assembly, including housing, hub, bearings and outer driveshafts – carriers known as Issue 18 castings and have '18' cast into them. Previous Issue 16 castings had no identifying marks. |
| | 1972/3 | Safety driveshafts introduced |
| | From chassis no 710101335L, 7011150087M, 7012160068N | Later-style bonded metal and rubber Rotoflexes introduced |

| | CHANGE POINT | DETAILS |
|---|---|---|
| ENGINE | | |
| | From chassis no 1280 | Stromberg carburettors introduced |
| | From Jan 1971 | S 130 Big Valve Sprint-spec engine introduced |
| | From Mid 1972 | Dellorto carburettors introduced |
| | From chassis no 1280 | Super SE Stromberg cams (ie, Sprint-spec but pre-S 130) introduced on engine type 'M' |
| TRANSMISSION | | |
| | S 130 | Fitment of differential stiffening bracket with introduction of S 130 |
| | From chassis no 72.10 ... (October 1972) | Five-speed gearbox offered as option |
| WHEELS | | |
| | From chassis no 0929 | +2S black and chrome steel road wheels introduced |
| | From around chassis no 0929 | Alloy wheels introduced with the +2S model, but does not seem to have been generally available until later |
| STEERING | | |
| | Up to chassis no 0928 | Ford steering column fitted. Replaced with Triumph type |
| BRAKING SYSTEM | | |
| | All Federal cars | Tandem master cylinder and attendant brake test lights, etc |
| | Federal cars from chassis no 1857 | Dual brake servos fitted |
| COOLING SYSTEM | | |
| | From chassis no 0928 | Narrow radiator with side plates and electric fan introduced |
| FUEL SYSTEM | | |
| | Federal cars | Federal cars fitted with closed-circuit fuel system with catch tank |
| ELECTRICAL SYSTEM | | |
| | From chassis no 1086 | Electrical system changed from positive to negative earth |
| | From chassis no 0929 | Alternator fitted to all +2S cars |
| | Up to chassis no 0177 | Carello units fitted originally. Replaced with Lucas items |
| | From chassis no 72050732L (UK), 72050235M (Export), 72050272N (Federal) | Electrics revised:<br>Fail-safe headlamp system fitted<br>New dash with fuse box replacing ashtray<br>Deletion of anti-theft switch<br>Deletion of lighting relays and fuses, replaced with thermo cut outs. New under-bonnet light<br>Separate switching of red warning lights in door edge and deletion of white puddle lights<br>Fog lamp switch mounted on fascia<br>Handbrake warning light combined with fluid level warning light<br>European-style single plug alternator wiring |
| | Up to chassis no 0928 | Ford single-stalk column switch replaced with Triumph twin-column switches |
| | Federal cars | Fitted with red side marker lights, reflectors and all-amber front light lenses |
| HEATING AND VENTILATION | | |
| | No significant changes | |

| | CHANGE POINT | DETAILS |
|---|---|---|
| **CLUTCH** | | |
| | No significant changes | |
| **FINAL DRIVE AND PROPSHAFT** | | |
| | No significant changes | |
| **EXHAUST SYSTEM** | | |
| | Up to chassis no 0928 | Transverse silencer replaced on introduction of the +2S with longitudinal unit on right-hand underside of boot floor. Bodyshell modified to fit |

## CAM COVERS: EUROPA-SPECIFIC TIMING CASES AND CAM COVERS, STROMBERG CAM COVERS

The most distinctive feature of the Lotus Twin-cam engine when viewed in situ is the cam cover. This was Lotus-branded from the word go, but the design was changed a number of times throughout the life of the unit. In addition, the colour of the cam cover was also used to denote the various specifications of engine throughout its life. The first cars had 'Lotus' written in raised script along each cam tunnel. The finish on these covers varied; some were painted all over, others had the 'Lotus' script polished.

When the Lotus Cortina evolved and grew a large air filter that covered the top of the engine, Lotus redesigned the cam cover to have 'LOTUS' written in capital letters across the cam chain bridge, to be read from the front, so the engine's origins were still visible when the Cortina's rear-hinged bonnet was opened. This cover was also

The Lotus Twin-cam was initially fitted with this type of cam cover.

With the introduction of the Mark II Ford Lotus Cortina, the 'Lotus' lettering on the top of the cam cover was obscured by the large air filter, so Lotus redesigned the cover with 'LOTUS' cast in at the front of the cover.

The second type of cam cover.

There were two types of the final 'Big Valve' ribbed cover. In the first version the writing was upside down when viewed from the side, as seen here.

used on the Elan and +2, replacing the original design. The change appears to have come during 1967, with early +2s and most Elan S3s being fitted with the original-style covers.

The final cosmetic change to the cam cover came with the introduction of the Elan Sprint and the +2S 130 'Big

The second type of cover, when used for Stromberg-equipped cars, was modified to have a small bolt-on bracket over the inlet camshaft to carry the throttle cable.

The cover design was quickly reversed so that the writing was the right way up when viewed from the side in the Elan and +2, as seen here. Note also the ribbing along the top of each cam tunnel.

Valve' models. This featured a series of six ribs cast into cam covers, and the script on the cam chain bridge was changed to read 'LOTUS BIG VALVE.' Initially this could be read from the front of the engine (forward facing), as on the previous version, but the casting was rapidly changed so that the lettering read from the rear of the unit, making it easier to read in the Elan and +2, with their forward-hinged bonnets. The surface of the ribs were polished, as was the lettering and its surround, while the rest of the cover was painted.

There were two more engineering changes made to the cam cover. The second type of cover – with the 'LOTUS' on the front of the cover – when fitted to Stromberg-equipped units, had a small bridge piece cast into the centre of the inlet cam cover to take the two threaded holes needed to fix the central throttle cable bracket. Europa cam covers have a semicircular cut-out at the rear on the exhaust camshaft side, to allow the extended camshaft fitted to the Europa to drive the alternator. While these *will* fit on an Elan head, you will need to seal the hole with something ...

From the factory, the cam cover was painted in various colours depending on its application. Today many cam covers will have been repainted or swapped, so the colour is not a good indication of the engine fitted! However, the following table summarises which cam cover was originally fitted by the factory to the Elan and +2.

| CAR AND MARKET | ENGINE SPECIFICATION | ENGINE PREFIX | CAM COVER TYPE | CAM COVER FINISH | DATE |
|---|---|---|---|---|---|
| Elan Standard, Domestic and Export | Standard spec – Weber | D | 'Lotus' script over both cams | Green | From 1963 |
| Elan SE (S1, S2, S3) Domestic and Export | SE spec – Weber | C | 'Lotus' script over both cams | Blue | From 1963 |
| +2 and +2S Domestic and Federal | SE spec – Weber | F | 'Lotus' script, quickly changed to Lotus on cam chain bridge | Red | From 1967 |
| Elan S4 Federal | Stromberg Federal | G | 'Lotus' on cam chain bridge | Red | From 1969 |
| Elan SE Domestic | Super SE Weber (high compression) | H | 'Lotus' on cam chain bridge | Red | Early 1968 |
| +2 Federal | Stromberg Federal | I | 'Lotus' on cam chain bridge | Red | 1969 |
| Elan S4 Domestic | Stromberg Domestic | K | 'Lotus' on cam chain bridge | Black | 1969 |
| Elan S4 Domestic | SE Stromberg | L | 'Lotus' on cam chain bridge | Red | 1969 |
| +2S Domestic | SE Stromberg | M | 'Lotus' on cam chain bridge | Red | 1969 |
| Elan Sprint Domestic | Big Valve Weber | N | Ribbed, 'Big Valve' | Black | Late 1970 |
| +2S 130 Domestic | Big Valve Weber | P | Ribbed, 'Big Valve' | Black | Late 1970 |
| Elan Sprint Federal | Big Valve Stromberg | T or W | 'Lotus' on Cam chain bridge initially, then Ribbed 'Big Valve' | Red | Late 1970 into 1971 |
| Elan Sprint European | Big Valve Dellorto | EN | Ribbed, 'Big Valve' | Red | From 1972 |
| +2S 130 European | Big Valve Dellorto | EP | Ribbed, 'Big Valve' | Red | From 1972 |

Finally, various tuning firms produced their own versions of the cam cover, with their name cast into it to advertise their wares. These included BRM, which, under Tony Rudd, produced a range of tuned engines for fitment in (amongst others) the famous 'BRM Elans' marketed by Maidenhead-based Lotus dealer Mike Spence. Holbay Engineering (based in Martlesham Heath, Suffolk, until it closed down in 1992) was a long-term Ford and Rootes group engine tuner, and also produced a tuned version of the Twin-cam, which gave 135bhp and was fitted to 13 Lotus Super Sevens produced by Lotus in 1970 and fitted with 'Lotus Holbay' cam covers. Tuning firm Piper Cams also produced its own cam covers, and can still supply camshafts for the Lotus Twin-cam.

## LOTUS CLASSIC CERTIFICATE OF VEHICLE PROVENANCE

Owners of Elans and +2s are lucky that the original manufacturer is still in business in Hethel, Norfolk, and still making cars in the spirit of the Elan. While some records were lost when the building in which they were stored suffered a flood, Lotus does have an archivist, Andy Graham, and is building up the factory records when time and money allow. While Lotus' records are only partially complete, it can provide a Classic Certificate of Vehicle Provenance, which confirms the actual build date of any Lotus, along with any other details of the build, including the original vehicle identification number, engine number, model, variant, colour, trim, and any options fitted, as well as the original dealer. It is a great source of information, and will form an important addition to any classic Lotus' history file.

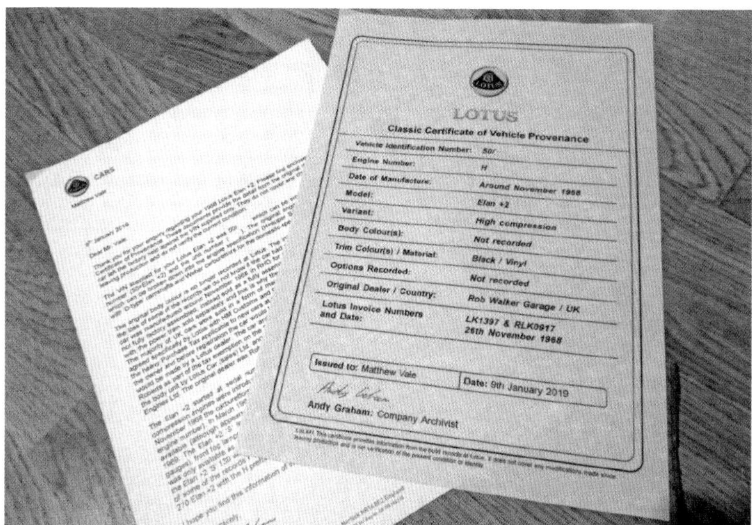

LOTUS

Classic Certificate of Vehicle Provenance

| | |
|---|---|
| Vehicle Identification Number: | 50/ |
| Engine Number: | H |
| Date of Manufacture: | Around November 1968 |
| Model: | Elan +2 |
| Variant: | High compression |
| Body Colour(s): | Not recorded |
| Trim Colour(s) / Material: | Black / Vinyl |
| Options Recorded: | Not recorded |
| Original Dealer / Country: | Rob Walker Garage / UK |
| Lotus Invoice Numbers and Date: | LK1397 & RLK0917 26th November 1968 |

Issued to: Matthew Vale | Date: 9th January 2019

Andy Graham: Company Archivist

Lotus runs a scheme that issues certificates of vehicle provenance along with an accompanying letter, which give all the details known about the car that the factory possesses.

## ORIGINAL PHOTOGRAPHS

The following pictures were taken in the 1960s and 1970s, mainly by Lotus, and are a good source of original details of the cars. However, while they were taken at the time of the cars' manufacture, they may not be actual production cars; rather, they could be prototypes and development mules, or press cars that may have minor deviations from the actual factory specification. This is especially evident in brochure pictures, as the brochures would have been designed alongside the

This Lotus factory picture shows the Series 1 Elan in standard trim. (Courtesy Lotus Cars)

A shot of an Elan Series 1 taken by its original owner back in the 1960s.

Taken at the Cheshunt factory in the mid-1960s, this is another view of the early coupé and drop head.

The last of the Elans was the Sprint, here seen in a factory photograph from 1971.

Another Lotus press picture, this time of the newly-introduced Elan Series 4 drop head from March 1968. (Courtesy Lotus Cars)

The author's +2, which – while it started life as a standard +2 – has been restored and up-specced by previous owners to S 130 specification.

Rear view of the new Series 4, showing the large Lucas rear lights. These were also fitted to the +2 from the 175th car, but were reversed and turned upside down when compared to the Elan.

development of the cars and may well have gone to press before the final specification of the model was finalised.

## CASE STUDY – 1968 +2

### INTRODUCTION

At the time of writing, the author owns two +2s: a +2S manufactured in September 1969, which is currently undergoing a nut and bolt restoration, and a running +2 manufactured in November 1968, which was supplied as a kit to the original owner. This second car is an interesting mixture of standard parts, later Lotus parts and aftermarket parts, and probably represents a typical +2 or Elan that is on the road today after an eventful life.

This section will take a close look at the car and will identify what is standard, what is from a later car, and some changes using non-Lotus parts. It will be an interesting exercise and will demonstrate to the reader how far an apparently standard car can be from original factory specification. The good news is that the car actually drives really well, has scintillating performance thanks to a tuned engine, and the interior actually allows you to feel quite comfortable and cosseted. So, a non-standard car can be as good to own and drive as an original.

## DOCUMENTATION

There is a note in the service book that the car was 'totally restored,' dated 29th February 1980 – not long after the engine was replaced. In addition, there is a massive history file with lots of receipts detailing work carried out and parts bought for the car. This is always a good thing, as it not only shows that work has been done, it also shows the previous owner(s) knew the value of documenting the work.

## ENGINE

The good news is that the car has a Lotus Twin-cam engine, which has a standard L-block and looks to be standard from the outside. However, inspecting the engine bay raises some issues. The cam cover is the second type, with 'LOTUS' written on the front over the cam chain. The factory moved to this type of cover in late 1967, so it would be expected in a 1968 car. The cam cover is a Stromberg type, evidenced by the screw holes for fixing the throttle cable in place on the carburettor side. This is not original, as the Lotus heritage certificate indicates that the car was originally equipped with Webers, although Strombergs were fitted to +2s from November 1968. The head is a +2 Weber or Dellorto unit, with the vacuum take-offs on the front and rear of the inlet manifold. The certificate shows that the original engine was a Super SE specification Twin-cam, equipped with Weber carburettors and D-type (ie, Sprint specification) camshafts and a high compression of 10.3:1. Looking at the documentation that came with the car, there is an invoice from Vegantune for a new engine tuned to Lotus Big Valve standard that was fitted in 1979, at 40,000 miles, and judging by the performance of the car the engine is still going strong! The replacement engine was fitted with Dellorto carburettors which are still on the car – again non-standard, as the original would have had Webers. However, it is possible that the head is the original unit, but there does not appear to be any numbering on the head to confirm this.

▲ A large history file came with the car that confirms much of the work done. This is what you should get with any Elan!

▲ Under the bonnet the car is tidy and largely oil leak-free. Dellorto carburettors have replaced the original Webers, and the engine has been up-specced to Big Valve S 130 spec by noted tuners Vegantune.

## ELECTRIC SYSTEM

One immediately obvious change from standard is the replacement of the originally-fitted Triumph Herald-type stalk switches with later 1970s Triumph units, as fitted to the Stag or Dolomite, which incorporate a headlamp flasher and horn functions.

Another change is the fuse box. The standard +2 should have a simple Lucas four-fuse box mounted in the engine bay; this car has a foreign unit, still with four fuses but a significantly different design to the Lucas unit. A second change is to the headlight operating system. Originally the car would have had a three-position toggle switch that would turn on the side lights then the headlights, and a separate pull switch to operate the vacuum to pull the lights up. The car's current setup only has the three-position toggle switch, and the headlamps come up when the switch is turned on or the headlamp flasher on the steering column is used. The original pull switch for the vacuum is no longer fitted, and a late-type solenoid-activated vacuum switch has been fitted in the engine bay to switch on the vacuum in order to raise the headlamp pods. The system has also been converted to fail-safe operation; a vacuum failure will result in the pods rising.

▲ Much work had been done on the car, including the fitment of later Triumph stalks as used on the Stag.

▲ The original Lucas fuse box had been replaced with a unit of undetermined origin.

## INTERIOR

The car has been fitted with a later interior from a +2S. Rather than the standard black basket-weave vinyl seat covers and cabin trim, and the one-piece plastic transmission tunnel cover, it is all upholstered in plump beige textured vinyl with cloth inserts on the +2S seats. Apart from the standard +2 dash, with its four minor gauges and toggle switches, probably the only original pieces in the cabin are the black door pulls, which do jar a little!

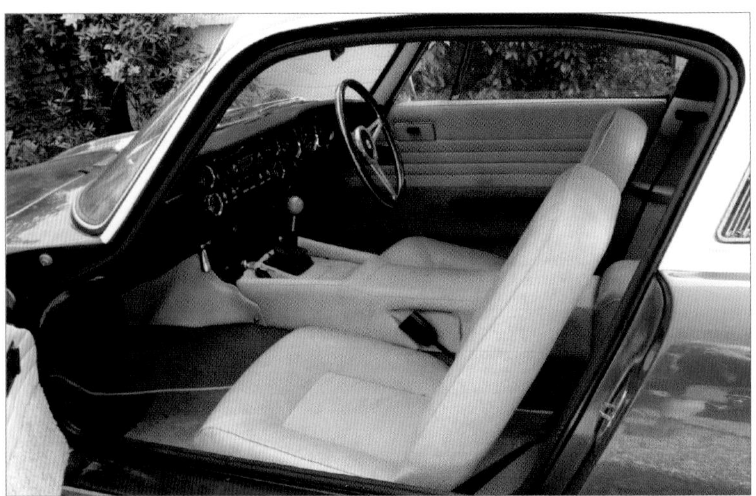

▲ The original black seats and trim have been completely replaced with an Oatmeal interior from a +2S, but the dashboard is the original +2-type with four minor dials.

Although not original, the interior is from a +2, and is actually a nice and comfortable place to be.

The car has been resprayed to give the impression of a later metal flake-style roof. It was done in metallic white and, while it is done to a high standard, is not to everyone's taste.

The wheels have been refurbished and powder coated. The black should extend around the rim, but this style of finish is actually quite attractive.

## PAINTWORK

The paintwork is not original, but Lotus records do not reveal what the original colour was. As it is now, the car tries to replicate the two-tone finish seen on +2S 130s from the early 1970s, with their silver (or gold) metal flake roofs and a contrasting coloured body. The bodywork below the roof is painted in a fairly accurate rendition of Lagoon Blue, and actually looks pretty good. However, the roof was resprayed in a metallic metal flake white, which was a brave decision by the previous owner but to the author's eyes doesn't quite work. It will be resprayed metallic silver in the future.

## DRIVE-TRAIN

The car is fitted with Lotus knock-on alloy wheels, when it would have originally been fitted with steel units. The alloys are also painted incorrectly: the black should cover the inner lip of the rim, while it has been left silver in this case.

At the rear of the car, the driveshafts and their associated Rotoflex flexible rubber joints have been replaced with sold shafts, fitted with Hooke's-type universal joints and a sliding spline. This is another sensible modification, when taking into account the price and availability of decent quality Rotoflex donuts.

A useful mechanical upgrade is the fitment of solid driveshafts, which use Hooke's-type universal joints rather than CVs. They work well, and the UJs are fitted with grease nipples, so can be maintained.

+2S 130 badges are fitted. Despite its beginnings, in the light of the tuned engine, they are not lying!

The car on the author's drive, ready for another adventure!

## BADGING

The rear wing badges have been replaced with a pair of later 'S.130' shields on the rear quarters, there are no rear badges apart from 'LOTUS' lettering across the boot lip, and the front wings each correctly carry a rectangular 'LOTUS' badge.

## SUMMARY

To summarise, ORJ is not an original car but that does not detract from what it is: a well-sorted +2 with a tuned engine, and a number of mechanical and cosmetic changes that have resulted in a quick, comfortable and reliable car that gives its owner a great deal of pleasure!

## MELODY AND HENRY KOZLOWSKI'S EARLY ELAN +2

Based in Cornwall, the far south-western region of the UK, Melody and Henry Kozlowski are the custodians of a very early +2 – the 60th made – that first hit the road in October 1967, a month or so after the new model was announced. It is a very original car, and as such it is probably unique and forms a useful reference for the +2 enthusiast, displaying all of the early features of the model. Many of the pictures of early +2 features in this book are from this car. They bought it in June 2011, after Melody had read an article about a long distance charity classic car rally – the Grand Tour Cape to Cape Classic Car Rally, which ran from Cape Wrath in the far north of Scotland, down to Cape Cornwall, the farthest point in South West England, and supported the Macmillan Cancer Support charity. The official route was 1580 miles long, and with a duration of seven days, the daily average mileage for the event was just under 226 miles – so it was a tough and gruelling event in its own right, and not a gentle trundle around the British Isles! Also bear in mind that there was an 800-mile trip to get to the start point in the first place. The car was bought with the intention of participating in the 2012 event, so Melody and Henry had plenty of time to prepare the vehicle ...

Melody and Henry's +2, ready for the off at Cape Wrath. (Courtesy Melody Kozlowski)

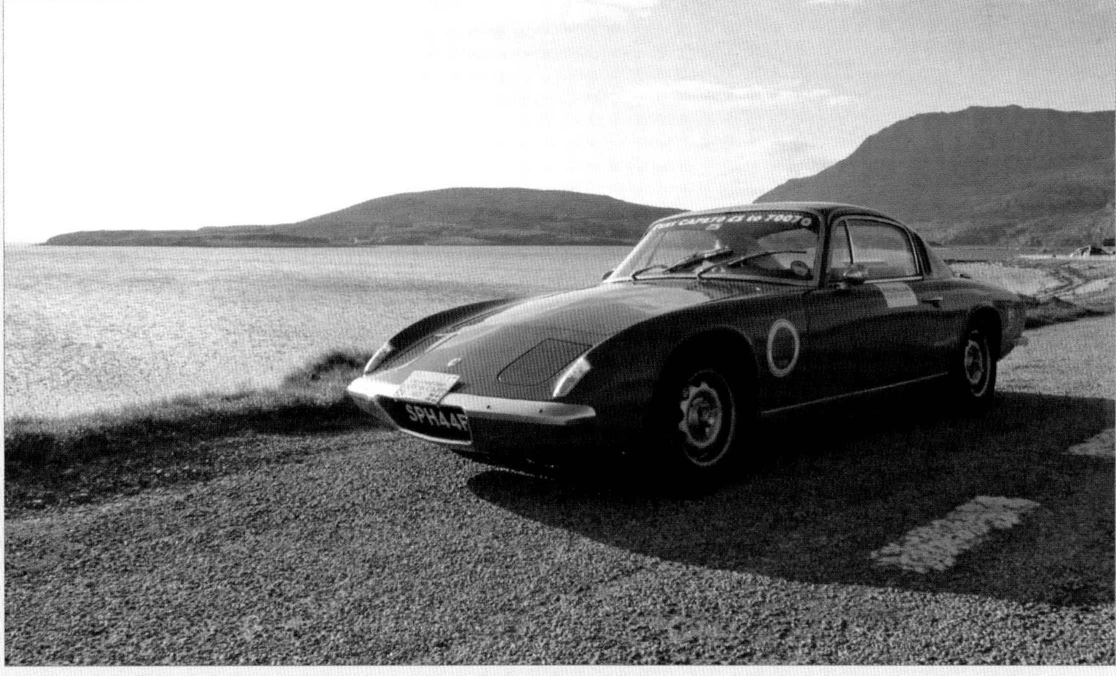


The +2, still in beautiful Scotland, after the start of the Cape to Cape. (Courtesy Melody Kozlowski)

The car, as bought, had been fitted in the past with a Lotus replacement chassis, was on the road with a current MoT, and seemed to be running well. However, as the clutch was obviously on the way out, they pulled the engine and gearbox out in January 2012 to replace it and, of course, thought that a quick look at the engine wouldn't go amiss..

Luckily, the engine's insides were all in pretty good shape, and so received a precautionary change of main and big end bearings, a new timing chain and sprockets, and some new valve guides. The guides threw up a problem – the valve seats were pocketed, which made it impossible to fit reasonable-sized shims to get the correct valve clearances. They ended up having to have the base circles on a new set of Sprint cams re-profiled to allow enough space for the shims. This took a little time to achieve, but luckily while the head was being worked on they were able to replace the rebuilt engine in the car, along with a new clutch and replacement universal joints on the propshaft. While waiting for the head, they replaced the dashboard – the old one was tatty and the veneer was badly cracked, letting down the rest of the car. Along with the dash, they sorted out the electrics. When the dash wiring was disturbed many of the terminals and connections disintegrated, necessitating a new dash and engine bay looms. The originals were fine when undisturbed, but, as is so often the case, failed when they were disturbed. At the same time, they changed from the original dynamo to an alternator. As Melody put it, "On cold, wet nights it meant we could have both the lights and the wipers on while slowing down to go round a bend ..."

Electrical fixes included fitting a Kenlowe electric fan, and a hidden electrical cut-out switch to protect against fire and theft! A few other problems appeared: the steering column was slightly bent and had to be straightened, the alternator bracket was wrong and had to be 'adapted' with various spacers to fit, and it proved difficult to find a properly dimensioned fan belt.

Still on the Cape to Cape, having traversed the length of the country. Here, the +2 takes a ford at speed on Exmoor, in Devon. (Courtesy Melody Kozlowski)

Melody and Henry's +2 has a very original early dash, with two main and four small ancillary dials. The toggle switches were later outlawed by the US Federal regulations, and replaced with recessed rocker switches.

Back home in Cornwall, the Kozlowskis' +2 is still in fine fettle.

The Kozlowskis' +2 retains a great level of originality – the engine bay is largely as the car left the factory.

The front and rear suspension was overhauled, and while doing the rear they found out that it was not a good idea to leave the car jacked up at the rear with no carburettors fitted; an overwhelming smell of petrol, a wet garage floor, and an empty fuel tank showed the error of their ways! Mismatched rear springs, some missing parts, and a lack of instructions turned what should have been a simple task into a bit of a marathon, but the rear end was eventually sorted. They were not going to replace the donuts, as on first inspection they seemed to be in good condition, but while rebuilding the rear suspension one of the donuts just broke apart for no apparent reason. So, the credit card came out and a set of CV driveshafts were procured, rapidly followed by a set of steel inner driveshafts – on one of the originals the spider was bent, so did not line up with the new driveshaft's flange.

Melody and Henry successfully completed the tour, and wrote up their experiences in *Club Lotus* magazine – suffice to say that they completed the course, gaining only six penalty points, the car ran pretty much faultlessly, and raised over £1000 for Macmillan. A great achievement by them and the car.

Today, the car is being used a little less intensely, but that does include runs to the Club Lotus Castle Combe track day and, in 2018, a visit to the factory at Hethel for the Lotus 70th Anniversary celebration. This latter trip, along with the classic tour, ranks as one of Melody's and Henry's best trips in the car. All in all, Melody thinks she's a little bit in love with the car, and even her worst moment in the car – when someone pulled out of a side turning and hit them, with luckily not too much damage – hasn't shaken her faith in the car. Melody says she can't imagine not having a Lotus, and is spoilt for choice as it shares the garage in Cornwall with a rather nice S1 Elise!

# Owner's Guide

## OWNING AND RUNNING AN ELAN OR +2

### INTRODUCTION

This chapter will seem to be a litany of disasters, but no one said that owning an Elan or +2 was going to be easy. The point of this chapter is to give an owner the inside knowledge they need to understand and maintain their Lotus, give suggestions for maintenance routines, as well as hints and tips derived from years of Lotus experience by the author and many other experts. Full details on how to carry out the actual mechanical methods and processes identified in this chapter are defined in the Lotus handbook and workshop manuals for the cars, and these should be followed. Owning a 1960s-technology low-volume sports car, with a race-bred pedigree and state-of-the-art (for the time) underpinnings requires a degree of commitment from the owner. The Elan and +2 are not sports cars that are based on heavyweight, lightly breathed-on saloon car components – such as the Spitfire, Midget or MGB. Neither are they robust and heavy old-school hairy-chested sports cars like the TR or Austin-Healey. The Elan and +2 are relatively highly-tuned cars that rely on a combination of good power and torque from the Twin-cam engine and a light weight to deliver performance that exceeds that of the competition – but at the expense of the increased need for careful maintenance and handling.

Back in the '70s and '80s, Elans were still enthusiasts' cars and a good run out was always welcome. This is John Humfryes' Elan Series 4, out for a day with his mates and their Elans, a brace of +2s and a Europa, in the New Forest in the 1980s. ➤

So, an Elan or +2 is not a rough, tough machine that can take abuse and neglect and still come back for more. It is a finely-tuned, delicate and poised thoroughbred, which will repay rough handling and neglect with unreliability and breakdowns. However, if treated well and handled sympathetically, it will reward the owner with an unparalleled combination of handling, roadholding and performance.

## APPROACH TO OWNERSHIP

Running a Lotus Elan or +2 need not be traumatic, but an owner needs to approach the car with their eyes open.

There is a thin line between character and pain, and '60s mechanicals and electrics are adept at straddling that line – an Elan sitting on the character side of the line is a marvellous machine, but cross over the line and you are due a world of pain. Problems with Elans don't come singly, there are invariably more than one that will conspire to cause an owner grief. Top of the list are the electrics; an Elan is capable of producing a variety of the most obscure electrical faults, which appear unconnected but probably involve a single misplaced earth wire. These electrical issues are compounded in the +2, where its increased sophistication in the electrical department over the more basic Elan is a recipe for additional problems. The Elan and +2 are pretty basic mechanically, so faults are easy to identify and surprisingly easy to fix, but, again, one problem often leads to another.

As an example, an oil leak from the cam cover could contaminate and soften the engine mounts, which results in the engine dropping on one side, thereby straining the exhaust to manifold joint, causing air leaks that give pops and bangs on the overrun, and which look like a carburettor fault. So, very often, forensic and thorough fault-finding skills are needed to properly diagnose problems. Don't just cure the symptoms, you need to establish the source of the issue.

However, looking on the bright side, the engine is generally robust and reliable, the suspension is basic, simple, and has few inherent faults – as long as the

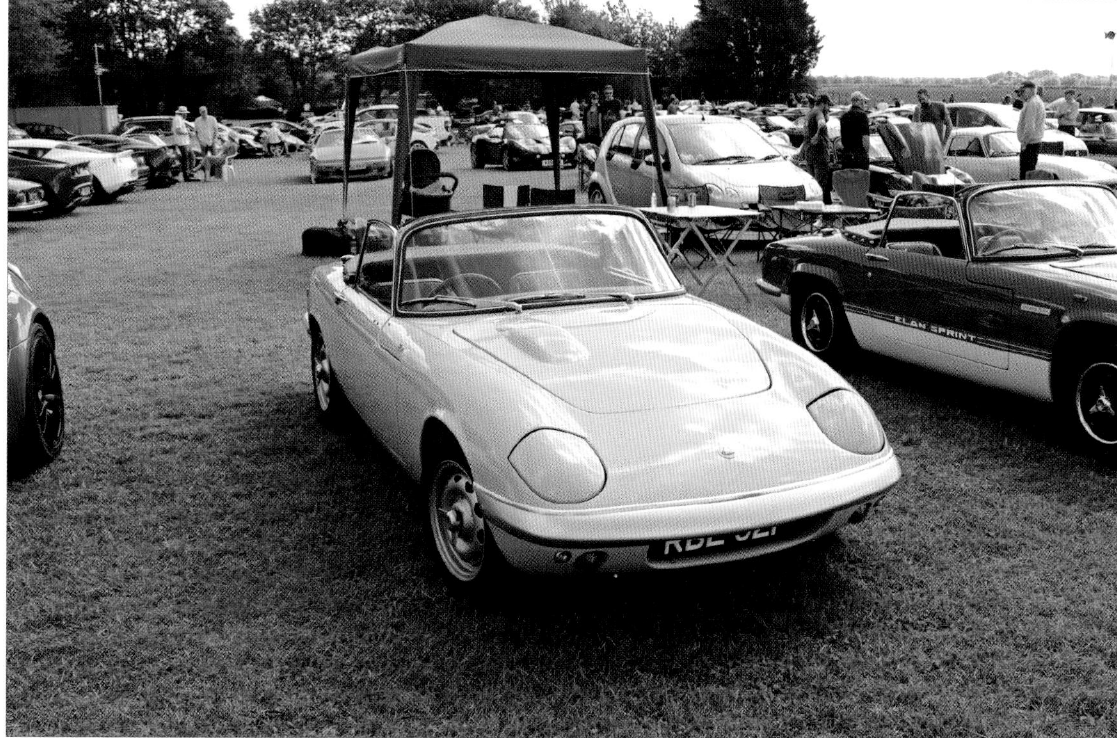


Pictured at a Club Lotus track day at Castle Combe in Wiltshire, an Elan SS and a Sprint sit happily among a fine assortment of other Lotus cars, old and new.

The backbone of the Elan and +2 is the chassis. This is a Spyder spaceframe version for the +2, from a car currently being restored by the author.

The +2 has a great combination of good looks, performance and handling. This is Jon Bradbury's lovely Roman Purple +2S 130/5 – one of the last of the line.

lubrication of the front trunnions is not neglected. Suspension wishbone bushes are metalastic items, which are long-lived and easily replaced when required, with poly bushes readily available. The gearbox and differential are robust and reliable, and it is only the driveshafts and rear hubs that can be problematical. The rear wheel bearings can have short lives, and the quality of new rubber donuts for the driveshafts is sometimes questionable. The good news is that a full wallet and hard work can ease the crossing of that line between unreliable old heap and dependable companion.

The owner has to accept that an Elan or +2 will never be like a modern, jump-in-and-drive day-after-day car needing just a simple yearly service. It is a finely-tuned instrument that craves attention and care, just like a thoroughbred horse. The owner has responsibilities, and if they don't want to take them up then they should buy a Mazda MX-5, Audi TT, or Mercedes SLK; or a Lotus Elise. The author also hastens to add that the MX-5, TT and SLK are brilliant little cars, any of which will give its owner a great experience – but they are not an Elan. While it still isn't an Elan, maybe an Elise is as close as a modern car can get to an Elan today.

## DEMANDS AND REWARDS

So why are the Elan and +2 so demanding and yet so rewarding? It's due to a number of issues, some of which are outlined below.

Firstly, we are dealing with 1960s technology. This is a *good thing*, but also presents some challenges. Service schedules for a Lotus are intense compared to today's company car culture, with its 20,000 miles between oil changes and sealed-for-life components. An Elan makes demands on its owner, which have to be met to keep the car in good fettle. Maintenance – little but often (and sometimes big) – is the key, along with a conscientious, knowledgeable, considerate and sensitive owner. The car needs to be used enough for the owner to be able identify problems before they become major. So, has the car used a bit more oil than usual this week? Does the steering seem a little bit heavier than last week? What's that new clonking noise from the rear end when accelerating? Is the battery charging correctly? Has something electrical stopped working? All these are signs that the car is telling you something is going wrong. In addition, the lifeblood of the Elan is its fluids, so the owner must monitor and maintain them. A sudden change in consumption of water, oil or petrol points to a

⅄ Under the bonnet of the Elan and +2 was Lotus' own engine – the famous Twin-cam. Although based on a cooking, or low-tuned, Ford Kent unit seen in the Anglia and Cortina, the Lotus head endowed the unit with excellent performance.

⅄ Independent suspension front and rear was rarely seen on British sportscars in the 1960s. The Elan and +2's wide wishbone and Chapman strut system was simple, but gave an excellent ride and roadholding.

new issue emerging that needs investigation. However, two areas where the Elan is definitely *not* stuck in the '60s is in the exemplary performance given by its state-of-the-art Twin-cam engine, and the ride and handling courtesy of the long-travel, softly sprung suspension. These two factors give the Elan a much more modern feel than any of its contemporary competitors, and make the car remarkably comfortable on today's roads.

Secondly, the cars were carefully engineered to be light. Again this is a good thing, but as before introduces possibly unintended consequences. These cars are delicate, precise instruments designed to scythe through traffic on A and B roads at top speed and the least interference – giving the driver maximum performance for minimal engine size; a simple function of weight, or rather lack of it. While lightness gives the car much of its character and performance, it is also its Achilles heel. Components are engineered to do their job and not much more, so additional strains and loads will lead to failure. For example, the suspension is designed to take the power and weight of the car; more power or additional weight will impose greater stress and decrease the life of bushes and bearings – witness the need for stronger rubber donuts on the Sprint and +2S 130 models. The chassis/subframe is lightly built from folded sheet steel, and is easily distorted by impacts (such as accidents or curbing the wheels) or even by incorrect jacking.

Its relatively lightweight construction, and lack of any significant rust proofing from new, means the unit will rust, usually in the front turrets that form the suspension mounts. Finally, age can take its toll, with stress cracks developing, often in the rear structure at the end of the transmission tunnel. Many Elans have had their chassis/subframes replaced with factory units, or spaceframe Spyder offerings, but there are a significant number that retained their original unit, and which are starting to be sought after by owners wanting to preserve originality.

The glass fibre body is lightly built and prone to cracking in the gel coat due to misuse – be careful how you close the doors – or the small knocks that cars suffer through general use. Bear in mind that the car's rigidity is derived from the combination of the body and chassis/subframe when they

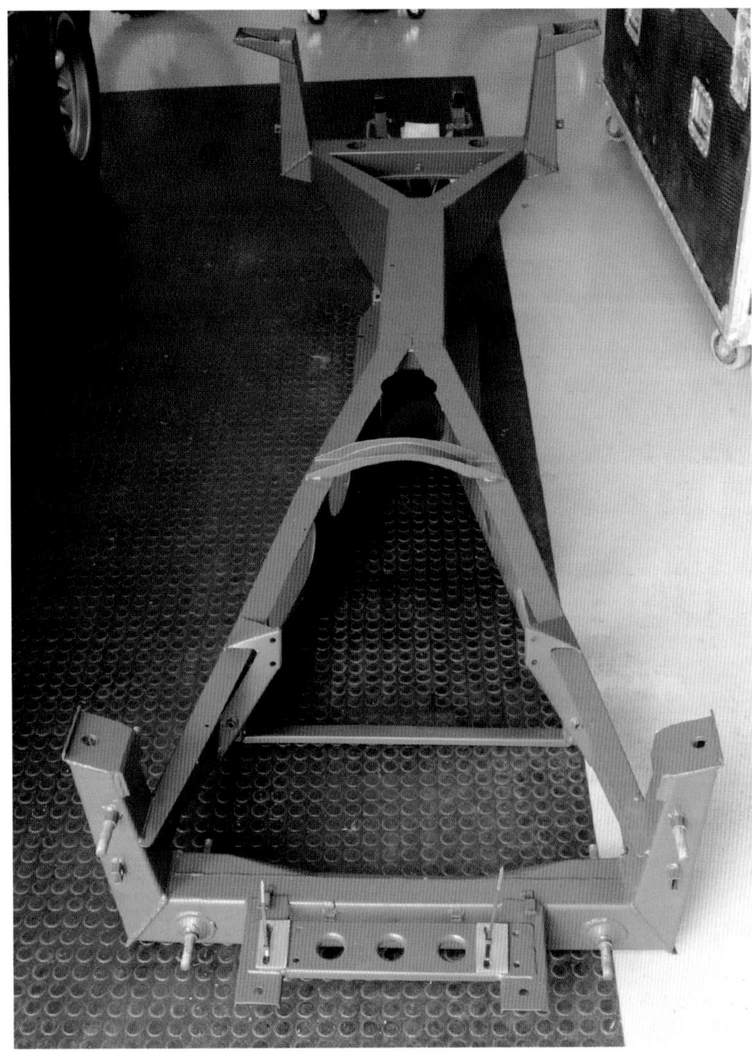

⮝ The original Elan chassis was simple and lightweight. Made from folded steel sheet, its only fault was that it could rust. This view shows the front turrets, the bases of which are often rusted out.

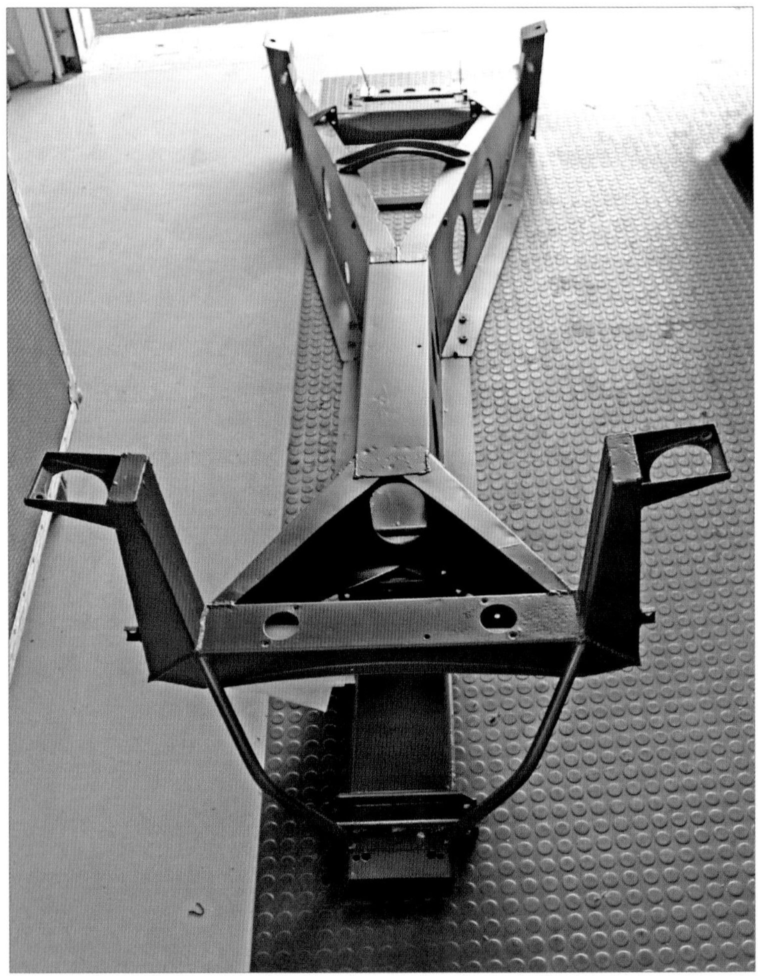

⮝ The rear view of the Lotus chassis shows its simple construction and the rear turrets that carry the rubber 'Lotocones,' which locate the tops of the rear struts.

are firmly bolted together. While damage to a corner, or the front and rear of the body, will be unlikely to damage the chassis, it may strain the body-to-chassis mounting points. However, an impact to the wheels or suspension components could, and usually will, result in damage to the chassis, which may also cause damage to the bodyshell around its mounting points.

Thirdly, the cars are used differently today than when they were new or descending into 'bangerdom.' While today they are usually used sparingly, and not as a daily driver, this lack of use introduces unreliability – connections corrode, bushes seize, grease dries out, and oil drains down from the top end of the engine. So, one way to get a car of the Lotus' ilk to be reliable is to use it – sparingly is okay, but often is the key. Back in the day the cars were used (and often abused), and when they became just another cheap secondhand sports car, maintenance often appeared low down on the owner's priorities. Spending just enough to get through the yearly MOT test, keeping them reliable enough to get the owner into work to earn the cash to pay the rent,

Early Elans are relatively rare. This is Jim Clark's original Series 1, which was subject to an epic restoration some years ago.

The Elan and +2 bodyshell is glass fibre, so does not rust. However, don't underestimate the amount of work it takes to restore the body if you want a good result! This is one of the author's +2s whilst being prepared for painting.

and otherwise having a good time was the norm. Today, if an owner uses the car regularly and often and maintains it properly, it will reward the owner with a surprisingly high level of reliability. Use is good.

Fourthly, while the glass fibre bodywork removes, at a stroke, the main concern of most British (and Italian) sports cars of that era – rust – it does introduce a whole raft of new problems that a lot of professional restorers and body shops do not understand. An Elan's body is built lightly. If you compare a Lotus body to a contemporary TVR or Reliant, the latter are built using a lot more material, the body sections are significantly thicker, and, while they are heavier, they are also a lot more robust. Lotus bodies are undeniably delicate, a corollary of being both light and cheap – why use more resin and glass fibre than is strictly necessary, when just enough is enough? A top quality final finish for any respray is the result of a lot of careful work, and in the case of an Elan the preparation of the glass fibre body is key. Any poor repairs will quickly become apparent once the car is painted, to the detriment of the its appearance. Even the best paint job will be affected by the inherent instability and flexibility of the body, and the life of an Elan paint job is significantly shorter than that on a metal-bodied car.

Fifthly, safety. The Elan was in production long before the advent of the built-in passive and active safety items of modern cars – there are no airbags, crumple zones, anti-lock brakes, active roll-over protections, or any of the other myriad of driver and passenger protection measures seen on modern cars. The first inklings of passive safety were introduced on the Elan Super Safety/S4 models and the +2S, all of which gave some thought to passenger safety by eliminating the worst protrusions in the cockpit – the most obvious change being the replacement of toggle switches with rocker switches, but also evidenced by the flat instrument bezels on the +2S and the British Leyland-derived flush inside door handles. However, the Elan does have a steel lattice bonded into the body around the door apertures, and the +2 has a steel beam running the length of the side sills, both of which afford some protection from side impact. The cars' glass fibre body also deforms progressively in a crash, absorbing crash energy while limiting the extent of damage to the car. It is in the active safety aspect that the Elan and +2 are probably better than any other contemporary vehicle – light weight, responsive engine and good brakes give the cars a very high level

⅄ The Elan's interior is fairly simple but good quality, reasonably roomy, and comfortable.

of performance, handling and manoeuvrability which can (hopefully) be exploited to enable the driver to avoid crashing in the first place. However, even an Elan cannot defy the laws of physics.

Finally, we have to confront the age of the cars today. Major components are pretty reliable, but an engine will probably need a rebuild after some 60,000 miles (100,000km), or ten or so years. The differential and gearbox, meanwhile, should last about twice that distance and time before needing attention. Suspension and brake components also have a limited life depending on how the car is driven, so expect to have to overhaul all the suspension probably twice as often as the engine.

Added to these issues is the age of the many other minor components that make up a large proportion of the car. The youngest cars in 2020 are nearing 50 years old, and when they were built their lifespan was expected to be a decade, maybe two if lucky. Today's survivors will have probably had

⅄ The +2 interior is a bit more sophisticated, and – while much more luxurious than the Elan's – usually needs more effort to restore. This rare Hexagon convertible +2 gives a unique view of the well stocked dash.

their engines, gearboxes and suspension rebuilt at least once, but are relying on components such as wiper, heater, and window motors, relays, wiring looms, fuse boxes, switches and instruments that were never intended or designed to last until today, and any of which could fail! Age also affects the interiors. From the spartan rubber mats and few creature comforts of the Elan Series 1 to the exceptionally well-appointed +2S 130/5, the interiors were designed down to a price, and can quickly look tatty and tired – especially if the soft top or door seals have been leaking.

The shortcomings of the Elan are all too easy to describe, and a prospective owner needs to be aware of what they are taking on. The cars are – in today's terms – high maintenance, but the rewards that the cars provide are beyond price and, in the enthusiast's mind, far outweigh the disadvantages. A well-sorted Elan or +2 is capable of covering a high daily mileage while keeping the driver and passenger comfortable, safe, warm (sometimes too warm), and dry, while carrying sufficient luggage for two; you can even add a couple of small children to the equation in the case of the +2. With the Elan and +2, the point is to enjoy the journey to your destination as much as the destination itself. You will aim to take the back roads, planning a route to avoid motorways, seeking out the twisty roads that the Lotus will relish. Every trip in an Elan or +2 is special, and the cars reflect the ideals of Lotus founder Colin Chapman – the driving force behind Lotus' unparalleled success in Formula 1 – to give the owner maximum performance at minimum weight. To someone used to a traditional British sports car of the time – such as the Triumph TR 4,5, and 6, or the MGB – the Elan is a quantum leap forwards in performance, handling and comfort, while remaining slightly higher-strung and possibly a bit less tolerant of ham-fisted handling. Owning and running an Elan is not a one-way street; the cars demand dedication and commitment from the owner if they are to give their best. So, if you don't want to make the commitment, then don't buy one. Make the commitment, however, and the Lotus rewards its driver with an unmatched package of handling and performance, along with the knowledge that you own and drive a car created by one of the geniuses of British industry.

## RUNNING AND REGULAR MAINTENANCE

### INTRODUCTION

When the author's father bought his first Lotus in the 1980s (a ten year old, well-used Éclat), he asked an engineer friend what he needed to do to keep it in fine fettle. The reply was initially "Don't buy it," but when appraised of the fact that he already had bought it, the advice was to "Check all the fluids before you use it, and keep them all topped up." Following this stricture resulted in a surprising degree of reliability from what was undoubtedly a car which was on the verge of 'bangerdom,' and the advice is valid and particularly apt for any aspiring Lotus owner and Lotus car, including the Elan and +2.

At the risk of 'teaching Grandma to suck eggs,' fluids are – by definition – the lifeblood of any car, and changes of level or colour over time can be used to diagnose problems before they result in breakdowns. Oil, coolant, brake fluid, clutch fluid, and petrol levels will all give clues as to the state of health of the car's systems. Engine oil levels usually drop, indicating the engine is burning some or it is leaking out: both common issues with the Twin-cam, and unless excessive are not too much to worry about, unless you value a clean driveway. The upside of leakage means the chassis will have a decent coating of waterproof gunge, which will slow down the inevitable rusting! Most Twin-cams will burn a little oil on start-up, but a continuous blue haze when running is not so good. The oil level rising is usually caused by one of two things: if it is accompanied by a falling of the coolant level, then the head gasket is probably failing; if not, then fuel is probably leaking past the pistons into the sump, due to carburettor float valve failure. Drops in coolant without a rise in oil level may still indicate problems with the head gasket, which may also result in white 'mayonnaise' in the oil filler. Otherwise, the coolant is being lost from a leaking hose, water pump, radiator, or heater matrix. Petrol use can be revealing – excessive fuel consumption implies a carburettor issue, or fuel leaks. A fuel fire in a glass fibre car can be extremely dangerous, both to the car and the occupants, so any leakage should be investigated, and the source of the leak found and fixed. If the body catches fire it can be very difficult to put out and damage will be extensive, while the risk to the driver and passenger is obvious and potentially fatal. Oil leaks from the gearbox and differential can be hard to discern, especially if the engine is leaking. If you suspect there is a problem, then check the levels regularly by adding oil to the units – when correct, the oil should be level with the bottom of the filler holes, and the units should not use any oil between changes. The main sources of gearbox leaks are from the rear output shaft seal, which should be obvious upon inspection. More unusually, the front input shaft can leak, which would result in oil leaking out of the bellhousing and potentially causing a slipping clutch, although these symptoms could also indicate the rear crankshaft seal has failed. There is a small breather valve on the top of the gearbox that allows for the oil to expand when it warms up. It is worth checking this is operating correctly before assuming the seal is compromised, as a blocked breather will cause the box to pressurise as it warms up, and blow oil out of the front and rear seals. At the rear of the car, the differential input and output shafts' oil seals can weep. Drops in brake or clutch fluids merit immediate investigation, as they indicate a failing in the brake system or the clutch release mechanism.

A pair of Elan Sprints rub shoulders with an M100 Elan, an Elise, and an Esprit at the Lotus day at Brands Hatch in 2014.

As well as regular inspection, the cars need regular servicing. The original Lotus service schedule for the Elan was an A-type service yearly, or every 5000 miles (8050km), and a more comprehensive B-type at two years or 7500 miles (1200km). However, today's owner probably only uses the car periodically and covers a low mileage so a yearly service will probably suffice.

## UNLEADED FUEL

The valve seats fitted to the Twin-cam head by the factory were made from relatively soft cast iron, but had a high nickel content to ensure their thermal expansion was the same as the LM8 WP alloy used to cast the head, and add durability to the seat. General experience seems to indicate that a Twin-cam that undergoes normal road use will not suffer from excessive valve seat recession for many thousands of miles. However, engines used hard – with regular use above 6000rpm – can and will suffer from rapid valve seat recession, which results in the valve clearances tightening up. So, it is well worth monitoring your valve clearances as per the schedule that follows, and record what the clearances are when you do check them. If the clearances are getting smaller, then it indicates that your engine is probably experiencing valve seat recession.

If you are getting your head overhauled, it is probably worth having the valve seats replaced with hardened ones, on both inlet and exhaust.

## ENGINE OIL

Miles Wilkins makes the point that the Twin-cam engine is based on 1950s technology, and has relatively wide clearances. The use of modern thin oils – whether mineral or synthetic – should be avoided, as the oil will simply drain down the valve guides, increasing oil consumption and potentially lowering the oil pressure. Wilkins advises that you stick to 20/50 or 15/50 oils, and the author concurs.

## ANTIFREEZE

While it is okay to run the engine with just water in the cooling system for short periods of time – for example, if

The oil filter on the Twin-cam is well hidden under the carburettors. Neglect it if you dare – clean oil is the lifeblood of any engine.

you've just replaced the water pump and want to check for leaks, you should never leave just water in the system. The mixture of alloy and cast iron components in the engine make the head and block vulnerable to corrosion, which can block the cooling system and corrode the head and block. Always use a good quality antifreeze with anti-corrosion protection, or store the engine dry.

## SUGGESTED SERVICE AND INSPECTION SCHEDULE

### INTRODUCTION

The following service and inspection schedule is based on Lotus' own schedule, and predicated on the Lotus A and B services, but redefined for the less intensive use that the Elan and +2 tend to be put through today. It is based on time and distance, and the tasks should be carried out as soon as either the suggested time period or mileage is reached.

Various sizes of radiators were fitted to the Elan and +2. This shot shows the full-width type, which many owners prefer. There is plenty of room to fit an electric fan.

## ON USE

Each time you go out in your car, check the following and top up if needed:

- Engine oil level
- Coolant level
- Tyre pressure
- Brake pedal pressure
- Brake fluid level
- Steering play
- Fan belt tension (½in movement in centre of longest run)
- All exterior bulbs
- Windscreen washer fluid
- Check for any oil leaks from engine, gearbox and differential
- Check for any water leaks from cooling system

Top up any fluids that are needed, replace any dud bulbs, and make a note of anything else may need more investigation. If the brake fluid level has dropped then don't drive the car – find out why fluid is being lost first.

## MONTHLY OR 500 MILES (800KM)

In addition to the 'On use' items specified above, check the following every month or 500 miles:

- Brake pad wear
- Wheel bearings
- Clutch fluid level

## YEARLY OR 5000 MILES (8000KM): LOTUS A SERVICE

Carry out the full Lotus A service for the car. The +2 service items are outlined below, and these are also applicable to the Elan.

## LUBRICATION

- Drain and replace engine oil
- Replace engine oil filter
- Check and top up gearbox and differential oil
- Grease propeller shaft universal joints
- Lubricate front suspension lower trunnions
- Lubricate throttle linkage
- Lubricate distributor cam weights
- Lubricate door locks, boot and bonnet locks and hinges

## ENGINE BAY

- Check security and condition of exhaust system and manifold
- Check tightness of fuel feed pipe connections
- Check fixing and rubber mounting movement of carburettors
- Check fan belt tension
- Check tightness of dynamo or alternator fixing bolts
- Top up engine coolant, including level in recuperator bottle
- Check all vacuum pipes and water hoses for condition, leaks and security
- Clean or replace air filter element
- Top up screen wash reservoir
- Check engine for oil and water leaks
- Set slow running (idle) mixtures and idle rpm

## IGNITION

- Check contact breaker points condition and gap (if fitted)
- Clean and reset or replace sparkplugs
- Check and adjust ignition timing

John Humfryes' lovely Series 4 Elan, which he has owned for many years.

## BRAKES AND CLUTCH

- Check brake and clutch master cylinder fluid levels, and top up as necessary
- If fluid level is low then check for cause
- Check braking system, including handbrake for correct operation
- Check all brake pipes (including servo pipes) for condition and security
- Check clutch slave cylinder push rod to release arm clearance
- Check all brake pads for material remaining. Replace if less than 3⁄32inch (2.4mm)

## STEERING AND SUSPENSION

- Repack front hubs with grease and readjust front wheel bearings
- Check the steering system for security and all moving parts for wear
- Check the front wishbones, lower trunnions and dampers for condition and security
- Check front disc mounting bolts for security

The +2 can fit into any social occasion, from the race track to the grand house, as shown by this early +2.

- Check front wheel toe-in
- Check rear wishbone and damper attachments for condition and security
- Check Rotoflex couplings for condition and security of mounting bolts

## ELECTRICAL

- Top up battery electrolyte
- Check battery terminals for security
- Lubricate battery terminals
- Check battery attachments for security
- Check cooling fan operation
- Check heater system operation
- Check operation of tachometer, oil pressure, water temperature, fuel and battery condition gauges
- Check operation of all lamps, windscreen wash and wipers, windows and rear screen heater (if fitted)
- Check headlamp beam setting

## WHEELS AND TYRES

- Check all wheel nuts for security
- Check all tyres for condition
- Set tyre pressures (including spare)

## BODY

- Check door adjustment
- Check operation of all locks and catches

## GENERAL

- Check condition and security of engine mounting bolts, gearbox and rear axle mounting bolts and propeller shaft retaining nuts and bolts

## ADDITIONAL CHECKS

As well as the Lotus A service checks described above you should also:

- Check the condition of the rubber engine mounts, gearbox mounts and differential mounts and snubbing rubbers
- Check the condition of the rear suspension Lotocones

## EVERY TWO YEARS OR 10,000 MILES (12,000KM): LOTUS B SERVICE

Every two years or 10,000 miles, you should carry out the tasks specified in the Lotus A service described above and in addition do the following Lotus B service checks:

### LUBRICATION

- Lubricate steering rack pinion

### ENGINE BAY

- Check timing chain tension and adjust if necessary
- Check torque of cylinder head bolts and tighten if necessary
- Check valve clearances and adjust if necessary
- Clean petrol pump filter
- Clean air filter body

### IGNITION

- No further checks required

### BRAKES AND CLUTCH

- Renew brake servo air filter
- Check for wear on brake and clutch master cylinder linkage and pivots

▲ The Series 3 and Series 4 Elans had a much-improved hood, which was bolted to the body and easy and quick to put up. The frames around the side windows helped the hood to fit snugly and cut down on draughts and wind noise.

### STEERING AND SUSPENSION

- Check rear hub bearings for security and moving parts for wear

### ELECTRICAL

- No further checks required

### WHEELS AND TYRES

- No further checks required

### BODY

- No further checks required

### GENERAL

- No further checks required

### ADDITIONAL CHECKS

As well as the Lotus B service checks described above, you should also follow the Lotus recommendation that the brake fluid is replaced every 18 months, and that the brake system is completely overhauled every three years, or 40,000 miles. The brake overhaul should include the replacement of all brake hoses, washers and seals.

If you have fitted replacement driveshafts with universal joints, these should be greased yearly or whenever the manufacturer recommends.

## THINGS TO WATCH OUT FOR

As well as the servicing and inspection regimes described above, the owner needs be aware of things that can go wrong, many of which can gradually deteriorate over time.

### BODY

### BODYWORK

In general the bodywork is pretty resilient, and there is no need to worry about rust! The bodyshell on the Elan and +2 is also quite resistant to minor damage, such as car park dings. The main preventative maintenance task is to keep the bodywork clean and give the paint a good wax regularly. The chrome on both the Elan and +2 is minimal. The side window frames on the Elan Series 3 and 4 and the +2 are chrome-plated brass, and should be kept polished and waxed. Even if the chrome looks worn, it is surprising how well it will respond to a good quality polish. Thc +2's bumpers are chromed, and again will need polishing from time to time. There are stainless steel rear bumpers out there, and these just need a wipe clean and the occasional polish.

## STRESS CRACKING

Stress cracks are where the gel coat has been fractured due to some force or impact being applied to it, such as impacts against immovable objects, or continued use of a component that is loose. Stress cracks can appear practically anywhere on the body, but are common on the flanks, around the wheelarches, on the top of the front wheelarches, and on top of the doors. They can also appear around the windscreen wiper spindles, boot hinge bolts, the tops of the door skins, and the top of the headlamp aperture on the +2. Repair of stress cracks entails chasing the crack out completely, before reglassing the surface and finishing. Not chasing out any stress crack – for example by just filling the crack – before painting is a waste of time, as the crack will quickly reappear.

## PAINTWORK

The paintwork on the Elan and +2 will reward care and attention. The usual rules apply: keep the paintwork clean, and regularly apply a good quality polish to keep the paintwork from deteriorating. The good news is that stone chips will not lead to rust, but they should still be touched-in to keep the car looking good. A good paint job is expensive due to the amount of preparation and time needed to do the job properly, so it is well worth nurturing the car's existing paintwork if it is in reasonable condition.

⅄ This shot shows typical cracking around the top edge of the +2 headlight opening on the nose.

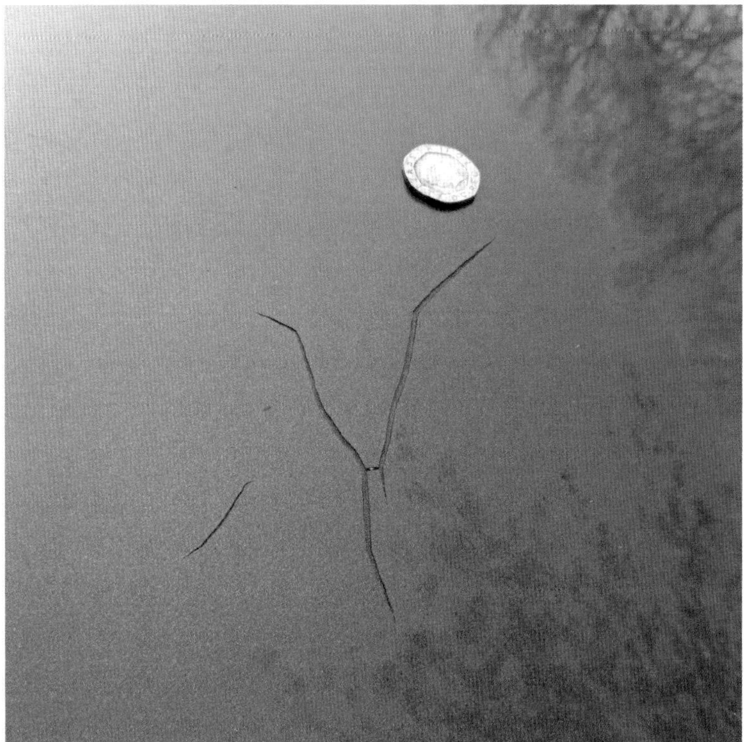

⅄ Too much paint will result in shrinkage and cracking – especially on areas that get hot, like the bonnet. A 20p coin (21.4mm) is included for scale.

## SUB ASSEMBLIES – DOORS, BOOT AND BONNET

On the Series 3, Series 4 and Sprint, it can be difficult to get the doors to fit in the body correctly – so that they fit flush on all sides – and no amount of hinge adjustment seems to make any difference. This is due to the doors' poor initial moulds producing poor-fitting doors, and the problem is compounded by the doors warping over time. The issue usually manifests in the lower rear edge of the door standing proud of the aperture. The solution is fairly major, and involves cutting a thin strip out of the rear of the door face, pressing the 'skin' inwards and glassing the skin back onto the door frame. Door skins can often exhibit stress cracks across their top face, where people have pushed against the skin to close the door, and around the exterior door handle if they have been used roughly – especially if they have been used to slam the door closed, or tugged on to try to open a locked door. Stress cracks can also form around the boot hinges if they are loose or too tightly bolted on. The bonnet can suffer from stress cracks if it has been slammed down on a foreign object left in the engine bay – for example a spanner left on the engine. The paint on the bonnet also has a hard time, as the engine bay gets hot. Too much paint on the bonnet will result in the paint cracking.

## HEADLAMP SYSTEM

Both the Elan and +2 signature feature is their pop-up headlamps. The movement of the pods containing the headlamps was achieved using a vacuum, with the front crossmember of the chassis acting as a vacuum reservoir. The reservoir was joined to the engine's inlet manifold via tubing and a one-way valve. Once the engine was operating, air was sucked out of the reservoir into the inlet manifold, and the vacuum maintained by the one-way valve. Each headlamp pod was attached by a rod to a vacuum cylinder, a rubber diaphragm enclosed in a steel casing, which would, when a vacuum was applied, pull the rod downwards, which in turn rotated the pod upwards. The 'light' switch on the dash was not electrical, but was in fact a vacuum switch that – when operated – connected the vacuum cylinders, causing them to lift the headlamp pods. The pods were fitted with switches that were flipped when the pod moved, and sent electrical power to the lights. The Elan Series 1 and 2 had spring-operated pull switches, while later Elans and +2s had micro-switches. If the pods do not rise when the engine is running, then this indicates a leak in the system – the worst case scenario is that the chassis crossmember has a hole in it. If the lights go down as soon as the engine is stopped, then this indicates that the non-return valve, usually fitted in the pipe from the manifold take-off, has failed.

The Series 4 Elans always suffered from poor-fitting doors. Poor quality moulds meant the rear edge of the door stood proud of the bodyshell, as seen here. ➤

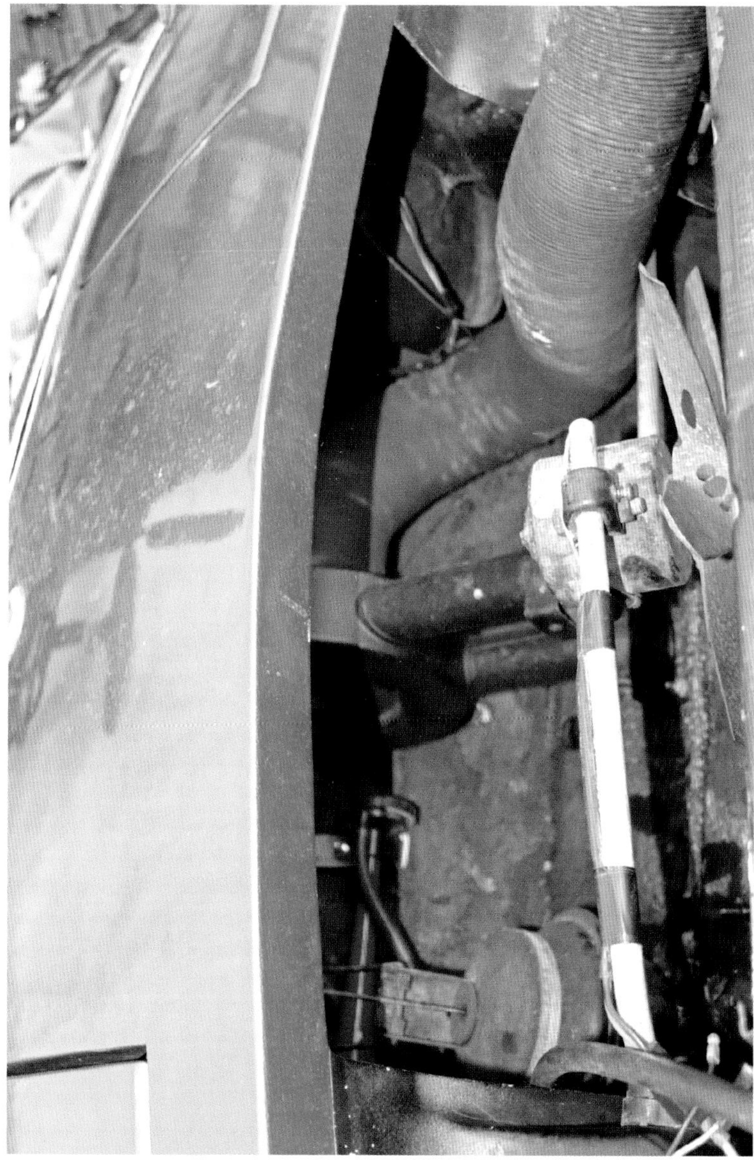

The headlight lift mechanism on the Elan and +2 was vacuum-operated, and relied on a complex system of pipes and micro switches to operate. To compound issues, the mechanism was buried in the nose of the car and is hard to access.

Early cars were fitted with 'fail-unsafe' systems, whereby the vacuum was used to hold the headlamp pods up, and springs were used to pull them down. Hence a vacuum failure – which was not uncommon – would result in the headlamps retracting. Federal legislation led to the lights being made fail-safe during 1972, with the vacuum used to hold the lights down and a failure making the lights return upwards – all in all a more sensible configuration. The fail-safe system had the two headlamp pods joined by a steel operating rod, and used a single vacuum cylinder to rotate the rod to raise or lower the pods. The vacuum control switch on the dash was replaced with a conventional electrical control switch, which operated a solenoid mounted in the engine bay to switch the vacuum on or off to the pods. The lighting circuit was protected with thermal overload switches to protect against shorts. Fail-safe systems are easily identified by the lights slowly raising themselves when the engine is off; this should take a reasonable amount of time to occur. If the pods raise quickly – ie between around five to ten minutes after the engine is switched off – then this indicates there is a leak in the system.

## FUEL TANK AND BREATHER SYSTEM

The +2 fuel tank is located relatively high up, and had its fuel filler pipe located in the middle of the side of the tank, connected to the fuel filler cap by a rubber elbow. This means the tank has to have a breather system, both to allow the tank to fill completely at the pump, and to let air into the tank when the engine is running. The breather system comprised a pair of large ¾in (1.9cm) diameter pipes running from each side of the top of the tank, up over the rear window, and sweeping down to exit holes in the inside edge of the sill just in front of the rear wheel. The design met two criteria – firstly, the tank would vent rapidly while being filled – stopping any blowback – and secondly, should the car turn over, the tank could not empty itself via the vent system. The system means that you may get a whiff of petrol from the rear side of the car if, for example, the car is filled up when it's cold outside, and then immediately placed in a warm garage. In normal use this should be slight and pretty much unnoticeable: any persistent smell of petrol in the boot or cabin will be due to leaks from the tank or the breather system. These could be from the rubber elbow to the tank filler, from the breather pipes themselves (which do harden and can fracture), a fracture in the brazed joint

The +2 fuel tank sits on top of the differential. Visible in this shot of a tank – taken from the rear – is the fuel filler, which is positioned half way down the side of the tank (red arrow), and the two vent outlets at the top of the tank (yellow arrows).

This is a shot of the chassis' nemesis – the front turret. As can be seen, the turret is open to the elements, and if the drain hole at its base gets blocked it will quickly rust out.

between the drain plug or banjo lugs and the bottom of the fuel tank, or rust on the top or bottom of the tank causing pin holes. Finally, the fuel feed banjo can leak, either at the through-bolt fixing into the tank, which must have good condition sealing washers in place, or at the olive fitting to the fuel hose itself, which must be tight. There are a number of modifications designed to replace this breathing system, which are described in Chapter 5.

## CHASSIS AND RUNNING GEAR

### CHASSIS

The Elan 'chassis' is more accurately described as a 'subframe,' as it is the combination of the frame and the body that gives the car its overall strength. UK owners should note that from the introduction of the Elan range, Lotus (and, later, Club Lotus) has an agreement with the UK vehicle licensing authorities that the 'chassis' is in fact a subframe. As such, it does not affect the formal identity of the car (ie its registration details) if the frame is replaced; nor does an owner have to inform the authorities if the frame is replaced. Alan Morgan at Club Lotus confirmed to the author that this arrangement was still in force at the time of writing.

While the subframe provided a relatively rigid sub-structure, the addition of the bodyshell added significant stiffness to the complete structure.

There is little regular maintenance to do on the chassis. Much of the structure is difficult or impossible to view or access with the body in place. The appearance of surface rust on the underside should be treated as soon as it appears; remember the main structure of the chassis is built from relatively thin steel sheet, and it does not take much rust to become serious. Luckily, the main area for rust – the front turrets – is accessible with the front wheels removed. Keep the drain holes in the base of the turrets clear, and keep a close eye on the state of them. It is well worth filling the turrets with oil-impregnated beads, or spraying oil or wax into the turrets on a regular basis.

### SUSPENSION AND BRAKES

The Elan and +2 share the same sophisticated all-independent suspension design, featuring a twin wishbone setup with combined coil spring and damper on the front, and at the rear a wide-spaced lower wishbone or A-frame with coil-sprung Chapman strut. This gives both cars relatively long wheel travel, which was softly sprung

⅄ The Elan and +2's front suspension uses Triumph Herald/Spitfire uprights with Spitfire disc brakes. Lotus used its own wishbones, which were longer on the +2 to provide the increased track over that of the Elan.

and progressively damped to give a compliant and well-controlled ride, along with excellent wheel control. The system as standard was non-adjustable, and with the exception of the front trunnions was very reliable and pretty much maintenance-free on a day-to-day basis.

⅄ At the rear, the wide-spaced bottom A-frame acted to locate the wheel longitudinally and transversely, while movement was controlled by the long-travel Chapman strut. Rear disc brakes were rare on British sports cars of the time.

There are a couple of areas that merit scrutiny while the car is in use. There should be no knocks coming from either end of the car; at the front, prime candidates for causing obvious knocking are the front anti-roll bar bushes. These are rubber, and suffer if they get coated in oil from the engine. The other source of knocks are worn nylon 'top-hat' bushes in the front trunnions. If the steering starts to stiffen, then it is likely that the trunnion swivels are dry of oil. Front wheel bearings are taper-type, and so are adjustable.

At the rear, the main issue is the rear wheel bearings. These have a relatively hard life, so do wear; the symptom is a whirring noise and – in extreme cases – knocking. They are not adjustable, so replacement is the solution.

With disc brakes all round there is little to go wrong or adjust. Keep an eye on pad wear and replace when required. There should be no fluid leaks, so if you start to lose brake fluid do not use the car until you fix the problem. The actual handbrake mechanism mounted on the callipers is reasonably robust, but the operating rods and the pivot tree on the chassis are quite flimsy. All parts of the handbrake mechanism are prone to seizure through corrosion.

## ENGINE

The Lotus Twin-cam unit is a relatively robust and reliable engine, with a propensity for being a bit oily and smoky, and has a 'between overhaul' life of around 50,000 to 70,000 miles (80,000 to 110,000km). The valve guides are relatively short and do let some oil into the combustion chamber, and as standard there are no rubber seals on the tops of the valve stems, so smoking on start-up is relatively common and is nothing to worry about. Smoking on acceleration and/or the over-run means a top end overhaul is needed.

The timing chain should be checked at the relevant service interval, and adjustment is simple, using the adjuster screw on the side of the timing case. The chain should be quiet when the engine is running; clattering from the timing case suggests a loose chain, while whirring implies a too tight chain – both of which are not good!

The water pump can be damaged by over-tightening the fan belt. If there is a leak from the pump, then the standard pump can only be replaced properly by removing the front timing cover, which will mean removing the head and the sump.

## CARBURETTORS

Through its life – and depending on the version – the Elan was fitted with a pair carburettors from one of three types: twin-choke Webers, twin-choke Dellortos, or constant-velocity Strombergs. All three types were rubber-mounted, and should have some movement present when fitted correctly. The movement helps to isolate the carbs from engine vibration, which causes frothing at higher revs, and if they are too rigid then bad running or a high speed misfire will occur.

⋏ John Humfryes' Elan Series 4 sports a fine pair of Weber carbs.

≺ The alloy timing case was unique to the Twin-cam and bolted directly on the front of the Ford block. The cam chain adjuster is arrowed – this engine has a new chain and sprockets, so the adjuster has plenty of play left.

A major cause of poor running is badly set-up carbs, and the Webers and Dellortos have much less tolerance of cack-handed owners than the Strombergs! The adjustment possibilities on Webers and Dellortos are many, and it is all too easy for an inexperienced or incompetent owner or mechanic to cock-up the balance and tuning of the carbs. So, owner beware: there is an apocryphal tale told regarding the average owner's ability to set up Webers. When Chapman was asked why the Elan did not have adjustable suspension, he replied that, considering the damage the average owner was doing to their Weber settings when armed with a simple screwdriver, making the suspension adjustable was just asking for trouble!

## TRANSMISSION

There is not much regular maintenance needed for the robust gearbox and differential – the main task is making sure the oil is in good condition, and has not all leaked out. Regular inspection should show if there is a problem with leaks.

Jon Bradbury's +2S 130/5 has very neat wiring, with a host of extra relays carefully positioned in the front of the engine bay, ahead of the radiator.

## ELECTRICS

The electrics on an Elan or +2 (more so on the +2) have a notorious reputation for unreliability. They do not have to be; some intelligent upgrades and careful maintenance will result in a reliable system, but 'as found,' many cars will display a myriad of strange and elusive electrical maladies. There are usually two simple cure for these – sort out the earths, and get rid of excess resistance by cleaning all the contacts!

Earths are the usual source of obscure electrical problems. A simple test is to run a new earth wire from the recalcitrant component to the battery terminal or one of the three main earthing points and see if the problem disappears. If it does, then it's time for that fun game that all Lotus owners get to play eventually: chase the earth. In general, the Elan and +2 electrical systems are fairly basic and the components that are used in them are still surprisingly reliable, considering their age. Problems are frequently due to poor connections rather than failed components, and the simple act of unplugging a connector will often clean off corrosion and restore a component to life. A dose of switch cleaner can also come in handy: a clean-up of connectors with a bit of emery paper and some electrical grease on old connectors helps to keep problems at bay.

The three main earth points are: in the boot, at the bobbin that bolts the body to the chassis, which should have the main battery lead attached to it; the bolt on the right-hand side of the tunnel, at the bottom of the dashboard; and one of the turrets in the engine bay.

Probably the major source of problems is the attempts by previous owners to bypass issues using extra wires and connectors, and the poor wiring-in of additional components such as radios, extra lights, and exotic electronic ignition systems. These 'fixes' typically use the ubiquitous blue snap-on 'scotch lock' connectors to feed power to the new components, which breach the original wires' insulation, can cut through the original wires, and only lead to problems. Strip them out, repair or replace the original wire, and use proper connectors.

An alternator produces more power than the original dynamo, and is a worthwhile upgrade, especially if the car is used in traffic or at night.

One point that is worth making, which was originally described in Brian Buckland's *The Rebuilding of a Lotus Elan – Addendum Engineering Workshop Manual* (see Bibliography). The Elan and +2 doesn't have a single fuse protecting all circuits. If you are doing work on the car's electrics, it is worthwhile to insert a fuse between the main feed wire into the loom and where it is connected onto the solenoid. Then, if disaster does strike and you get a direct feed to the earth side, the fuse will blow before the loom goes up in smoke – or the car suffers an electrical fire.

Poor charging is usually caused by a loose fan belt or tired dynamo. Worn brushes, corrosion in the connections to the field coils and output feed, and worn bearings will gradually reduce the dynamo's output, and electrical upgrades made to dynamo-equipped cars can lead to poor battery charging, as the dynamo is only rated at 22amps (264 watts). The dynamo's charging rate can be marginal if you are driving on a wet night with your uprated 60w headlamp bulbs blazing, heater fan on full chat and wipers doing overtime, especially if he dynamo is tired. The charging system on alternator equipped cars can pump out 36A (432W), can handle the maximum demand thrown on them, and while it will suffer from poor connections and mechanical wear, it tends to either definitively work or fail. The Lucas electro-mechanical regulators fitted to cars equipped with dynamos are all getting on, but usually just carry on working. Replacements are available, but some foreign-made items have a poor reputation. However, if sourced from a reputable dealer they are usually fine. Most alternators have a reliable solid-state rectifier and regulator incorporated into the body of the alternator. These tend to either work fine or fail completely, and, while repair is possible, complete new alternators are readily available and reasonably cheap.

## MISCELLANEOUS HINTS AND TIPS

### INTRODUCTION

Despite 'Lotus' often being quoted as standing for 'Loads Of Trouble, Usually Serious,' a well-maintained example is no more problematical than any other car; well, maybe a *bit* more problematical, due to Lotus' high state of tune and carefully engineered components. Be that as it may, as with all cars, the Elan and +2 have little quirks that a savvy owner can apply to save them both time and effort when fixing or avoiding problems. This section gives a summery of all those known to the author, and which have not been covered elsewhere in the book. Many of these tips have been documented on the fantastic lotuselan.net forum.

## DRIVING

When you start the car, does it take longer than usual for the engine to fire? Are there any unusual noises from the starter motor, or does the engine turn over a bit slower than usual? While things do change over time, a noticeable difference could indicate a developing fault. Slow turning over could be a failing battery or starter motor, while more churning than usual could be dodgy sparkplugs, or a fuel leak that has drained petrol from the feed pipe or carbs while the car was standing. Reluctance to fire when hot could be a failing coil.

Keep a wary eye on the instruments. If anything changes – say the water temperature seems to go up a bit higher than before, or the car takes longer to get up to temperature, or the oil pressure drops a little, or the voltmeter or ammeter reads a bit lower – don't ignore it, as it is likely to be a symptom of an emerging problem. If you catch it early, it should be cheap and easy to fix.

Try to be aware of any changes from drive to drive – if the noise level in the car goes up, or the suspension doesn't seem so compliant over the same stretch of road, or the steering seems stiffer, again, it is likely to be a symptom of impending problems. Find out why something has changed before it becomes obvious when something breaks or wears out!

Stiff steering, or steering failing to self-centre, is often due to lack of oil in the lower trunnions on the front suspension and causing them to seize up. If left and not addressed, the upright can snap just above the trunnion, which is both dangerous and expensive to fix.

Steering in the Elan and +2 should be reasonably sharp and responsive, but there should be minimal kick back. If the steering does react badly to bumps by kicking back, then it is likely that the level of steering rack in relation to the chassis is incorrect. The rack mount level is determined by shims under the mounts, and is chassis dependant. See Chapter 4 for details of measuring and setting the rack height.

This is a shot of the author's +2 dash with all the instruments registering. You can learn a lot from keeping a close eye on the instruments – strange behaviours here may be the first indication of a problem.

## BODY AND TRIM

The self-tapping screws that fix the bonnet clips to the bulkhead on the Elan should be screwed on from inside the car. It doesn't look as neat under the bonnet if they are – and they are awkward to fit – but if the bonnet cable seizes or breaks, then you can unscrew the catches from the bodyshell from inside the cabin to release the bonnet.

The windscreen frame on the convertible Elan is not the strongest of items, but it is light and does the job. There should be a wire connecting the top of the frame to the dash, which is in fact a bicycle wheel spoke. Make sure your car has this fitted, as it stops the top of the frame lifting at speed when the roof is up. If the frame does lift, the screen can pop out and land on you and your passengers laps, or worse.

Closing the doors should be done by gently pushing on the door skin with your palm – using the door handle concentrates the stress around the relatively small mounting holes, and may cause gel coat cracks.

If your +2 leaks fuel from the filler cap onto the rear wing when cornering, it is likely that you have the wrong filler cap, with a vent hole in its sealing disc. Pop the filler cap and look for a small hole on the steel disc inboard of the rubber seal. If there is one, then the cap is vented and the

This is the Elan's bonnet catch. Note the screws that fix it to the bulkhead have been put in from the interior, so the catches can be removed if the cable breaks.

The windscreen brace fitted to drop head Elans is a vital piece of equipment, and is not there just to provide a mount for the rear-view mirror. It keeps the top rail of the windscreen frame in position; without it the rail can lift, and the screen could pivot backwards into the car.

The filler cap on the +2 should not be vented. If the cap is vented (see the hole highlighted by the red arrow) then it is incorrect, and fuel will leak from the cap onto the rear wing when cornering.

Typical +2 air vents that have lost their chrome coating on the centre knob.

wrong type. You can fix it by plugging the hole with a petrol-resistant adhesive, or buy a complete seal refurbishment kit from the cap's original manufacturers: the cap is a Presto 75 Non-vented, from Ceandess of Wolverhampton.

If the cable-operated boot lid mechanism fails or jams on a later +2, then one way of getting the boot to open is to reach over the rear wheel, on the side where the pull lever is in the door jamb, locate the cable outer, and give it a tug. If the cable has slipped at the catch, and so is out of adjustment or broken, this may be just enough to trip the mechanism.

If this does not open the jammed boot, then the workshop manual details where to drill a 0.1875in (4.76mm) diameter access hole, behind the number plate, to gain access to the mechanism. This is sited 2.5in (63.5mm) down from the top edge of the boot opening, on the centreline of the car, then measure 1.75in (44.5mm) horizontally – to the left of the centreline on a right-hand drive car, and to the right on a left-hand drive car. Insert a thin screwdriver upwards at about 60 degrees, push down on the boot lid, and operate the slide sideways with the screwdriver. It is worth checking that the number plate can be removed with the boot closed – if it is fixed on by bolts with non-captive nuts then change the fixings before the boot jams.

If you are storing the car outside, then use a soft cotton cover over the bodyshell and then cover with a waterproof tarpaulin. Make sure air can circulate around and under the car, and remove the covers when the atmosphere is dry to air the car as often as possible.

Another lotuselan.net tip: the plastic eyeball dash vents in the +2 are now getting old, and the chrome-plated centre knobs have often lost their chrome. There is a two-stage solution to 'rechrome' them using a pair of products – google them for suppliers. First, use Molotow Liquid Chrome to paint the knobs, then use Liquitex Professional High Gloss Varnish to seal the finish. These products can also be used to refurbish any other plastic chrome parts, such as the chrome ring around the air vents.

The seats in the +2S are a lot plusher and have more moving parts than those in the Elan and the early +2. The mechanisms usually work seamlessly, but can seize up through lack of use and dried-out grease. It's well worth taking a bit of time to carefully grease the pivots and runners once a year or so.

Gordon Sauer on lotuselan.net recommends the use of hook and eye Velcro pads, rather than the usual self-tapping screws, to address issues like the fixing the under dash bolsters in place, securing the carpets to the floor, and also to persuade a loose +2 map light to stay parked!

+2 door hinges pivot on a pair of nylon 'top-hat' bushes, which are the same parts used in the front suspension's lower trunnions.

The experts on lotuselan.net named the two bolts that form the +2's bonnet hinges as the two most frustrating bolts on the car. To ease the hassle of taking off and replacing the +2's bonnet, grind a bevel on the end of each bolt to make them easier to get the thread started in the bobbins. Then, weld a washer at 90° to the head of each bolt so it acts like a wing bolt, so you can screw them in or out by hand, which is easier than getting a socket or spanner on them.

It is awkward to get at the clevis pins that are used to attach the clutch and brake pedal to the master cylinders. There are two fixes: either drill a pair of holes in the top of the pedal box, to give access to the pivots and cover with rubber grommets; or cut a hatch in the top of the pedal box, and cover the hole with a panel secured by self tapping screws or rivet nuts. Make sure you fit a gasket to make the hatch waterproof, otherwise you may have water leaking in via the pedal box when it rains.

In the Elan and early +2, the seats are bolted directly to the floor and have a limited range of movement. However, there are two positions they can be bolted in that give greater or lesser legroom. An Elan should accommodate the full range of driver sizes, so if it seems you have too little or too much legroom, check the seat position and the seat mounts.

It is worth painting all surfaces of the car, inside and out. Paint blistering is common on the Elan and +2, and can be caused by damp permeating the body panels through the unpainted interior panels. Painting the inside face of all body panels can help to stem the flow of moisture and cut down on blistering, but make sure the shell is totally dry before painting.

The faces of the rocker switches in the Series 3 and 4 Elans and +2S can fade and go grey. Various solutions have been suggested to bring these back to the original finish. Proprietary plastic cleaners such as Armor All or Autoglym Vinyl and Rubber Care will restore the finish, but may not

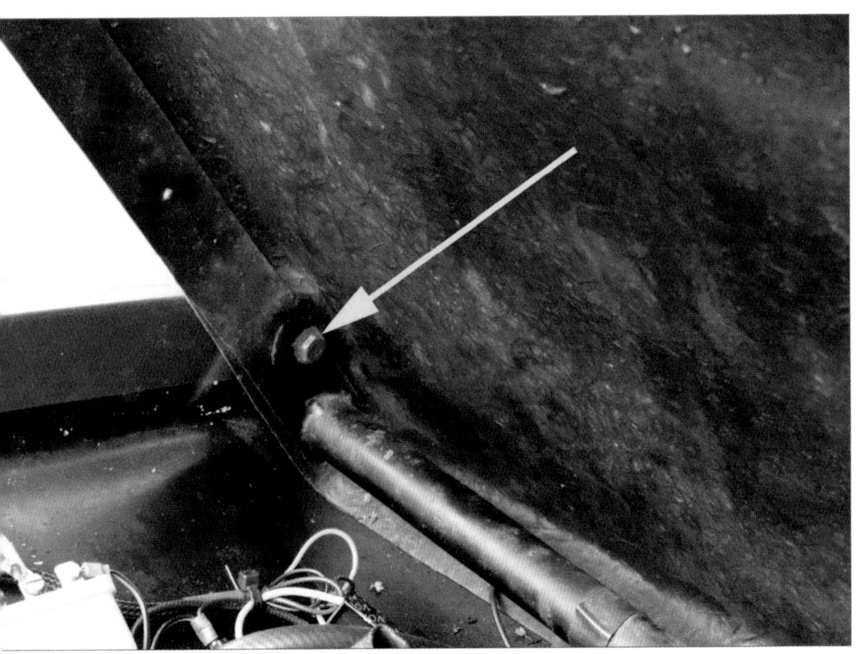

The worst bolts on the car – the +2 bonnet pivot bolts!

Jon Bradbury swears by baby oil to renovate switches and instrument faces. Here is the evidence that it works – the restored dash of his +2S 130/5 with gleaming rockers.

last more than a year or so. Some people advocate that you use brake fluid, which – again – will restore the finish but may not last, and baby oil has been used successfully by some owners – Jon Bradbury also used baby oil to successfully restore the faces of his instruments. Finally, you can clean the switches and spray them with black paint for a more resilient finish.

## WHEELS AND BRAKES

When putting on or taking off wheels, bashing the eared spinners – even with a hide hammer – can result in dents and damage to the chrome. Over the years, various suppliers have produced three-eared leather-coated 'grips' that not only protect the chrome from damage, but also allows the use of a torque wrench to accurately tighten the spinner.

There are sockets available for the octagonal 'safety' spinners, that allow you to use a torque wrench to tighten them to the correct torque, rather than Lotus' own rather crude 'ring' spanner.

Do not use spinners marked 'alloy wheels only' on steel wheels. The taper angle on the eight-sided alloy wheel nut is different to the three-eared type, so may not seat correctly on steel wheels. Also, if used with steel wheels, the thread inside the octagonal spinner may bottom out on the hub before it actually clamps the wheel in place against the hub.

Make sure all your wheels and tyres are balanced; an imbalance can throw up some strange noises and vibration.

Check the age of your tyres, especially if you've just bought the car. All tyres should have a four-digit age stamp showing the week and year of manufacture. If the tyre hasn't got one, then it's very old! Replace tyres once they reach about ten years old.

The ratchet handle for the standard Lotus +2 jack was also used by contemporary Jaguars.

Never jack up the car on the chassis, as it will bend. If you can't use the standard jacking points then spread the load from the jack using a large flat off-cut of wood, placed between the jack and the floor of the car.

## ENGINE, GEARBOX AND DIFFERENTIAL

The cam cover gasket on the Twin-cam engine is a large cork affair, that is easily damaged. When fitting a new one, stick it onto the head with a thin smear of silicone sealant,

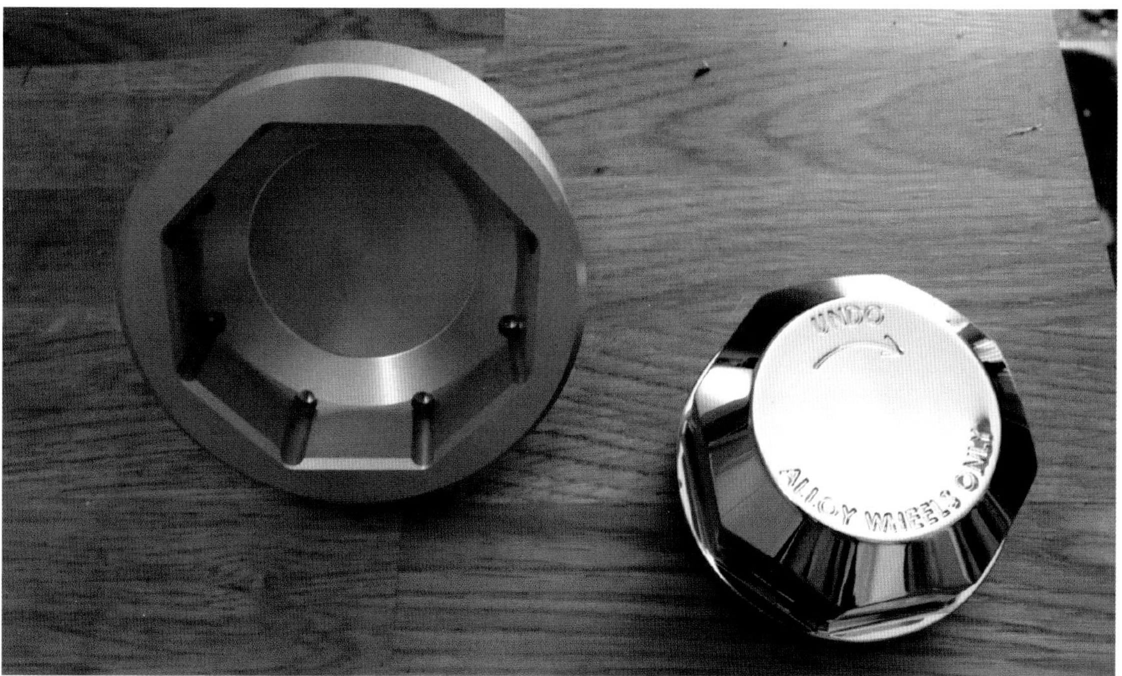


◄ Octagonal wheel nuts marked 'alloy wheels only' should not be used on steel wheels, as their threads may bottom out on the hub before fully tightening the wheel. Note the neat alloy socket, which can be used with a torque wrench and will be gentle on the chrome.

then lightly coat its surface with grease before fitting the cover. This should mean it stays in place on the head when the cam cover is removed and will separate from the cam cover, cleanly avoiding damage.

The cam cover gasket should be a about 3mm thick, and should have some 'bounce' in it. If it hasn't, then it's time to replace it.

Make sure you use the special rubber sealing washers under the cam cover nuts. If you don't, oil will leak from around the studs.

On Weber and Dellorto carbs, don't over-tighten the carb-to-manifold joints – the rubber O-rings fitted either side of the carb-to-manifold spacer are there both to seal the inlet tract and to isolate the carb from engine vibration. There should be a gap of 40 thou (1.01mm) between the coils of the spring washers on the carb studs, and the carbs should have some play, and so can be moved up and down. The spring washers should be in good condition so that they lock the fixing nuts in place.

Stromberg carbs are also mounted using O-rings between the carburettor-to-flange assembly, and there should be a consistent 70 thou (1.78mm) gap between the parts. Again, as long as the spring washers are in good condition they will prevent the carbs falling off!

There is an engine breather pipe running from the cylinder head into the air box. You should check periodically that the pipe is not blocked, and that the air box isn't full of oily gunge.

Remember that, when up to temperature, a standard Twin-cam will have a running oil pressure of around 35-40psi (2.4-2.8kg/cm$^2$). While this seems low when compared to other engines, it is normal. Higher pressure may indicate that a high-capacity oil pump has been fitted.

Make sure that the foam rubber seal running across the top of the radiator is in good condition. It is there to help to duct cooling air through the radiator.

Sprints were fitted with a blanking panel fitted below the radiator, designed to improve airflow through the radiator. These can be retrofitted to earlier models to improve cooling.

▲ The breather pipe on the back of the head connects the crankcase to the air box. If blocked, you will have oil leaks and potentially a drop in performance.

Remove the inefficient pressed steel fan blade fitted to the crank pulley, and replace it with a thermostatically-controlled electric fan mounted on the radiator. This will enable you to run the fan belt slightly looser, as it is doing less work, which will increase the life of the water pump bearing, as well as saving a bit of power and improving the cooling system's efficiency.

Engines fitted with Stromberg carburettors will run up to 5°C hotter than the equivalent Weber or Dellorto cars. This is due to the different port shapes and the carburettors giving a leaner mixture, and is nothing to worry about.

Stromberg dash pots should be filled with thin (SAE 20-grade) oil, up to ¼in (6.4mm) from the top of the damper tube. If the oil level is too low, then a flat spot will occur if the throttle is snapped open.

Stale fuel can stop an engine from starting – always try to use some new fuel if the car has been standing for a while.

It is well worth numbering the sparkplug leads – getting them round the wrong way is embarrassing, irritating and can be tricky to fix!

The Twin-cam's sparkplugs are easily accessible in the well between the cams. It is well worth numbering the sparkplug leads.

The first port of call in tracing a misfire is the sparkplugs. Modern plugs soot up a lot easier than they used to, and can be difficult to clean. Buy new plugs from reliable sources, as there are a lot of fake Champion and NGK plugs out there.

The second port of call for misfires is the 'anti-theft' cut-off switch in the glove box. These are now over 50 years old and can fail, cutting off power intermittently to the coil. Replace or isolate!

If the car is misfiring repeatedly due to fouled plugs then try running the next hotter grade of plug. A hotter plug dissipates less heat into the head, so remains hotter and burns off deposits better than a cooler plug. With NGK plugs this means decreasing the plug number, so an NGK B6 is 'hotter' than a B7, and with Champions it's the other way round – so a Champion N4 is 'hotter' than an N3. If you do change the grade of plug then check the engine is not running too hot by doing a plug chop and checking the plug's colour – light brown is good, white means the plug is too hot.

Fitting an electric fuel pump can be helpful if the car is only used periodically, and saves cranking the engine over to fill the carbs using the standard mechanical pump. Fit an impact switch to the pump's power supply so it is electrically isolated if the car is crashed. A hidden manual

Cutting a hole in the body under the fuel tank gives access to the differential filler plug and the handbrake mechanism. Make sure the cover is waterproof.

cut-off switch for the pump is a useful anti-theft device.

If you do not have access to a ramp, then drill or cut a hole in the rear of the boot to give access to the differential level and filling plug. This makes changing the differential oil easy. Either cover it with a flat steel plate, or cut a round hole and use a large rubber cover from a marine chandlers or similar. Make sure the cover is watertight.

## SUSPENSION

Check that the plate that closes off the bottom face of the lower trunnion on the front suspension is oil tight. Lotus recommends the use of EP90 gear oil for the trunnion, and if the plate is loose then you will rapidly lose the oil, resulting in rapid wear and – in the worst case – stiff or even seized steering and a broken front upright. You may be able to seal the plate with solder or epoxy resin if it is loose or leaking.

Worn out front anti-roll bar bushes are a common source of knocks from the front suspension. While they do wear, they are more usually contaminated and softened by oil leaking from the engine.

The rear suspension should have a cylindrical rubber AEON buffer fitted on the damper tube. This acts as an additional progressive spring when the suspension approaches its full travel, and must be present. On the +2 there is an alloy spacer that should sit on the bottom of the damper rod, below the AEON buffer, again to limit suspension movement.

When refitting wishbones using the original-style metalastic bushes, tighten the front spindle bolts and rear chassis bolts when the car is sitting level on the ground and fully assembled. This will ensure the rubber in the metalastic bushes is neutrally 'tensioned' when the car is level and at rest.

If you want to get some wire rope restraints made up for limiting suspension movement when fitting CV driveshafts, then a ship's chandler will often be able to make up a limiting strap using stainless wire and fittings usually used for making stays for yacht masts.

When you are replacing the rear wishbone bolts with the body removed from the chassis, make sure you put them in the right way round so you can remove them with the body on the chassis. The bolts should be inserted from between the wishbone ends with their heads facing each other, so the nuts are on the outside face of both wishbone ends.

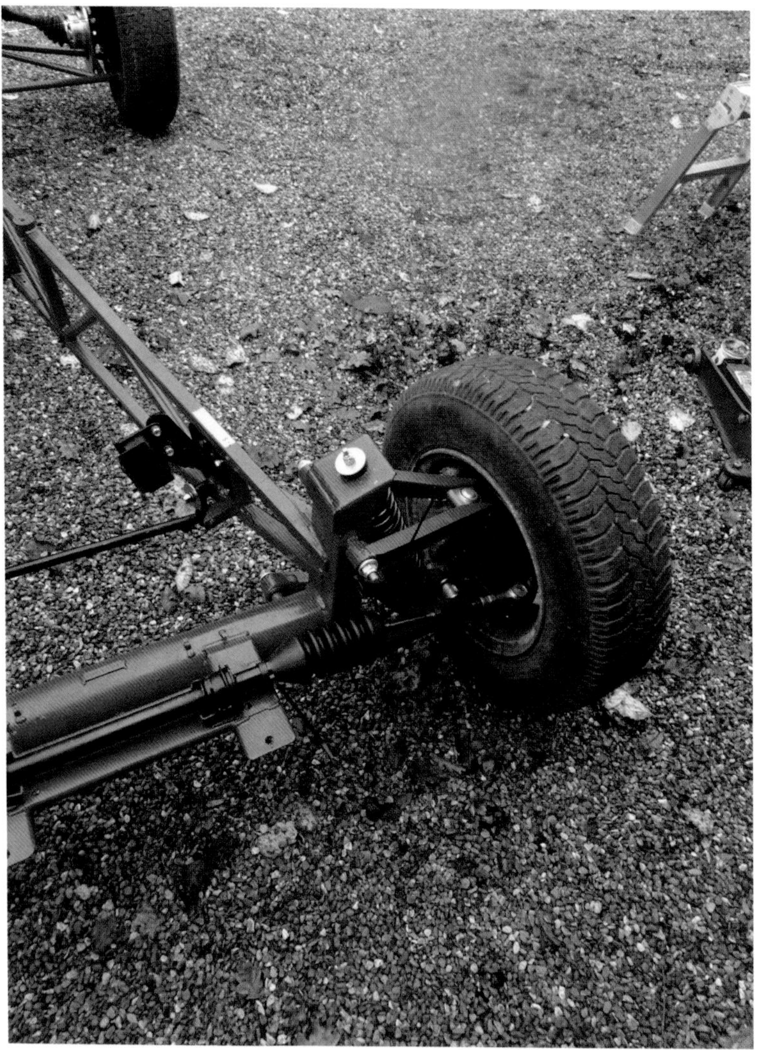

The anti-roll bar bushes on the drop link are often the first suspension bushes to wear, as they are often contaminated with oil. They make an alarming 'clonk' when they are worn.

Removing the rear hub requires a special tool to pull it off the outer driveshaft. You can often get away with using an alloy spacer to butt against the shaft – being careful not to damage the threads – and then screwing a spinner onto the hub so that it pushes the against the spacer, and draws the hub off.

Particularly tight nuts can usually be persuaded to undo with an impact driver. These can be either air- or battery-powered, and have helped the author dismantle several assemblies without damage.

The rear wishbone or A-frame to chassis bolts should be put in with the heads facing each other, as seen here. Put them in the other way round, and they cannot be extracted with the body in place.

## ELECTRICS

Always buy good quality ignition and electrical components such as coils, relays, HT leads, distributor caps, rotor arms, etc, from trusted sellers. There are too many low quality pattern parts out there.

The standard electrical setup has only a few fuses. It is relatively easy to fit a new modern fusebox with individual protection for more of the original circuits. This will allow the use of the correct fuse rating for individual circuits, and simplify fault finding at the cost of originality.

Rewire the headlamp feed wiring with relays – this both avoids running relatively high current through the headlight switch and dash wiring, and will also help to feed the full 12V to the lights.

Remember that most engine running problems that seem to be carburettor related are usually electrical, and vice versa.

Replacing the original dynamo with an alternator will provide reliable charging and more capacity for other electrical improvements. Replacement alternators that look like dynamos are available if you want to keep the engine bay looking original.

Jon Bradbury's fitment of relays shown close up – note they are all labelled, which helps fault finding.

If you do fit a standard alternator you will also need a new fixing bracket that bolts to the engine block, and an adjuster strap that bolts to the timing chest. It is also advisable to fit the steel reinforcement strip that is bolted to the timing cover, to spread the load caused by the new adjuster strip.

LED-based instrument bulbs can be an improvement on the standard festoon type, giving more light for less power, and increasing the visibility of the instruments at night. They also come in a variety of colours to jazz up the car's interior at night!

The various small electrical instruments such as the temperature and fuel gauges are designed to run on a 10V feed rather than 12V, to allow accuracy in the face of variations in battery voltage. They are all powered through a voltage regulator. The standard item is electro-mechanical, and will be getting old, which will result in the instruments registering low (or possibly high). It is viable solution to change the regulator for a readily-available semiconductor-based unit.

As has been said many times before: if there is an electrical problem, the first thing to do is check the earth!

## CONCLUSIONS

A well-maintained and looked after Elan or +2 is a rewarding and enjoyable classic car, and, like any classic, rewards careful handling and regular preventative maintenance. All Lotus cars have their quirks and character; these are part and parcel of ownership, and should be embraced. Elan and +2 ownership is a learning curve, and even experienced users can be caught out! Even an impeccably maintained and driven Elan or +2 may let you down, but care and attention will reduce the chances of that happening.

Finally, probably the most satisfying hint and tip is to join lotuselan.net. It is free and friendly, will save you both time and money if a problem arises with your Elan or +2, and is a marvellous source of tales and stories about the Elan, as well as a great place to post up your Elan-based triumphs and tribulations.

## JON BRADBURY'S 1973 +2S 130/5

Jon Bradbury has owned his +2 since November 2017, and in that time has carried out a large number of improvements, fettles and fixes to make the car reliable, mechanically sound, and look good cosmetically. The car is a March 1973 +2S 130/5, and it is now resplendent with the original Carnival Red paintwork replaced by Lotus Roman Purple, which sets off the silver metal flake roof brilliantly.

Jon took the process of buying the car seriously. He wanted a hobby, and started to consider a classic car as retirement approached. He originally thought about getting a Triumph Spitfire, as he had owned some in the past, but was put off by the high prices being asked for mediocre cars. He came into the Lotus fold after he realised what good value +2s were – especially when compared to baby Elans and Europas – and did his research on the lotuselan.net website. He even viewed a car owned by a forum member before taking the plunge with his car.

Since he has had the car, Jon has treated it to a 'rolling restoration,' with many replacement parts and repairs carried out to bring it up to an acceptable standard – a not-uncommon situation today, as +2s creep out of the realms of 'bangerdom' and become desirable cars in their own right. Along with a full suspension refurbish, including rear wheel bearings and a new outer driveshaft, other major jobs carried out by Jon included fitting Sue Miller CV-jointed driveshafts, fitting a new clutch, overhauling the differential, updating the electrics (fitting relays where possible), fitting an electric fuel pump, and generally tidying up the car. The end result was a car in which everything works – even all the electrical gubbins. Jon was particularly pleased with his fix for the clock, which incorporated a protection circuit that prevents the clock self-destructing when the car's battery is low.

The car's handling and roadholding, once the suspension had been sorted out, is great. In Jon's own words:

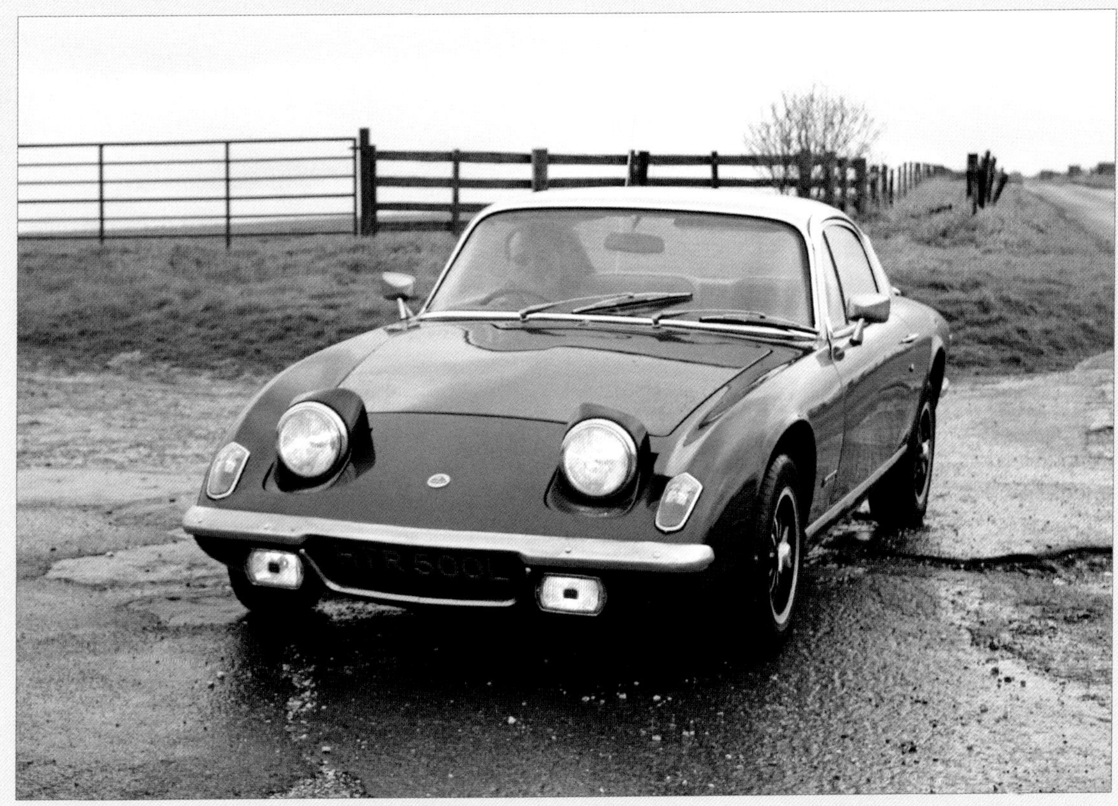

◄ Jon Bradbury's +2S 130/5 is a fine example of the breed. It is unusual to see a shot of a +2 with the lights on and spots blazing.

"Steering is very sensitive to input. This is quite different to modern cars that have high castor angles and power steering. There is very little self-centreing force on the +2, but once you get used to this it is very nimble. Turn-in is lightning-quick, and it can catch you out if you are not familiar with it. For a 47-year-old car, it is amazing (and this coming from someone who used to own an Elise). The Lotus handling DNA is very much present, and I think this is down to the suspension overhaul. Prior to the overhaul, the car was overcompensating when turned in; it would dive into corners scarily, as if it had roll steer (I later found out this was because the anti-roll bar bushes were shot, and there was a few millimetres of play on the joints). Another problem it had was vagueness in a straight line; this was caused by having overinflated tyres. The suspension geometry on these cars is very sensitive to out-of-range parameters! Grip is good, and I rarely encounter tail happiness, despite being an enthusiastic driver. When it does start to slide, it is progressive and can easily be corrected. Body roll feels quite pronounced, but this is by design and once the car has reached a certain point (this being when the rubber bump stops are reached by the shock absorber), the car adopts a set stance and just carries on round the bend. I recall the Elise being like this as well. It is very confidence-inspiring. The only thing to be aware of is wet braking performance is not great. The car is very happy to lock up the front wheels in the wet, especially under emergency braking. Whether that is due to the low weight, tyre pressures or braking system imbalance is unknown."

Jon's experience matches closely to the author's findings in his +2, and serves to reinforce the excellence of the +2's suspension package. Finally, after several years of ownership, Jon has the following 'top tips' for current and prospective +2 owners:

The interior of Jon Bradbury's +2 is standard and shows the high level of refinement and comfort that these cars offer. ➤

"First off, as soon as you buy a car, check the front suspension's trunnions. Disconnect the bolt that holds the trunnion on to the lower wishbone, then unscrew each trunnion off the bottom of the uprights. Check the threaded kingpins for rust or other damage. If you find any, replace them. There are many true stories of these vital parts shearing off at low speed due to rust and/or poor manufacturing causing 'stress risers' (microscopic cracks in the metal) which can cause sudden failure. Also, ensure the trunnion is oiled regularly per the service schedule, using EP90 gear oil, injected into the grease nipple on the uprights with a grease gun, until you see clean oil oozing from the top of the trunnion. There is debate about lubricating this joint with EP90 or grease. Use EP90, that is what Triumph [the original users of the uprights] recommended, and do it regularly. The service interval is 12 months. If on first inspection you

⮝ Jon's careful maintenance, and the attention to detail he lavishes on the car, is shown in the appearance under the bonnet. As is the case with both the Elan and the +2, the Twin-cam dominates the engine bay.

Taken on a somewhat damp day on the South Downs, this shot shows Jon's +2 ready for another blast across the countryside.

find cracked seals or soap-like deposits of old grease, dismantle and inspect immediately.

"Get rid of the rubber Rotoflex couplings on the rear half shafts and replace with CV-jointed shafts. This is not a cheap option – they cost £650 at the time of writing – but they are 'fit and forget.' Apart from the 'winding up' effects you encounter with the rubber joints, they can fail spectacularly, leading to huge damage to the underside of the car. There is much debate about the quality of modern replacement Rotoflexes, and a full set is almost as expensive as a CV-joint conversion, so for peace of mind it's a 'must have' to go for the CV joints.

"On the later S 130 models, Lotus deleted all the relays from the wiring loom, apart from the air horn and starter relays. To protect the lighting circuits, it fitted thermal cut-outs, which seem to be very close tolerance. On my car, I have halogen headlights, and these would trip the cut-outs – plunging me into darkness without warning (this happened once on a dark lane at speed; fortunately I was able to safely pull the car into a lay-by). One of the first things I did after this event was to wire in fused relays for the main and dipped beams, using the old main/dip power wires to trigger the relays and laying a new +12V line to provide power. I feel that this is the very bare essential work if you have one of these models, as it is a matter of safety. I later revisited this wiring and fitted fused relays to the radiator fan, spotlights and horn (replacing the original). This was well worth it, especially as I'd also laid in a new ground wire, which helps greatly with electrical performance.

"I fitted an electric fuel pump. The reason being, that fuel will evaporate from the carburettor float bowls when the car is left for a few days, leading to the need (with the mechanical pump) to turn the engine over excessively when starting, in order to refill the bowls. This, in turn, causes increased wear on the starter motor, its gears, and the starter ring. When doing this conversion, you need a safety cut-out switch – I used an inertia switch from a Ford Ka. Choose the pump carefully – you need a low pressure pump suitable for your carburettors. Mine is a Huco model 133010.

"Check the main chassis earth in the boot. This is the bolt that the negative side of the battery is connected to. You need a good earth connection here, as the rest of the car depends on it. Take the negative wire off the bolt end and clean the bolt, washers, and wire end tab with a wire brush, then reassemble with copper grease."

Jon's +2 is a credit to his maintenance skills and runs and drives just as a +2 should. Its spectacular Roman Purple paintwork complements the silver roof perfectly, and the car really epitomises all that was great with the 1970s Lotus.

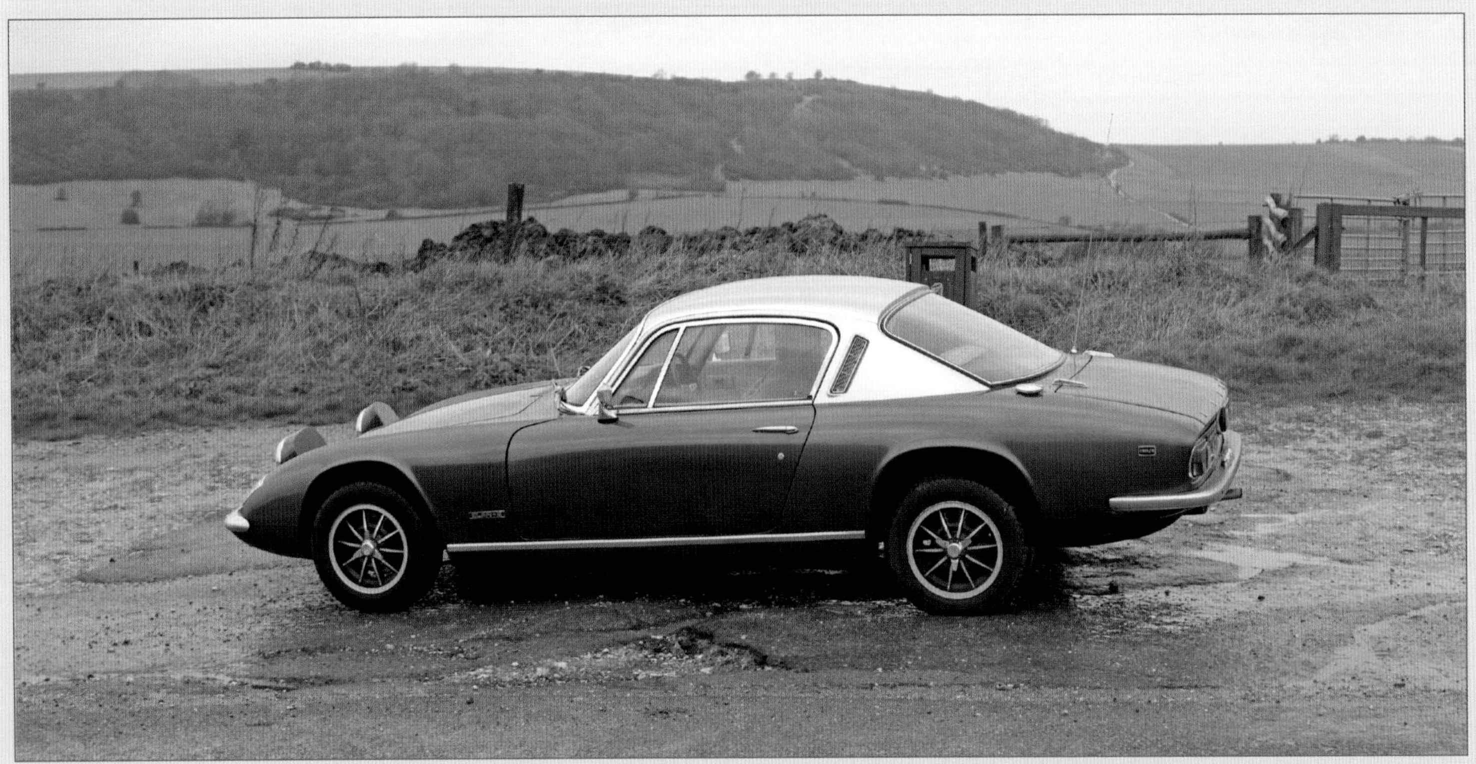

The contrast between the silver metal flake roof and the Roman Purple paintwork is shown to good effect in this shot. All in all, a rather nice '70s colour scheme.

# Restoration Guide

## INTRODUCTION

The restoration of an Elan or +2 is well within the capabilities of anyone with a modicum of common sense, some mechanical knowledge, and a willingness to learn new skills. Unlike some exotica, there is only a little mechanical complexity in an Elan; the Twin-cam engine bottom end is all run-of-the-mill Ford, as is the gearbox, and while the rear suspension is all Lotus, the front (apart from the wishbones) are mainly proprietary parts from Standard Triumph. The chassis or subframe means that any metalworking – ie, welding and fabrication – is limited (or the whole unit can be replaced), and the glass fibre bodyshell can be repaired using easy-to-learn skills. Finally, the strong market for the Elan and +2 means that virtually all parts needed to restore a car are available off-the-shelf, and the value of a well-restored car will be equal to, if not exceed, the cost of doing a home restoration where you do the majority of the work.

The last version of the Elan was the Sprint. Seen here is Tom Featherstone's super example in red, driving with the lights on.

Two books that will make life a lot easier in any restoration are the official Lotus workshop manual and service parts list. There are separate volumes for the Elan and the +2, and these are available from the suppliers shown in Chapter 6. The workshop manual does what it says on the can – it describes the processes and procedures for removing, repairing and reassembling all aspects of the car. The service parts list shows every component and sub-component of the car in 'exploded' diagrams; not only does this give you the original Lotus part number of a component, but it also shows the order of assembly of components. Finally, the part number of the many nuts, bolts and screws incorporated a code that describes the specification of each standard nut, bolt and screw fixing. The parts lists and manuals are supplied in ring binders – this makes it easy to copy individual pages for use in the workshop, which avoids getting the originals mucky.

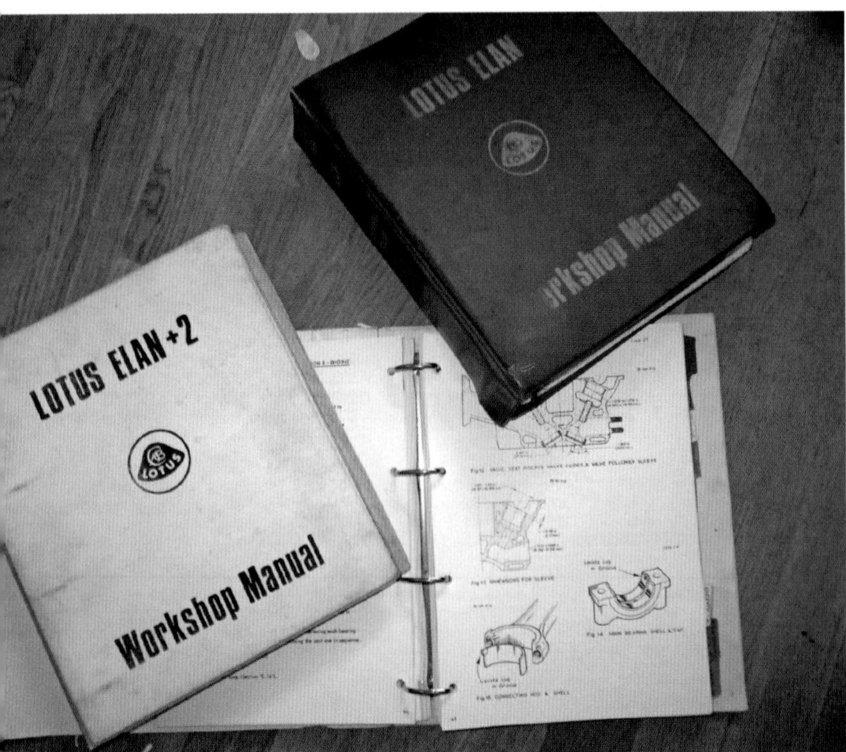


Restoring an Elan and +2 is straightforward, but you are strongly advised to purchase copies of the official Lotus workshop manual and parts lists. They are not cheap, but are full of useful information.

## GENERAL RESTORATION CONSIDERATIONS

### INTRODUCTION

When embarking on a restoration project, there are a number of considerations that the restorer should consider before starting. These not only cover what the end product should be, but also include the facilities available to the restorer, the start point of the restoration, the skills that the restorer possesses (or needs to learn, or outsource), and the planning of the restoration. This section addresses each of these points in detail.

### ENDPOINT: RESTORED, RENOVATED OR PRESERVED?

Broadly speaking, there are three 'classes' of cars recognised in the classic car scene. These are, firstly, a car that has been fully restored: stripped back to bare metal or glass fibre, and refinished to a standard better than the factory; an all-new interior; all chrome redone with no imperfections; and a mechanical refurbishment. This results in a car that has the finish, performance, handling and roadholding that an original car fresh from the factory should have had.

Secondly, a car which has been renovated: has had various repairs and modifications made to it, where some modifications could be 'in period,' and others taking

The author's +2 has had a long and eventful life and is nowhere near standard. It is, however, a drivable and usable +2.

advantage of modern technology, to produce a car that is improved to a degree unheard of in the original.

Thirdly, a car that has been preserved in a mostly original state: which has never been resprayed, and so retains the factory original paint; with an original and possibly worn, but neat, interior; factory mechanicals that are mostly original and have been well-maintained and repaired when required; and bears the scars and patina that make up the evidence of a long and active life.

This is the conundrum that faces the proud new owner of a classic. Should they:

- Restore – ie, bring back, reinstate or return to a former state, usually the state it left the factory.
- Renovate – ie, restore it to a good state of repair, possibly with some contemporary or period modifications.
- Preserve – ie, maintain it in its original or existing state.

Preservation really only applies to conserved or 'survivor' cars, which have been an interesting aspect of the classic car scene for some years, and the trend is gaining traction in Lotus circles. Typically, these are well-preserved cars, perhaps barn finds or very low mileage original cars that have had very little work done to them to disturb or alter the factory specification. These cars are often still in use, but have not had any work done to them other than what was necessary to keep them safe and mechanically sound – hence conservation, rather than restoration. These cars will typically retain their factory finish – including paint, interior trim and all factory-fitted stickers – and, mechanically speaking, will be as original as possible within the bounds of safety, so are both rare and precious. Unfortunately, an original car is difficult to restore – once the original finish or patina has been removed, it is gone forever. The touching up of original paintwork and cleaning of components is probably as far as you can go if you want to preserve the car – basically do the minimum that the car needs to be

▲ How not to buy a restoration project. The author's other +2, as found: mostly dismantled, with parts spread across several locations, and some work already done. I like a challenge!

▲ Melody and Henry Kozlowski's +2 is a very original early car that, while needing some work when purchased, is now an eminently usable and practical car – as evidenced by the completion of the Cape to Cape charity rally.

safe and presentable, while preventing further decay. Truly original Elans and +2s are few and far between, and are starting to command higher prices than cars that have already been restored or renovated, and certainly deserve to be preserved.

Assuming a car is going to be renovated or restored as opposed to preserved, the restorer first needs to think about what sort of use the finished car will be put to, and, secondly, what form they want the end product to take. There are a number of end points for a restoration: a 100-point, museum-quality car that is completely factory standard (but probably better finished than when it left the factory); a re-engineered working car that will not be 100 per cent original, with sensible modifications – new and old – that enhance the car's driveability and makes it safer in today's traffic; or a standard, but used, car that is how the owner remembers (or imagines) the car was when it was someone's daily driver, with a few faults, and maybe a non-standard paint colour and some period mechanical modifications.

## PLANNING

Planning a restoration, while not compulsory, can be useful. Some people like to plan their work down to the finest detail, others will have a general overall scheme of work, and some simply address jobs as they arise. At a minimum, a plan should provide an overview of the tasks to be done and an order in which to do them, and should break the car down into the basic components. The most basic plan is simply to strip down, refurbish, rebuild, and reassemble in some sort of order.

With the body off, all of the Elan and +2 mechanical parts are exposed and easy to work on. This is Glenn Moules' very original early Elan coupé's chassis with the body off and engine removed.

Good planning can minimise expense, duplication of effort, and delays – especially when having external work done by specialists. For example, if you want to have the suspension wishbones sandblasted and stove-enamelled, then it is usually more economical to get them all done together, rather than having the fronts and rears done separately.

As can be seen from the large number of unfinished projects that are available for sale, the easy part of a restoration is the strip down. It is all too easy to pull a car to pieces, and then be faced with a pile of parts that have not been catalogued and properly assessed, resulting in a huge job just to sort out what is what, where it goes, and what is needed to refurbish it. You must be methodical when stripping the car down: label all the parts taken off and store them using some sort of system, so you know where – for instance – all the front suspension parts are. Plastic boxes are good for storing large parts, plastic freezer bags are good for small parts, and indelible markers are good for labelling the boxes and bags. Some parts may benefit from having labels applied to them – masking tape is good unless the parts are oily or greasy, in which case tie-on card labels (written on with an indelible marker) are good.

Another tip is to avoid dismantling things too far until you are ready to refurbish and rebuild them. It's easy to forget how a part fits together if you pull it apart and don't rebuild it until six months or a year has passed! Reference to the parts list can help, but remembering how it came apart is the best method!

The author has found that the main advantage of having a plan is the ability to arrange the work so that there are tangible goals all the way through the restoration. In the case of his +2, the first goal was to refurbish and paint the secondhand chassis he had bought, then rebuild the front suspension and brakes, fix the front suspension onto the

➤ The Sprint was the final incarnation of the Elan, and was usually painted in two-tone schemes. This lovely example is in the very attractive yellow over white.

chassis, rebuild the rear suspension and brakes, fix the rear suspension onto the chassis, and get the (refurbished) wheels on the chassis. This resulted in a rolling chassis, which had two benefits: it was a significant goal achieved, and the chassis was mobile, so could be moved in and out of the garage at will to provide additional space. The second goal was to restore the power train, dismantling the engine, sourcing all the parts needed, having the block and crank machined by a specialist, and then rebuilding the unit with all-new bearings. Fitting the refurbished gearbox to the engine, along with a new clutch, meant that the whole unit could then be installed in the rolling chassis – getting them out of the way and making the workbench clear for other jobs. Finally, with all the other ancillaries attached to the chassis (including new brake lines, the differential, and refurbished propshaft), there was a complete rolling chassis that was ready to take the body sitting in the garage – another tangible goal achieved.

## SPACE AND FACILITIES

Having the space to carry out a restoration is vital, and, in the case of an Elan or +2, there is the issue of storing and working on both a chassis and a bodyshell. In the best case scenario, you will have room to store the body off the chassis inside your garage or workshop. Luckily, as the shell is glass fibre, it can be stored outside and – if properly waterproofed and protected – it will be fine. Miles Wilkins, in his book *How to Restore Fibreglass Bodywork* (see Bibliography), recommends standing the shell off the ground on bricks or blocks (the author uses old tyres – non-porous to water and gentle on the body's underside), covering the bodyshell with cotton sheets and then a loosely-fitting waterproof tarpaulin. There should be room for air to circulate, and the covers should be removed on warm days, if the air is dry. Wilkins claims that treated in this way, a shell will not suffer any deterioration, and in the author's experience this is the case.

Regarding facilities, there are actually very few specialist tools needed to restore an Elan or +2. First off, a good solid bench is invaluable, and a decent quality medium-sized metalworking vice firmly attached to the bench is also a necessity. You should also buy a set of soft jaws for the vice, to hold delicate items. Decent lighting over the bench also helps immeasurably.

One of the joys of owning an Elan or +2 is attending shows and meets. This is Paddy Byers' Series 1 Elan at a Brooklands New Year's Day meet.

A good set of AF spanners, a socket set, torque wrench, and an assortment of screwdrivers are, of course, needed. A bench press is useful for fitting rear wheel bearings, various bushes and new universal joints, but the vice can also be used if it is big enough. It is convenient to use an engine stand when rebuilding the unit, but it can be done on a bench. The main facilities needed when rebuilding any part of a Lotus are patience, cleanliness and care.

## SKILLS

The main skill an individual needs to take on an Elan or +2 is a willingness to learn and a 'can do' attitude. There is very little mechanical work that a person with a basic knowledge of car mechanics can't undertake, with the proviso that you should read the manual and fully understand what you are attempting. The bodywork, being glass fibre, is actually relatively easy to work on. The great thing about glass fibre bodywork repairs is that if you make a mistake, it is easy to undo the work and fix it. The main disadvantage of doing it yourself is that, as you learn on the job and gain the requisite skills, you may want to go back to the first repairs you did and re-do them!

Some operations which may require outside help include:

- Chassis repairs – unless you are a competent welder and able to jig the chassis accurately.
- Brake component rebuilds, including calliper, master cylinder and servo refurbishment – these are relatively skilled jobs with safety implications.
- Engine part machining, including crank grinding, main and big end shell grinding, and block and head truing – these jobs require specialist equipment, which would be pointless to buy for a single rebuild. However, there is nothing to stop the owner from measuring up the relevant components to work out if they do need to be rebored/reground, or if they just need new bearings or piston rings.
- Gearbox rebuilds – again, specialist knowledge and skills are required to setup a gearbox.
- Differential rebuilds – again, specialist skills are needed to measure and set up the unit.
- Electrics – often owners have a bit of a blank spot about electrics, and Lotus electrics can be challenging! Sometimes it is worth getting an auto electrician in to chase down problems.
- Paint – This is the main part of a restoration that everyone sees, so is worth getting it right. It is perfectly possible to paint your Lotus at home, but remember that the main part of painting a Lotus is in the preparation, so even if you do go to outside help then there is plenty you can do to prepare the shell first.

## TAKING ON A BASKET CASE

A 'basket case' is a project car that has already been dismantled, hence it can be taken home in baskets or boxes. They tend to be cheap, but there is a reason for this; basket cases are, by definition, dismantled. There is no guarantee that all the parts in the baskets make up a complete car, or, indeed, if all the parts in the baskets are from the same car. While purchasing a basket case is the cheapest way of getting a project started, it can also be risky – especially if this is the first Lotus the new owner has owned or restored. The most important thing to do if you start with a basket

In contrast to the author's +2 basket case: *this* is how to buy a project. Everything needs doing, but everything is present and still on – or in – the car.

The author's +2 project, on collection, showed evidence of previous but unfinished preparation work: a driver's door from another car, no engine or gearbox, and a well-rotted chassis.

case is to sort everything out and identify three things: which bits belong to the car, which bits are from another project altogether, and which bits are missing. This will usually take a bit of work to achieve, and may well involve a fair bit of detective work to sort things out. It is the obscure brackets, fixings and spacers that usually present the biggest challenges, but if you use the parts manual for the car you should be able to sort things out.

## GLASS FIBRE

### INTRODUCTION

Glass fibre work is quite straightforward, and a lot easier than welding. However, it involves a number of potentially harmful chemicals and chemical reactions, so you must make sure you read, understand and follow all health and safety instructions that come with the products.

### GENERAL GUIDE TO GLASS FIBRE WORK

#### PAINT REMOVAL

One important thing to remember with glass fibre is to not use chemical paint strippers. These will probably attack the gel coat as well as the paint, and may permeate into the

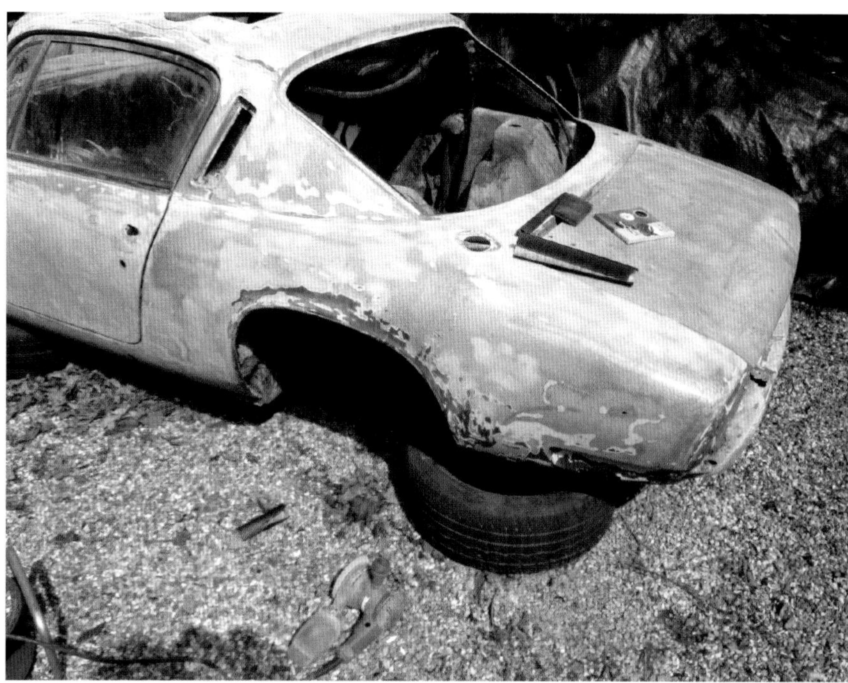

Even with lots of the paint already removed, getting the last of it off the car is a long, dusty and tedious job. It is not advisable to use chemical strippers on glass fibre bodies, as it is hard to remove all traces of the chemicals.

body, making it very hard to remove entirely. While some people have used chemical stripping successfully, the author strongly recommends removing old paint manually, using scrapers and abrasive paper.

## RESIN

There are two types of resin that you will need when working on your Lotus. Polyester lay-up resin is used to 'wet out' all types of glass fibre used in repairs. Available from all good suppliers, it is a liquid but is generally sold by weight. A gallon (4.5L) weighs about 10lb, or 4.5kg. The second type of resin is gelcoat, which – while similar in chemical composition to polyester resin – contains additives to stop it running on vertical surfaces. Originally intended to be the first coat added to the mould, it is not really needed for general body repairs. Both resins are usually supplied with a hardener, which, as the name implies, is added to the resin to kick off a chemical reaction that will solidify the resin. The supplier will be able to tell you how much hardener should be added to the resin; various percentages can be used to give various setting times. Finally, Acetone is good for cleaning tools and brushes after use, and cleaning glass fibre surfaces. Be warned that the addition of hardener to resin results in an exothermic chemical reaction that generates heat. Too much hardener generates a lot of heat, and may even set the mixture on fire.

## GLASS FIBRE TYPES

There are four types of glass fibre that you will need to use for body repairs on your Lotus. The main type is Chopped Strand Mat, which is supplied in rolls and comes in various weights, ranging from 300g/m$^2$ up to 900g/m$^2$. The mat comprises a layer of randomly-oriented lengths of glass fibre, which is held in position by a glue to form a flexible sheet that can be cut using scissors to the size required. The glue is designed to dissolve in the resin. In general, you should use 300g/m$^2$ mat for all your repairs. Woven Roving is a plain weave sheet fabric that is often used for sheathing a product, but is strong and can be used in an area that needs strength – for example, creating a reinforcing patch where you want to bolt something through the bodyshell. Glass fibre tape is made from woven roving, and comes in various widths. It is good for providing local reinforcement in areas like wheelarch lips, or covering string or rolled cardboard strengtheners. Finally, tissue is fine glass fibre in a sheet, with the consistency of tissue paper. It has a weight of only about 30g/m$^2$ is used as a surface finisher for repairs.

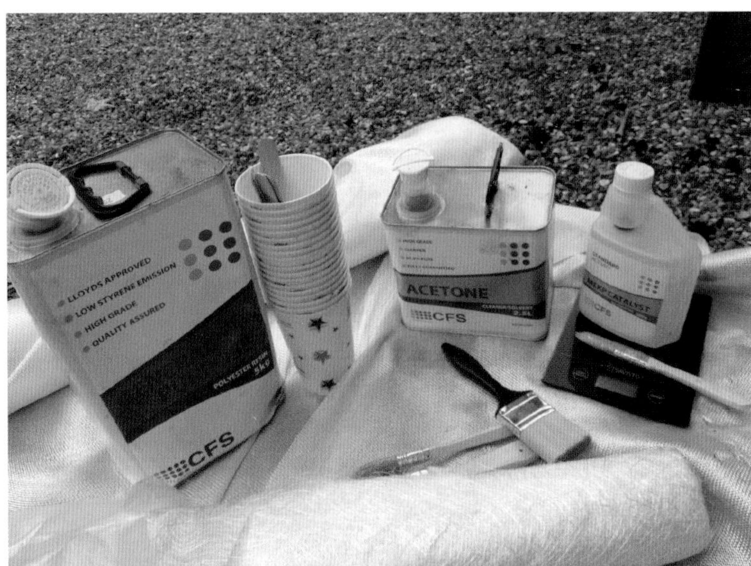


▲ A selection of typical glass fibre repair materials, including resin, mat, paper cups and wooden tongue depressors to mix the resin and hardener, electronic scales to weigh out quantities of resin and hardener, and paint brushes to apply the resin.

## TOOLS

There are a number of tools that you will need. Firstly, 500ml disposable cups are the perfect receptacle for mixing resin and hardener. Do not use glass vessels, as the heat generated when the resin is hardening may crack it. For mixing, wooden tongue depressors are cheap and effective. To apply the resin to the mat you should use a suitably sized paint brush.

Finally, a cheap electronic scale with a 'zero' function is very useful to measure the amount of hardener needed to add to the resin. Place your mixing cup on it, zero the reading, add the resin, read the weight, then calculate how much hardener is needed, zero the scales and add the required weight of hardener. It is not advisable to use the kitchen scales, as there will be spills which may be difficult to explain away.

## COMMON PROBLEMS AND HOW TO FIX THEM

### INTRODUCTION

There is not enough space to give an in-depth description of glass fibre repair techniques. This section will describe the common problems you will come across on an Elan or +2, and give a summary of how to carry out a repair. For further details consult the Lotus workshop manual or one of the specialist glass fibre repair books in the Bibliography.

### GEL COAT CRACKS

The most common glass fibre issue with an Elan is cracking of the gel coat. The problem with cracks is that they will often have penetrated through the gel coat into the resin and mat. Just filling a crack will not work, the correct way to repair is to instead grind down the area around the crack until it has been completely eradicated – washing the ground down area with acetone will expose any residual cracks – then glass over the area with mat, and finish with tissue.

### MICRO BLISTERS

Micro blisters are caused by moisture in the glass fibre wicking through to the surface of the body and accumulating under the paint layer. Also known as osmosis in the boat industry, the only cure is to eradicate all moisture from the shell, and then seal it against further penetration. This means sealing both the inner and outer body surfaces; while the outer is already sealed thanks to the paint, the inner surfaces are often completely unpainted – for example, the inside face of the doors. A total cure is expensive and time-consuming, but the problem can be minimised by thoroughly drying out the car – which should temporarily cure the problem – then painting all surfaces. Companies such as Option 1 have developed processes to minimise the effect of blistering.

▲ This shot shows typical gel coat cracks on the rear wing of a +2, as well as other damage around the badge mounting holes. All the cracks must be ground out completely, properly filled with mat, and topped off with tissue if they are not to reappear.

### DAMAGE REPAIRS

Local damage to the car is relatively easy to fix. If a panel is cracked then you need to grind out the crack, getting rid of all cracked or loose material, and then feathering the outside edges back to solid material and cleaning up the rear face of the damage. Then, stabilise the damage by screwing flat metal strips across the crack on the outside face. These strips will hold the bodywork in position and allow you to put a couple of layers of mat behind the crack to produce a strong and accurate substrate. Once the repair to the back of the panel has hardened, remove the strips and fill the resultant groove with mat, and finish with a layer of fine tissue. Finish the repair by sanding back and, if necessary, use the minimum amount of filler to complete the repair. The same technique is used to fit repair panels to the original body. Once the panel to be replaced has been cut off, trim the repair panel to size, and then feather the top edges, clean the rear, fix the panel on using strips of metal, and then glass from the back. Remove the strips and glass the outer side with mat, again finishing with tissue and minimal filler.

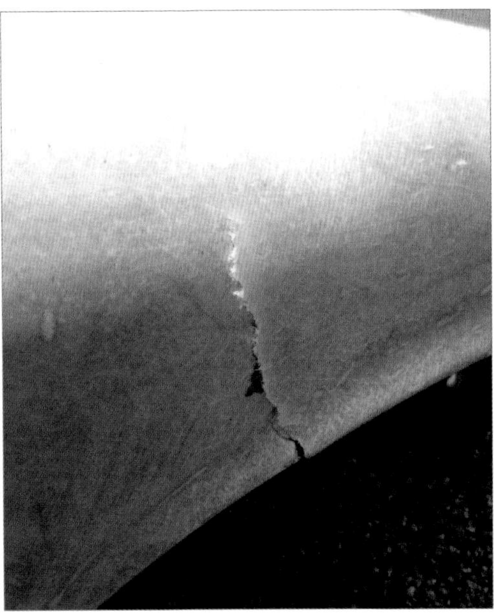

This is a typical result of an impact on a wheelarch, resulting in a tear in the bodywork. Repair is straightforward, but involves several steps.

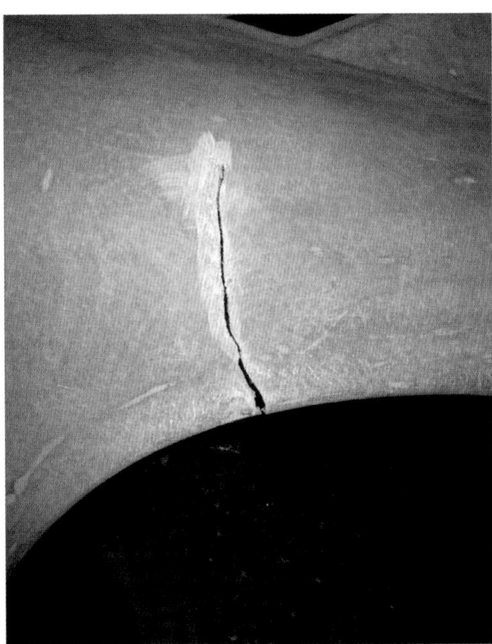

Step one is to grind out the edges of the damage on the front and rear sides, taking it back to solid glass fibre.

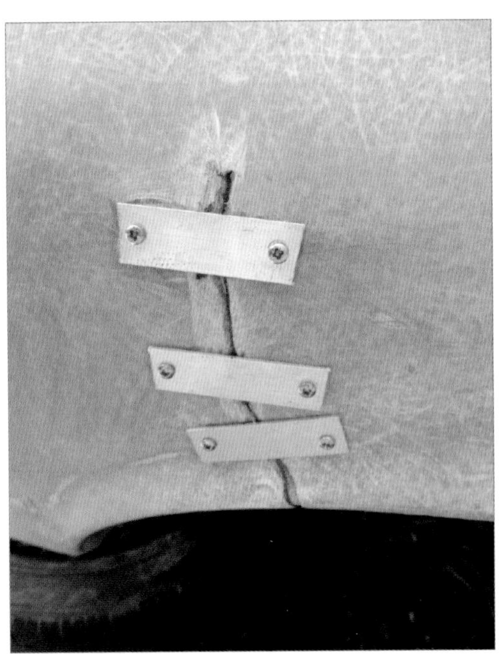

Stabilise the crack by fixing metal plates across it to hold the two halves of the shell in the correct position.

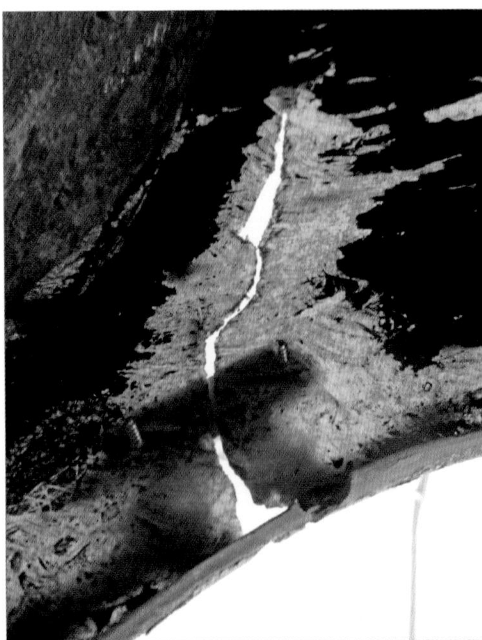

Use mat and resin to coat the area behind the crack. This fixes the break, and reunites the body panel.

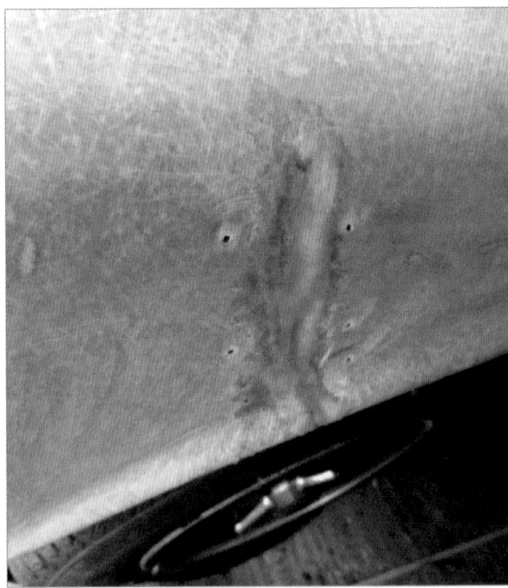

Remove the metal plates and fill in the gap on the outside with mat. Fill the holes from the screws that held the plate on with resin and tissue, and finish the overall surface with tissue. Finally, sand back to finish.

Areas that have suffered damage, with significant chunks of loose glass fibre bits, can be repaired by joining the damaged parts back together using the metal strip method outlined above. If you can get behind the area to repair, such as on the boot floor, then you can make up a backing piece from cardboard covered in cling film, which you can fix behind the area to be repaired and then glass over. The cling film will not stick, and will give a smooth finish to the repair.

### BOBBIN REPAIR

Bobbins are small circular or oval drilled – and sometimes threaded – fixings, made from soft alloy, which are positioned in the bodyshell. The bobbins are used to position the bolts that attach the shell to the chassis/subframe, or to reinforce specific areas of the bodyshell where components are bolted together. For example, the headlamp pods are pivoted on bolts that pass through bobbins on the body and the pod, and there are two threaded bobbins at the rear of the +2 bonnet that fix the reinforcing frame in place. The point of the bobbin is to provide an accurately-positioned mount that is more resilient than a simple hole drilled in the glass fibre, and to spread the load of the attachment over a larger area of the bodyshell than such a hole would be able to. Bobbins may need to be replaced if the hole becomes enlarged, the thread is stripped, or the bodywork around the bobbin is damaged and needs repair or replacement. There are two issues around the replacement of bobbins in the bodyshell: the first is to get the positioning correct, and the second is to glass them in place correctly.

As standard, a bobbin is very strong and will not pull out of the body; the body structure around a correctly-fixed bobbin will fail before the bobbin, and its glass fibre fixing, is pulled out. Lotus started using structural glass fibre on the Elite – so already had many years' experience of bobbin design and fixing before the Elan was in production – but fixing the bobbin in place is critical. Lotus carried out a series of tests for the strength of bobbins in 1961. The subsequent report documented that, if glassed in correctly, then for oval bobbins subjected to shearing, the bolt or bobbin will fail before there is any glass fibre damage. For bobbins in tension, a force of around half a UK ton (1120lb, 508kg) was needed to pull the bobbin through the glass fibre. Detailed instructions on the repair or replacement of bobbins are in the relevant workshop manual. Basically, each bobbin needs to be fixed in place with a minimum of five layers of mat. The bobbin should be glassed into the surface of the panel, with the mat running up the sides of the bobbin. Then, a reinforcing ring of extra laminations of mat is added to surround the bobbin.

## BODYSHELL

### BODYSHELL REMOVAL

The bodyshell is fixed to the chassis by 16 bolts on the Elan and +2. It is relatively easy to remove, and just needs either a two-post lift, or five or so strong people, to lift the shell off the chassis. The highest part of the chassis is the rear turrets, and sit about 1m high.

### ELAN BODY REINFORCEMENT

The Elan's steel latticework reinforcement – that is positioned around the door aperture in the body – is bonded in place, and should be corrosion free. This has two functions: it gives extra rigidity to the bodyshell, and it provides limited side impact protection. However, if the glass fibre covering the steel latticework has been damaged and water has penetrated, it will rust and 'blow' the body skin. Replacement is fiddly and time-consuming, as it involves cutting the old steel out from the inside of the shell, and then bonding a replacement or repaired latticework in place.

The only other steel reinforcements in the Elan shell are two steel strips running up the inside of the windscreen pillars.

### +2 BODY REINFORCEMENT

In each of the +2's sills sits a fabricated steel beam that is designed to protect the passenger space from sideways intrusions, provide secure outer seatbelt mounting points, provide jacking points, and add rigidity to the bodyshell. The protection they provided from new is not great; while they will provide some resistance to intrusion if the car goes into a tree or lamp post sideways, they are set low down, so do not offer much resistance to a larger vehicle 'T-boning' the +2. The member is completely enclosed between the inner and outer sills, and is fixed in position with three rectangular plates, which are mounted in the cabin on the front, centre, and rear, on the vertical edge of the sill, and each plate is bolted to the member through the glass fibre using four bolts. These sill members, and the fixing plates, were originally made from mild steel, and were poorly protected against corrosion from new.

Unless a car has been used almost exclusively in the dry, the likelihood is that an original sill member will be corroded, and many by now will be non-existent; the author removed most of his project +2's members with a vacuum cleaner and brush. Bearing in mind the safety aspects of the sill members, close inspection is vital. Replacements are available from most parts suppliers, either to original specification, in stainless steel, or redesigned tubular galvanised types.

## BUMPERS, LIGHTS AND DOOR FURNITURE

The brightwork on the Elan is relatively limited. There are chromed door handles, locks, boot hinges, light bases and bezels and – on the Series 3 onwards – the side window surrounds. The +2 shares these items, with the addition of chromed steel bumpers and roof gutters, although later cars had polished alloy gutters.

The Series 1 and 2 Elan's door handles and boot hinges were different to those on the Series 3 onwards, the handles being quite chunky and the lock being incorporated into the round push button, and the boot hinges having a recess to accommodate and fix the hardtop.

The Series 3 Elans had new door handles that incorporated the locks into the casting, below the door press button. The design changed again with the Series 4 cars, which used the same handles as the +2, with separate locks positioned below the handle. These last handles were used on a range of common British cars of the 1960s and '70s, and replacements are available. The door handles were

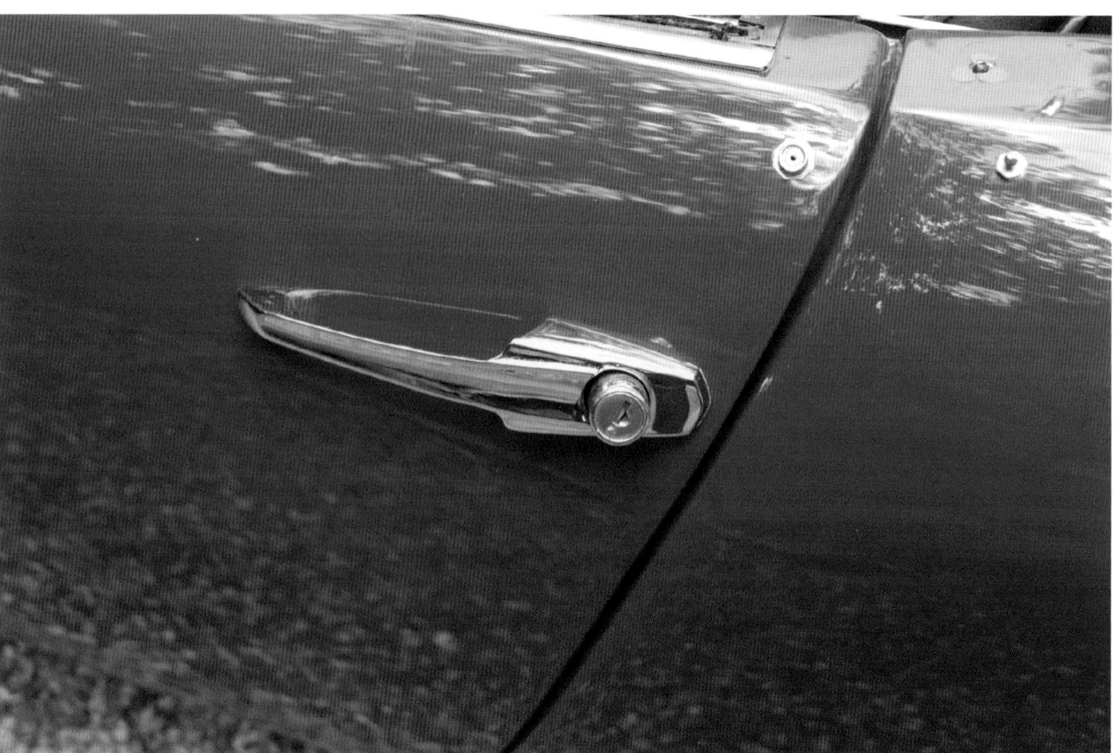

Elan Series 1 and 2 cars had this design of door handle, which incorporated the lock barrel in the knob on the handle. ➤

made from brass and then chromed, so can be rechromed if pitted. Various suppliers have reproduced the Series 1 and 2 handles in polished light alloy. Rear light bases are cast zinc alloy, generally referred to as Mazac or pot metal. Rechroming pot metal is a bit of a specialist art, but can be done. Window frames on Series 3 and 4 Elans, and the +2, are made from brass channel and the chrome will often polish up nicely. The +2 bumpers, again, can be rechromed unless they are very heavily corroded.

### PAINT

The paint on an Elan or +2 is the crowning glory of a restoration, and it can be difficult to get a good and lasting finish. A great deal has been written about painting glass fibre cars, and Lotus in particular, and the quality of paint jobs can vary enormously, as can the cost. There are three fundamental issues with painting an Elan or +2. These are: doing the correct level of preparation to the surfaces to be painted, taking the time needed for the preparation to be completed, and not putting too much paint on the body at one time.

Restorers need to understand that glass fibre is not as stable as steel or aluminium, and painting it is a bit of a dark art. When exposed to heat or cold, a glass fibre body will expand and contract or 'move' more than an equivalent metal body, and this will have a detrimental effect on the paint – bearing in mind the paint is simply an extra layer of plastic on top of the body proper. In addition to movement, the paint will react to various factors such as retained thinners or solvents trapped in the shell, or the wicking of moisture through the shell from the inside (and often unpainted) faces. These give rise to many issues, from micro blistering through to sinkage. In many ways, the key to Elan and +2 paintwork is to treat it as a consumable, and expect to have a respray every ten years or so. The key to a long-lasting paint job is preparation, both in terms of proper repairs and making sure there is not any trapped moisture or solvents retained in the shell before the paint is applied.

From the Series 4, Elans had separate door handles and locks similar to those used on the +2S.

## INTERIOR TRIM AND HOOD

The interior trim of the Elan and +2 is fairly basic, and made from materials available at the time – mainly vinyl for the seats and soft trim, carpet for the floor (although the Elan Series 1 and 2 had 'Elephant hide' rubber mats on the floor), and reasonable quality perforated synthetic cloth for the roof lining. Later +2 seats came with cloth inserts in the seat faces, making them a bit more comfortable in hot weather. The wooden dash was originally oiled teak on the Elan, although with the introduction of the +2 a walnut veneer was introduced, giving the cars a very upmarket look. The hoods fitted to all Elans were made from a plastic material, as were the hood windows. The Series 1 and 2 build up hood are complex, and have a number of parts, including side rails, while the Series 3 and 4 hoods have the cover fixed to the frame, which bolts onto the body and drops into a well behind the seats when down.

The interior trim should not present a competent trimmer any problems, apart from sourcing original specification materials. While the 'basket weave' vinyl used on the seats and door cards can be matched, the cloth trim used in later +2 seats is hard to find. Door cards are backed with fibreboard, which deteriorates rapidly if wet, but replacements can be made using the originals as templates. Original Colin Chapman signature steering wheels are hard to find secondhand, and many cars have replacements, Moto Lita being common.

The Elan Series 1 hood was complex, involving side rails that fitted around the side windows, and transverse hood rails that clipped onto the rails.

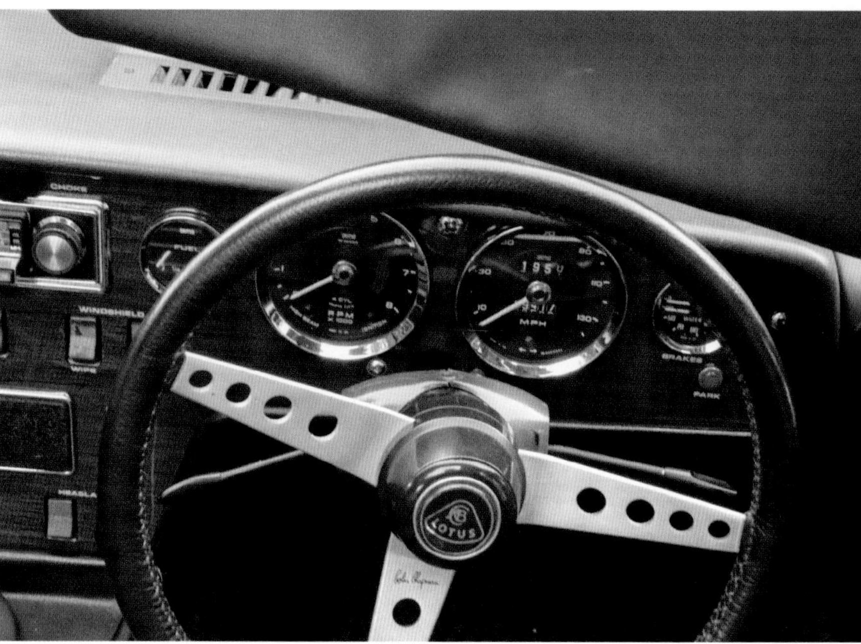

The Elan Sprints and late +2 models were fitted with the desirable 'signed' steering wheel, which had a facsimile of Colin Chapman's signature etched into the top of its bottom arm.

Once up, the Series 1 and 2 hood was pretty good, and reasonably water- and draught-proof.

## ELECTRICAL SYSTEM

The original Elan electrical system is simple and straightforward, and was only slightly more complicated by the time production finished with the Sprint. The +2 is another story; while the original +2 electrical system was relatively simple and similar to the Elan S3/S4, the +2S system was significantly more complicated due to additions made to the car to raise its comfort levels. The Elan S1-S3 loom came in two parts – a main loom that served the dash and engine bay, and a rear that handled the rear lights and the fuel tank sender. The +2 and Elan S4 loom has three components – an engine bay loom, dash loom and rear loom. So, the good news is that you may not have to replace the complete set of wiring looms on an Elan or +2 – but the use of two or three different looms introduces extra connections that can cause issues with age.

In the author's experience, there is little to be gained from trying to keep an original loom. These are now over 50 years old, have been subjected to many stresses and strains, and will very likely have physical damage to loom tape, insulation, and the wires inside the insulation. On top of this, the connections between the wires and connectors will likely be weakened and the connectors – be they bullets, spades or plugs – will be corroded. Finally, the ministrations of previous owners fixing problems and introducing extra electrical components may also introduce additional problems. The net result will be a cornucopia of faults in the old loom, which, at best, will cause intermittent faults, and at worst will result in a fire. It is common sense to replace an old loom, either with a new item or by remaking the original using new wire and connectors. The first option will save time but cost more than the second.

The electrical earth points on both cars are vital. The Elan and +2 have three, one on the front suspension turret, a second on the bottom of the centre of the dashboard, and the third on the rear body mounting point in the boot. All three double up as body mounting points – the connection is made through to the chassis with the body mounting bolts, and the chassis is used as the return. As such, the points where the loom is attached to the body must be clean and free from corrosion. Silicone grease or petroleum jelly should be used on the bolts and washers to ensure good electrical contact is maintained.

There was a factory option 'Radio Suppression Kit' designed to reduce radio frequency interference from the engine. It comprised a two-part clip-on – or single part bolt-on – alloy cover that fitted on the head over the sparkplugs, an alloy backplate that bolted to the rear of the head on the bellhousing, and an alloy screening plate fitted around the coils. Sparkplug leads were rerouted through the gap at the rear of the head. It is rare to see these kits still fitted today, mainly as they hindered access to the sparkplugs, and modern suppressors on the coil and sparkplug leads will cut interference down to an acceptable level.

## CHASSIS

### INTRODUCTION

The Elan and +2 chassis or subframe provides all the location points for the suspension, as well as supporting the other main mechanical components. As such, its condition

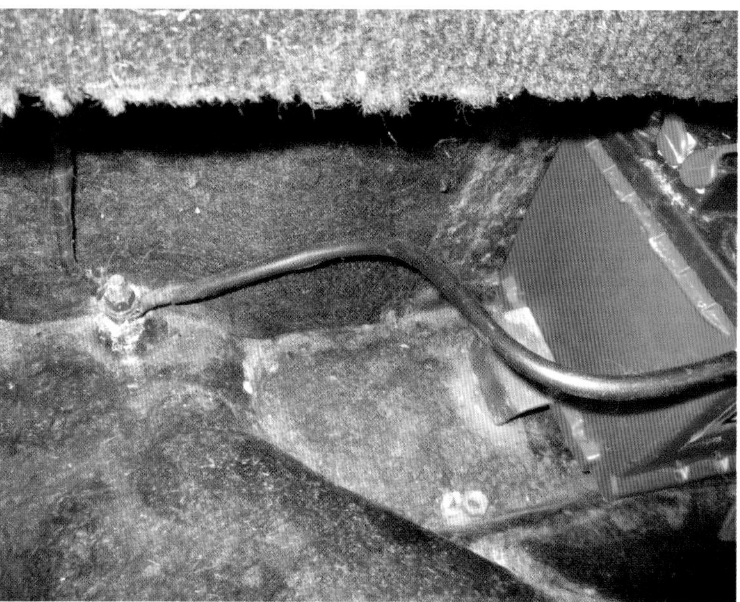

▲ The earth connections in the Elan and +2 are vital for the car's electrical health. This is the position of the +2's main earth, connecting the battery terminal to the chassis through the fixing bolt in the boot.

▲ Electrical interference from the HT side of the ignition system is a problem with the Elan and +2 due to the glass fibre bodywork. Lotus fitted a cover over the plugs to try to cut down the interference, with limited effect.

is vital to the integrity of the car, and, unfortunately, it is also prone to rust and impact damage.

## CHASSIS MARKINGS

An original chassis should have the vehicle identification number stamped on the top flange on the right hand side of the engine bay 'V', just forwards of the engine mount. There is also a second stamping on the top front of the tunnel which displays the part number – in the case of the Elan '26A701,' and the +2 '50A701.'

A genuine Lotus replacement chassis will have an etched or stamped number that will not match the original VIN, and is pre- or postfixed with 'LR' to mark it as a Lotus Replacement unit. An additional identification point for a Lotus replacement chassis is that they were galvanised (hot zinc coated) post-1982, but galvanising was dropped around the year 2000 as concerns about the process distorting the frame emerged. Most, but not all, +2 LR chassis have the number stamped on the left-hand (inlet) side on the flat face just behind the engine mount, while an LR Elan chassis will have it etched or stamped on the right-hand (exhaust) side. However, some have the number etched or stamped on the front crossmember.

Spyder chassis have a number stamped on the top of the front crossmember in the form 'SPY9999,' and usually have a riveted-on name plate on the top tube of the chassis, just behind the engine mount.

## COMMON CHASSIS/SUBFRAME PROBLEM AREAS

Problem areas in the chassis are the same for both the Elan and +2. The main issue is corrosion in the front suspension turrets; these square section boxes were designed with one fatal flaw – the side of the box was open to the elements, while the bottom was closed with a drain hole in it to let water out. This drain hole was small and easily blocked, resulting in water and road dirt accumulating in the lower part of the turret, which leads to rust. The rust starts on the inner faces of the turret, and is pretty much invisible until it breaks through to the outside surface. At this point, not only is the turret's structure compromised, but the end plate that closes off the front crossmember will also be rotten. This results in the crossmember's function as the air reservoir for the headlamps being compromised as well. In extreme cases the turret will collapse inwards, causing damage to the bodyshell in the engine bay and excessive camber on the front wheel.

▲ The Elan chassis usually had the Lotus part number '26A701' stamped on the top face of the transmission tunnel, just where the two sides of the engine bay meet.

▲ In this view of the front turret of the Elan chassis, the drain hole in the base of the turret is arrowed. Make sure it is clear of debris, otherwise water gathers in the base and causes corrosion.

➤ The ultimate result of corrosion in the base of a turret. This one is seriously weakened, and the inner plate that closes off the crossmember is also rusted through.

➤ The engine mounts are pretty flimsy and often crack. This mount has been somewhat crudely welded, and needs to be properly repaired and reinforced if it is not to crack again.

Corrosion can occur anywhere on the original chassis, as they were not well protected from new. The most likely spot, after the front turrets, is on the upper face of the bottom of the transmission tunnel, where the body bolts on. Water can gather here, and can also soak into the felt cover that sits between the body and chassis, causing corrosion where it touches the chassis.

The engine mounts are fabricated from relatively thin 16-gauge sheet steel, and are prone to developing cracks both on the top of the mount, and on the lower area where it is welded to the frame. See also Point 1 on picture 'Chassis 1' below.

The gearbox mounts are simply four captive nuts welded to the lower flange, and cracks can develop in the flange around these nuts, especially if the gearbox mount had been loose.

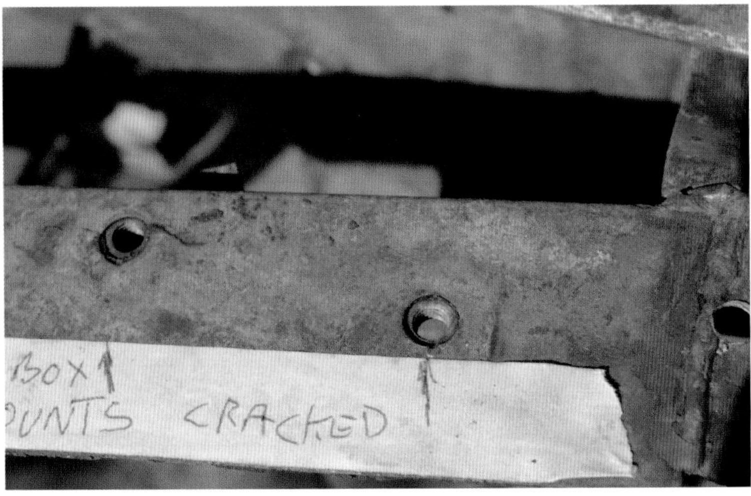


Here we can see how the metal around the captive nuts that the gearbox support bolts on to has cracked. Again, the cracks need to be welded to effect a good repair.

Chassis 1: this picture shows the engine mounts, front crossmember and steering rack platform, all of which are susceptible to damage (see main text for explanations on numbered elements).

The picture 'Chassis 1' shows the weak engine mounts (see Point 1); the bottom face of the front crossmember, which can be easily damaged or distorted if it has been used to jack up the car without spreading the load adequately (see Point 2); and the steering rack mounting, which is positioned on the forward face of the front crossmember, and can be damaged or distorted in a front end collision or through careless jacking (see Point 3).

Picture Chassis 2, below, shows the captive nuts that locate the forward ends of the differential torque rod mounts can break loose, which results in the holes becoming elongated (see Point 2).

Cracking can develop at the rear of the tunnel, close to the join where the side flanges extend outwards to carry the rear crossmember (see Point 1). The rear wishbone mounts are welded onto the flange on the steel sheet that makes up the floor of the tunnel. Cracks can develop in the flange around these wishbone mounts (see Point 3).

The front suspension's wishbone spindles can be bent if the car is run into a kerb or pothole, and it is possible to replace them. However, space is very limited with the body on the chassis, and there is the ever-present risk of fire when welding close to the bodyshell, so it is safest to carry out spindle replacement with the body removed from the

⅄ Chassis 2: this picture shows the centre section of the chassis, showing the differential mounts that can be enlarged, and the areas cracks can develop (see main text for explanations on numbered elements).

chassis. With the body off, it is also easier to measure and ensure that the spindles are correctly positioned as well.

The final issue with the chassis is crash damage. If a car has taken an impact that has bent or distorted the subframe, especially the front 'Y' or the tunnel, then replacement is really the only answer.

## CHASSIS REPAIR

Repairing a chassis takes significant metalwork and welding skill, as well as careful jigging to ensure an acceptable result. For many years, replacement chassis were readily available and relatively cheap, so it made little sense to repair a rusty chassis. Today, however, that situation has changed somewhat. New replacement chassis are no longer cheap, and there is an increasing interest in maintaining the originality of Elans and +2s where possible.

Chassis dimensions are given in the Elan and +2 workshop manuals, and can be used to jig a chassis for repair.

▲ The first point of the chassis that needs to be drilled and tapped is at the top of the front turrets.

## CHASSIS REPLACEMENT

Chassis replacement is relatively easy on an Elan, apart from one point. When the body is off and the mechanicals of the car exposed, it is also too tempting refurbish everything you take off the old chassis: suspension components could do with cleaning up and re-painting, engine mounts could be renewed, callipers could be rebuilt, brake lines should be replaced, new Lotocones would be nice, suspension wishbones could be re-bushed and painted ... The list goes on. And, of course, with the engine out it's worth taking a look inside to see what the bearings are like, it would be a good idea to change the clutch, and the gearbox could do with new bearings ... So, while it is possible to do a chassis swap quickly, things will typically get out of hand and a complete restoration of the car results!

Getting the body off is the first task. It is simply bolted on to the chassis with 16 bolts, plus the inner seatbelt fixing bolts. Six of the fixings bolt directly into threaded holes in the chassis (two on the front turrets, two on the rear suspension crossmember, and two on the central tunnel below the dashboard). Six are bolts that screw into threaded bobbins in the shell along the bottom of the transmission tunnel, and there are four nuts and bolts that bolt through unthreaded bobbins in the body, two at the front and two at the rear of the chassis. Once unbolted, the body can be lifted off, either by hand (you'll need at least four strong people to lift it off, but six is better), or by using a two-post lift, placing the lift arms at the front and rear of the sills. The main problem when lifting the shell on or off the chassis is raising the body high enough to clear the rear suspension top fittings on the rear of the chassis. To clear the chassis, the body has to be lifted a good three or four feet (1-1.5m) high so that the cabin and boot floors clear the chassis.

While you can leave the engine in place, you will have to take off the carburettors (and, in the case of Strombergs, the carb-to-manifold fitting) for the body to clear the engine bay.

When fitting a new chassis, you will need to drill fixing holes in the chassis, and cut threads in the new holes in the front suspension uprights, the rear body cross brace, and the intersection of the top flanges of the front sidemember on the top of the chassis. This last position is close to the

The second point is the top front of the rear turrets – you may need to use shims between the body and the chassis at this point.

The third area to be drilled and tapped is on the rear top of the engine bay Y-section, just to the front of the transmission tunnel.

join of the front Y section, just behind the bridge piece that sits over the gearbox. Use the body as a template to mark out the position of all the holes, spotting the new holes using the position of the bobbins in the body. Then remove the body, drill the holes and tap threads in the six that require it, and then you can bolt on the body.

When a body is replaced on a new or repaired chassis, it is possible for there to be a gap between the shell and the rearmost mounting brackets – those on the top of the rear suspension turrets. If this is the case, then the gap between the body and the turret should be packed out with 16swg washers. If you just tighten the bolt until it 'fits' you will strain the body, which will be likely to misalign the door openings.

## SUSPENSION AND STEERING

### FRONT SUSPENSION PROBLEM AREAS

While the front suspension is largely trouble free, there are two areas where trouble can occur. The threads in the trunnions or lower link on the upright should be kept properly lubricated. They work by having a coarse thread into which the upright screws, and when the upright is turned by the steering it moves by going up or down on the thread. As it is threaded there is a large area to take the load, and this is why the manual recommends gear oil for lubrication – grease will not flow back onto the bearing surfaces on the threads once it is displaced. If the trunnion runs dry, two things happen. First, the thread will no longer be lubricated, and so the steering will get stiffer and the threads will wear. The worst case scenario is that the threads will seize, and the upright will snap at the top of the thread. So, it is a good idea to keep the trunnion lubed. The bottom trunnion is fitted to the wishbone using nylon bushes, which allow the trunnion to pivot in relation to the wishbone to accommodate the suspension movement. The bolt that connects the wishbone to the trunnion runs in a steel bush that forms a bearing and a spacer between the trunnion's nylon bushes and the bolt. The second issue that can occur on the trunnion is that this bottom bolt can seize onto the steel bush. If the bolt is really solidly seized, the only way to get it out and disconnect the wishbones is to cut the bolt. You can either cut the head and end off

The Elan and +2 have similar front suspension, but the +2 has longer wishbones and slightly larger discs and callipers.

the bolt flush with the outer face of the wishbone, which may give you enough room to pry the wishbones apart and extract the trunnion, or – using a thin angle grinder or hacksaw – cut between the wishbone and the trunnion, through the nylon bush. This will mean cutting through the steel bush, which is hardened and so not easy to do! The only other alternative is to cut through the trunnion itself or the wishbone; in which case make sure you can source replacements.

The bolt holes in the top wishbone used to mount the top swivel can be enlarged if they are run loose – replacement or welding and redrilling is the cure. Later front wishbones had reinforcement in the form of a metal piece wrapped around the inner eye which holds the metalastic bush; it is a good idea to closely inspect all wishbones for cracks around the mounts at each end.

With the original metalastic-type bushes, the suspension movement is provided by the play in the rubber between the inner and outer steel tubes, as the inner tube is clamped tightly to the spindle or bracket, and the outer is a tight fit into the wishbone. When fitting new bushes, the spindle nuts and the inner rear wishbone bolts should only be tightened when the car is sitting on the ground with all its weight on its wheels. Failure to do this with the metalastic type bushes will 'set' the suspension height at full droop, resulting in incorrect ride height and reduced suspension travel and compliance, as well as a reduced life as the rubber bushing will be incorrectly tensioned.

## REAR SUSPENSION PROBLEM AREAS

The rear wishbone or A-frame is made from relatively thin walled tubing, and can be crushed or bent if the car has

At the rear, damage to the A-frame is not uncommon – it is fabricated from tubing and can be bent or dented, especially if it has been used as a jacking point.

The Lotocones at the top of the rear turrets are rubber, and can perish.

been jacked up on it. While they are easy enough to replace, it does indicate a lack of care and attention by a previous owner, or mechanics who have worked on the car.

As described in Chapter 1, the rear suspension's top location is achieved by mounting the top of the strut in a flexible rubber bush bolted onto the top of the rear chassis crossmember. These are known as 'Lotocones,' and are designed to allow for the strut's small amount of sideways movement when the rear suspension moves. Lotocones are rubber and, while they are long-lived, they can perish, so should be checked periodically for cracks and hardening. The other main rubber components in the rear suspension are the Rotoflex couplings or donuts. These are subjected to quite high forces, all the more so in tuned cars, and if one breaks up it can result in the driveshaft flailing around and potentially smashing the glass fibre at the rear of the cabin. So, Rotoflex condition is important, and they should be inspected regularly for cracking or de-lamination of the rubber.

The brakes on the Elan and +2 are simple and easy to maintain, but it is worth changing the brake fluid regularly – especially if the car is left standing for a while. Discs/rotors, front and rear, are solid and rarely give any problems other than general wear or surface rust if not used, and are easily available and not overly expensive. With the callipers, spares such as pistons and seal kits are readily available for front and rear, but only the front callipers are readily available new. The +2 had slightly larger front callipers than the Elan, and are a useful upgrade to an Elan. The handbrake mechanism and its operating 'tree' and rods is unnecessarily complicated and with multiple links is prone to seizing and wear, leading to poor handbrake efficiency; cleaning up, replacing worn pivots and proper lubrication of the moving parts will restore the mechanism.

## FRONT AND REAR SUSPENSION REBUILD

You should be able to push out the metalastic bushes in the front wishbones or rear wishbone A-frame using a bench press or vice, and sockets as mandrels. However, if they are firmly seized into the wishbone, then you will have to burn out the inner bush, using a blowtorch to remove the rubber. With luck this will have freed the outer element of the bush – check by trying to press it out again. If it is still stuck, then carefully cut a slot in the outer bush using a hacksaw before chiselling the remains out of the wishbone. Replacement of the rear metalastic bushes in the A-frames can also require a lot of force to press them in.

Heat and cold can be used to assist in the replacement of the bushes if they are very tight. Place the new bushes in the freezer overnight, and heat the ends of the wishbones – either in boiling water or with a blowtorch – before quickly pressing the bushes in. If originality is not an issue, then Polybushes are a sensible replacement which are much easier to install.

## REAR DRIVESHAFTS AND SUSPENSION UPRIGHTS

While the original rear drive, with its rubber Rotoflex donuts, did a fine job, good quality Rotoflex donuts can be

The articulation of the driveshaft that the Rotoflex couplings allowed is shown here on a lightly-loaded rear end. These old Rotoflex donuts are displaying classic cracking and deterioration, and are basically scrap. ➤

hard to find, and are almost as expensive as fitting a solid driveshaft conversion using either universal joints or CV joints. Rotoflexes should be regularly inspected for cracks in the rubber and any signs of delamination around the steel inserts. Any deterioration indicates that the joint is ageing and should be replaced.

### STEERING

The main issue that can occur with the steering is the setting up of the steering rack's rack mounts to minimise kickback. Every original chassis had its rack height set using shims under the rack mounts, and the shims would vary from chassis to chassis. The thickness of the shims required is usually stamped or engraved on the chassis close to the rack mounts; for example, if there is '140' engraved on the chassis, then this indicates the shim pack should be 140 thousandths of an inch (1.524mm) in total. Note that the required shim height may be different from side to side.

The objective of shimming the rack height is to compensate for the unequal length of the Elan and +2's wishbones, which means that there is some wheel camber change as the suspension moves. As the steering arms are not pivoted in the same plane as the wishbones, and are different lengths, when the wheel moves they describe a slightly different arc to that of the wishbones, which feeds back into the rack. The shims are used to position the height of the rack, so as to minimise the differences in movement between the various linkages. While you will never completely eliminate bump steer, a properly set-up rack will minimise it.

## ENGINE

### INTRODUCTION

The Lotus Twin-cam engine, while sophisticated and high-powered for its time, is actually relatively easy to strip and rebuild. Its entire bottom end is Ford-based, and is simple and robust with very few areas to trip up even a first time rebuilder. While this section is not intended to be a step-by-step guide to rebuilding a Twin-cam, it will give the amateur pointers as to what will need to be checked and renewed or machined. For full instructions on engine rebuilds, consult the Lotus workshop manual and Miles Wilkins' *Lotus Twin-cam Engine* book. Brian Buckland's *The Rebuilding of a Lotus Elan - Addendum Engineering Workshop Manual* also has lots of detail and helpful hints and tips.

### ENGINE AND GEARBOX REMOVAL AND REPLACEMENT

Removing the engine of an Elan or +2 with the body on the chassis is relatively easy, although there are clearance issues. If you want to use an engine hoist then there are a couple of considerations of which you need to be aware. In the Elan's case, there is limited clearance between the front wheels (approx 41in/104cm), so make sure that the engine hoist legs will fit between the wheels. The distance between the wheels of the +2 is wider than the Elan, so there is less of an issue with the hoist's feet. In the case of the +2, the reach of the hoist is important – the engine is relatively far back in the bodyshell, and you need to make sure the hoist can cope with this. Another issue is the angle needed to remove or insert the engine – it is worthwhile using a load leveller along with the hoist, so you can alter the angle of the engine to suit.

The engine and gearbox were angled about right, but Dave Groves and the author just could not persuade the unit to go in!

Replacing the engine and gearbox in one piece, in an Elan with the body on and with a standard chassis, can be challenging. Despite early accounts of achieving this feat while building the kit versions of the Elan, there are a number of parts of a standard Elan chassis that conspire to make the operation tricky. These are the clearances between the sump and the front crossmember, the top of the gearbox and the chassis top crossmember, and the entry into the transmission tunnel for the gearbox end piece. These three clearance issues are further complicated by the outer edges of the bellhousing being too wide to fit between the standard engine mounts, and having to be lifted over them before the engine and gearbox can be slotted into the chassis. Apparently, the trick is to move the engine and gearbox in at an angle of around 35 degrees and twist the engine and gearbox towards the exhaust side to get it in. In the author's experience, getting the engine and gearbox unit in one piece into an Elan is virtually impossible. However, other experts have replaced the engine and gearbox as a unit, and in the early articles on building up Elan kits the issue does not seem to arise. Having spent a day and a half trying to get the combined engine and gearbox into a late Sprint, and then spending only a couple of hours to get the gearbox in first followed by the complete engine, in the author's experience the second route is the easiest! The issue is less severe when a Spyder chassis is in use, as the engine mounts bolt onto the chassis and can be removed during installation, and the engine bay crossmember is removable.

⅄ Having removed the gearbox, Dave Groves and the author found that the Sprint fitted in the car really easily.

The author's brother-in-law, who has worked on Elans for upwards of 40 years and has taken many engines in and out, recommends putting the gearbox in first, followed by the engine without the head, and then fitting the head on the block in the car. This method also makes it a lot easier to fit the ancillaries, such as the starter motor and clutch slave cylinder, gives good access to the block-to-bellhousing bolts, and also means you can position the exhaust manifold in place beside the block before fitting the head.

## CHASSIS AND ENGINE MOUNTS

There are a few foibles regarding the Elan and +2 engine mounts. The mounts have two steel elements that bolt to the engine block and chassis (on the original car), which are joined by a rubber insert and are designed to be fail-safe. The half with the four bolt holes is U-shaped, and if the rubber fails the part with the two bolt holes will fall into the 'U,' and the engine will stay put – albeit sitting low on the failed side. The mount on the inlet side of the engine is spaced out from the block using four bushes – the mount on the exhaust side is bolted directly to the block. The Elan's two mounts are different from one another, and are identified as left-hand and right-hand, while the +2 uses a single design which is used on both sides. The Elan's mounts are designed to give a slight lift to the engine on the inlet side, to allow the carbs and air box to clear the body. The issue doesn't arise on the +2, which is why the mounts are identical. On a Spyder chassis, the mounts are bolted directly to the chassis using the four-bolt fixing, and dedicated engine mount brackets are used to join the mount to the block. Where the rubber mounts are bolted to the chassis they should have the outer U-shaped element facing downwards, so still being fail-safe. The Elan and +2 Spyder chassis both use an identical pair of the standard +2 mounts.

## ENGINE PROBLEM AREAS

The Twin-cam engine is robust and reliable, but can be a trifle incontinent with regards to retaining its oil. Earlier engines, with the flywheel fixed to the crank using four bolts (up to engine number 7799), had a rope-type seal on the rear of the crankshaft, which was not as efficient as the later rubber lip seal fitted with the six-bolt crank. Make sure the breather from the head into the air box is not blocked. If it is, then the engine will leak much more than 'normal.'

While the robust oversquare Ford bottom end is capable of delivering the power of a Sprint engine without any problems, the engine can be damaged through over-revving. The generally accepted limit for the standard crank and connecting rods is 6500rpm, with very occasional forays above. Any sustained use of higher revs will result in either the crank breaking, the main bearing caps cracking, or a con rod letting go. Hence, standard cars have a spring-loaded rev limiter incorporated in the rotor arm, and owners are advised not to exceed the limit. If an engine is being built to exceed the limit then stronger connecting rods, forged main bearing caps, and a forged steel crank are strongly recommended.

The main weak spot of the Twin-cam design is the water pump. While the pump itself is a reliable unit, it is not very tolerant of misuse, and over-tightening of the fan belt will take out the bearing, and lead to water leaks. Interestingly, on the Europa Twin-cam the water pump seems to rarely fail, which is probably because the drive belt is not adjustable – the Europa's alternator is mounted on the back of the engine, and driven by a separate belt mounted on an extension to the exhaust camshaft. On many ordinary engines the failure of the water pump is no big deal, but on the Twin-cam the pump is mounted in the front timing cover and it can be a big job to repair it, usually necessitating the removal of the head and sump. And, of course, if the head is off it's worth doing a top end overhaul ...

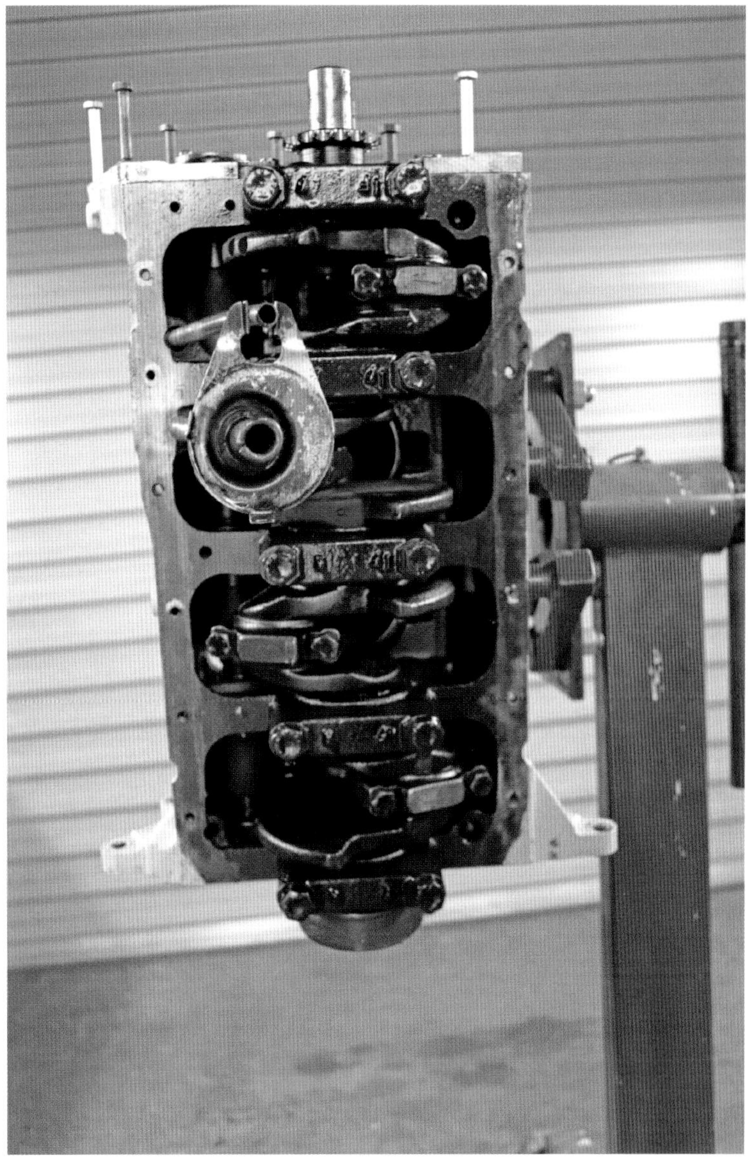

The bottom end of the Twin-cam is all Ford. With the sump off, the five main bearings and the oil pick-up pipe are visible.

Cam chain adjustment is important. A loose chain will produce rattling and rumbling noises from the front end and may hit the top of the cam cover, introducing alloy chips into the oil. This is serious if there is no adjustment left; check the length of exposed thread on the adjuster on the side of the engine – if there are more than about 10 threads exposed there is some adjustment left, and so some life left

Looking at the inside of the timing cover, you can see the water pump impeller, the crankshaft oil seal on the bottom, and, to the left, the rubber strip that protects the case from the cam chain.

The cam chain runs on four sprockets – one on the crank, one for each camshaft, and one for the ancillary driveshaft in the block. The condition of the sprockets is as important as that of the chain. Any wear and they should be replaced.

in the chain. Chain replacement is really a head-off job, and if the chain has been neglected it can cause wear on the sprockets, crank, jackshaft and camshafts. The classic way to check for wear on the sprockets is to try to pull the chain away from the sprocket while it is not under tension – it should not move much at all. A further check is to inspect the sprocket teeth. Looking at them from the side, they should be symmetrical and there should be a flat face on the top of the tooth; a point indicates excessive wear and that a new one is required. The cam chain must be endless – never fit a spring link.

Valve clearances on the Twin-cam engine are slow to go out of adjustment, and while they are relatively simple to adjust, it does require some careful measurement before taking the cams out, moving shims between valves, and the purchase of more shims as well. While it is time-consuming and exacting work, it is well within the capabilities of the home mechanic. Check all the clearances with the camshafts in place and the timing chain connected, then remove the cams, check the existing shim size, and

The cylinder head is a large alloy casting, and carries all eight valves, which are operated by the camshafts directly using bucket tappets over the valves. Each cam is fitted with five shell bearings. Note the inlet manifold cast as part of the head.

replace with the required size if necessary. Never rotate one camshaft independently of the other as a valve can potentially try to occupy the same space as one on the other camshaft, and a bent valve will be the result. Follow the instructions in the workshop manual to the letter.

## ENGINE REBUILDING THE BOTTOM END

Detailed instructions to dismantle and reassemble the bottom end are fully documented in the Lotus workshop manual. This book will give pointers, hints and tips as to what else needs to be done. The most important thing to achieve when rebuilding the engine is cleanliness. You should make sure the unit is reassembled in a clean environment, and that no grit, debris or other contamination is introduced during reassembly. A clean working environment and careful attention to tolerances and clearances will result in a smooth running, long lasting engine.

The first thing to do to the engine once it is out of the chassis is to give it a good clean. You need to get rid of probably years of accumulated oily muck, so use a proprietary degreaser and a paintbrush, and don't be afraid to hose or pressure wash the unit down – just make sure you seal off any openings. Having a clean engine to start with will make it nicer to work on, and will prevent contamination in your nice clean engine rebuild space.

Once the engine is in bits, it is important clean every individual component properly. Inspect each component for damage and wear, and make a note of what needs to be done to it before storing it carefully. Items like main bearing and big end caps, con rods and pistons should be replaced in their original positions, so mark them up accordingly and don't mix them up.

Once you have the block and crankshaft on the bench, then refer to the lubrication chart in the workshop manual to see where the various oilways are in the block and

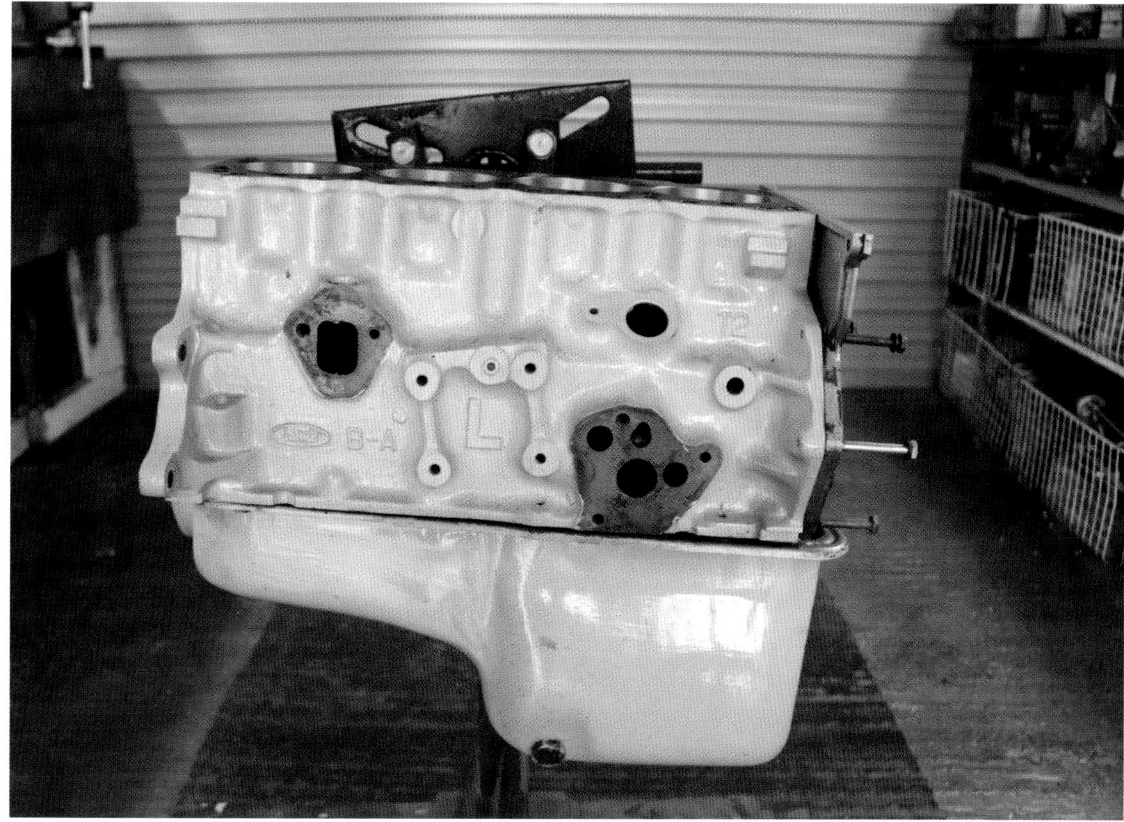

Later Lotus engine blocks had the capital 'L' cast into the block under the engine mount. The inlet side of the block carries the fuel pup, oil pump and distributor, all driven from the original Ford camshaft in the block.

With the main bearing caps and the connecting rods removed, the size of the plain bearings can be appreciated. ➤

From the top without the head, you can see the reasonable gap between the bores and the Lotus pistons, as well as the original eight holes for the pushrods used on the Ford engine. ➤

crankshaft, as these need to be cleaned. You can use a pipe cleaner in some of the more accessible holes, and then use a pump-action oil can to pump oil down each hole and continue until the oil coming out runs clear. This has two functions – firstly, you know the oilways are clean and any muck in them has been washed out, and secondly, by referring to the diagram you should be able to see if any oilway is blocked.

All the bearings in the engine – the main, big end and jackshaft bearings – are plain, and the main and big end bearings are split, and easy to remove and replace. The crankshaft is robust and is easy to take out and replace. The crankshaft bearing journals can wear in three ways. If the oil has been contaminated with metal particle grit, there can be grooves on the bearing surface that are easily found by running your fingernail across the bearing surface – it should be smooth. General wear of the journal will result in it being undersized, and the journal can also be worn oval; both of these types of wear will occur over time. While it is easy to buy a micrometer and learn how to measure the bearing journals for size and ovality, a good machine shop can do this for you and regrind the crank if needed. Specialists stock oversized main bearings in various dimensions to allow for regrinding of the crank to remove the wear. All this also applies to the big end bearings. When fitting the crank, make sure you get the end float within tolerance.

The other main area where wear will occur is in the cylinder bores. Again, your friendly local machine shop should be able to measure them for wear and ovality, but a simple test is to check for a ridge at the top of the bore by running your fingernail up the bore. If there is wear or ovality, oversize pistons are available. Lotus provided +020 and +040 thou (thousandths of an inch), and it is worthwhile to get the machine shop to bore the cylinder to the actual piston size rather than rely on the notional size of the replacements. If the bore is within tolerances, you should always renew the piston rings and have the bore roughened or 'glaze busted' to give the new rings a slightly roughened surface to bed in. Failure to glaze bust may result in low compression and high oil consumption.

Wear on the plain bearings will manifest itself as grooves in the bearing surface, the bearing surface starting to break up, or copper showing through where the white metal has been worn away completely. In the author's opinion, it is not worthwhile reusing bearing shells. While you can measure the wear on a plain bearing using a product such as Plastigauge, the bearings are relatively cheap and easy to replace. Also the old bearings will pick up impurities that embed themselves in the bearing surface, which will eventually cause wear on the bearing journal, so using new bearings will ensure you have maximum life built in.

When assembling an engine, the author uses a high graphite content bearing paste, such as Graphogen Assembly Compound, on moving surfaces such as plain bearings, pistons, cylinder walls and valve stems. Use of a paste like Graphogen protects the bearing surfaces, preventing rubbing or scuffing when the engine is first started, and also forms a long-lasting film on the surfaces that will not drain off and will inhibit corrosion if the engine is to be stored for a while. On first start-up, the paste protects the bearing surfaces until it is washed off by the circulating oil. Early crankshafts can be identified by the four-bolt fixing for the flywheel, and they use an old-fashioned rope-type seal on the rear of the crank, and this means the use of a different sump to the later six-bolt crank engine.

The original Ford camshaft is retained in the Twin-cam engine, and has a skew gear on it to drive the distributor and oil pump, while a lobe of the cam is used to drive the fuel pump. The three large diameter plain bearings it runs on are slow to wear, but should be replaced – along with the camshaft – if they are worn. They are supplied with oil from the pressure side of the system, and wear will result in lowered oil pressure and flow to the main and big end bearings. While the camshaft is out, it is worth inspecting the skew gear drive for the oil pump and distributor for worn teeth.

The Twin-cam's oil pump sits on the outside of the engine, and can be easily replaced in situ. Replacement pumps are readily available and surprisingly reasonably priced. One point to note is that the oil pump needs to be

The rear of the block, showing the six-bolt crank used on later engines. The three bolt holes around the crank are to affix the rear bearing lip seal carrier to the block. The earlier four-bolt engines used a rope seal, which could leak.

The front of the Ford block with the inner Lotus timing cover fitted. At the top is the hole that accepts the water pump impeller, then to the left is the original Ford camshaft now used to drive the ancillaries, and at the bottom the crank, with the cam drive sprocket on its nose.

properly primed before starting the engine. This can be achieved by hand filling the pump with oil before fitting it, and pumping oil into the oilways though the oil pressure gauge port, using a oil can or pressure pump.

While it is not critical, it is a good idea to have the engine balanced. This involves adding or removing weight to the crankshaft to offset the weight of the con rods and pistons, and makes the engine run more smoothly. It is a specialist job for your engine shop, but it is worth weighing each con rod and piston assembly and making sure they are all the same weight, or at least within a couple of grams of each other. Include the new big end bearings and the piston rings when weighing. Take off any excess weight by carefully removing material from the rough surface inside of the piston using a scraper or a file.

A couple of other points to watch out for: the author once had a BSA single-cylinder motorcycle engine explode dramatically because the machine shop that had reground his crankshaft had reused the bolts that fixed the flywheels to the crankshaft. When one of these let go, it went round the engine once – destroying the piston and barrel liner – before making a break for freedom through the crankcases, taking them out as well. So, be warned, there are several highly-stressed bolts in the Twin-cam that you should replace, especially if this is your first rebuild of the engine, as you have no idea what the previous owner(s) have been up to. The author, when rebuilding his +2's Twin-cam engine, automatically replaced the big end cap bolts, main bearing cap bolts, the flywheel bolts and the cylinder head bolts with good quality replacements from reputable suppliers. Never re-use gudgeon pin circlips – new ones are cheap and readily available, and if an old one fails than it will cause an impressive amount of damage to the cylinder bore. This normally means a rebore and new pistons, and may even cause the block to need to be re-lined in order to save it. Always use new gaskets when rebuilding an engine; it is a waste of time to try to reuse any bottom end gasket, as they are not designed to be used more than once and crush into shape. Finally, be sparing with any gasket goo you use, especially silicon sealant. Excess sealant is messy and doesn't look good, and excess use of silicon sealant may result in beads of the hardened sealant breaking off from the inner edge of the join and getting into the oil, where they will block oilways.

The cam caps on the head are line bored, and each cap is marked with a corresponding number on the head. Visible here are caps four and five.

### THE HEAD AND TIMING CASE

As with the bottom end of the engine, the cylinder head and timing cover should be cleaned and carefully inspected before reassembly. If they are going to be reused, the valves, camshaft bearing caps, cam follower buckets and each valve spring assembly should be replaced in their original position. Note that the camshaft bearing caps are line bored in place and are stamped with a number. There is a corresponding number stamped on the head, so it should be hard to get them wrong. If you buy a secondhand head without its camshaft bearing caps – or if you lose your existing ones – new caps are available, but will need to be line bored to fit the head correctly. If you do fit new caps, then make sure you mark their position in the head after line boring.

One major consideration for the head is how much it has been skimmed in the past. It is common to skim the head during a rebuild to make sure it is flat, but skimming will increase the compression ratio – sometimes up to an unacceptably high level. As a rule of thumb, a standard head should measure 4.640in between the bottom surface and the surface of the camshaft bearing cradle (which should be the same as the cam cover surface). A Sprint head was skimmed by 0.030in by the factory, giving a height of 4.610in. In general, you can skim a head 0.040in before the compression ratio gets too high, but a thicker head gasket can compensate. However, users have reduced the height to 4.520in – a skim of 0.12in – and the head was still usable. It appears that the limiting factor is the water jacket below the exhaust ports.

There are a number of other issues to look for when inspecting the head. As the head is alloy, corrosion is always a possibility, especially if the engine has been run without corrosion inhibitor in the coolant. Evidence of corrosion may be seen in the coolant ports on the underside of the head, and will need to be welded if it encroaches on the gasket fire rings.

The heads can exhibit cracking between the valve seats and the sparkplug holes. Small cracks can be ignored, but if a pressure test shows leakage they can be repaired by welding.

The hole for the pivot for the cam chain adjustment quadrant, which is sited on the front face of the head, should be inspected for damaged threads. It is a precision job to repair, as the pivot needs to be precisely aligned in the head.

Over time the head's aluminium alloy can get soft. Evidence of softness takes the form of recession around the head bolts, or where the head gasket fire ring has indented the head surface. If there is any, then you should get the head tested for hardness; if it has softened then, realistically, it is scrap.

Before you fit the valves, it is worth checking that the camshafts spin in their mounts without any sticky points. If they do bind it may just be the bearings, but also could be a bent or warped head or camshaft. A bent camshaft should be replaced, a warped head will need to be skimmed to restore the head to specification, and the cam bearings will need to be line bored to fix the problem – which will probably require new cam bearing caps. Sometimes it is simply time to replace the head with a new one.

The combustion chamber in the head is significantly smaller than the bore, giving a pronounced squish effect to the charge – one of the reasons the Twin-cam gives such good power.

The cylinder head, looking directly at the combustion chambers, showing how the piston is a larger diameter than the combustion chamber. While this is not a Big Valve head, the valves are pretty much as big as the combustion chambers would allow!

Valve guides will be worn unless recently replaced; they are relatively short, so do wear quickly. Replacement guides should be reamed in situ, to the valve stem size. Lotus tolerances are fairly close, at 0.003-0.0023in for the inlet and 0.0025-0.0030in for the exhaust. Any greater clearance will result, to quote Miles Wilkins, in "the well-known Lotus oil haze from the exhaust."

Valve seats wear slowly, so will hopefully be in reasonable condition and only need a light regrind. There is some debate over the use of unleaded fuel in the Twin-cam, but unless the seats show significant pocketing or wear, there is no need to replace them for normal use. The definition of 'normal' in this context is using the car as a cherished classic, driving on normal roads at normal speeds. In this case, the owner should keep an eye on the valve clearances: if they start to get smaller, then the valve seats are likely to be pocketing. If the engine is to be raced or subjected to continuous high revs it is worthwhile having the seats replaced with hardened seats suitable for unleaded fuel.

## CARBURETTOR CHOICES: WEBER, DELLORTO OR STROMBERG

Webers are the carburettor of choice for racers and performance chasers – a well set-up pair of Webers (or Dellortos) will be able to chuck bucket-loads of fuel into an engine, and are particularly good at feeding the engine at high revs, or when the throttle is snapped open. These are useful characteristics on the racetrack, and all the 26Rs were fitted with Webers. The Strombergs, being constant-velocity units, are excellent at providing the correct fuel-air ratio throughout the rev range, are probably better low down and at 'normal' speeds, and run slightly leaner than the Webers. Looking at the power outputs of the various Twin-cams and performance figures from contemporary road tests, there is little to choose between the carbs on a road car. However, the emotional pull of a pair of Webers (or Dellortos) under the bonnet trumps the slightly more staid-looking Strombergs, and so Weber heads command

➤ Weber carburettors are the most popular choice for racing and road use.

a premium over the Stromberg variety. So, for roads users, it is a choice between ultimate top-end performance and under bonnet bragging rights, or smoother, better behaved real-world performance. Racers will go for the Webers or Dellortos – this is mainly down to their ability to hose copious quantities of fuel into the cylinders when the throttle is wide open, and their accelerator pump gives a sharp throttle response.

Changing from Strombergs to Webers involves either replacing the cylinder head, or having the Stromberg inlet tracts cut off and a replacement Weber manifold grafted on. Either way is not cheap, and the cost only increases when adding the price of a new pair of carburettors and the associated linkages. If Webers are important to you, then I would advise buying a Weber-equipped car from the word go; Stromberg heads and carbs are significantly cheaper than the Weber alternatives and, in the author's opinion and experience, offer no significant loss of performance on the road.

## GEARBOX, DIFFERENTIAL AND FINAL DRIVE

### GEARBOX

The Elan and +2 were fitted with the Ford four-speed all-synchromesh gearbox from the word go, and while fitted with various gear ratios, they all shared the very direct and satisfying gear change feel. The gearboxes are robust and reliable with no inherent faults, and with regular oil changes

▲ The Ford gearbox is compact and has what is generally considered to be the best gear change feel!

will go on for ever. The only minor problem area is the degradation of the 'anti sizzle' fixing on the bottom of the gearlever, which can introduce noise into the cockpit, and wear in the nylon ball that the gearlever sits in, which will make the change a bit vague.

The Lotus five-speed gearbox is much maligned, but if properly assembled and looked after is a reasonable unit. It is essentially a repackaged Austin Maxi unit with a Lotus-designed case, bellhousing and tail all made from cast alloy. Originally intended to be fitted to the 1970s wedge-shaped Lotus Elite, the delay in getting the new car onto the market meant it could be fitted to a very few Elans, and was an option on the +2 from October 1972. While the box has a reputation for being less reliable than the Ford box, and indisputably has a poorer gear change feel, it is in general pretty reliable. This is down to it being designed to be fitted into the Elite, with its 160bhp Lotus 900 series power unit, so it can handle the Twin-cam's power easily. The main issue is weak synchromesh, especially on third gear, which results in a slow and potentially noisy change. Like all mechanical items, regular fluid changes and high quality oil will prolong its life.

## PROPSHAFT

The propeller shaft is reliable and long lasting. It has a universal joint at each end, and has a slide-in splined fitting at the gearbox and a four-bolt flange to attach it to the differential. A road speed-related vibration can be caused if a universal joint is failing, or the propshaft had become unbalanced. Some universal joints have grease nipples or plugs for nipples fitted, and it is worthwhile making sure they are kept greased. The universal joints are relatively easy to change, as long as you have a press or vice to remove and refit the bearing caps. If you do replace them, make sure you refit the yokes the same way round that they came off, otherwise you may unbalance the shaft, and bolt

➤ The propeller shaft has a universal joint at each end and a splined fitting into the gearbox, which allows for a small amount of flexing from the rubber mounts of the engine, gearbox and differential.

The differential is a Ford unit with a special Lotus cast alloy rear case. It is rubber-mounted to the chassis with two top mounts, and has a pair of torque rods bolted to the front of the chassis to resist twisting.

The torque rods are rubber-mounted on the lower front side of the diff, and bolt on to captive nuts on the chassis, which can break out of the chassis as shown here.

the flange onto the differential in the same position that it came off. The propshaft can be removed with the gearbox and differential in place using the access hole in the side of the chassis tunnel, but it is fiddly. You will have to unbolt it at the differential, then move it backwards to allow the spline to be pulled off the gearbox output shaft, then fiddle it forwards through the hole in the transmission tunnel into the footwell. Getting the shaft rebalanced is a job for the professionals. The old dodge of putting a jubilee clip on it and turning it around to rebalance the shaft is a bodge of the highest order and is not recommended.

## DIFFERENTIAL

The differential is a robust unit and should be quiet and smooth. It uses Ford crown and pinion but the rear case is an alloy casting unique to the Elan and +2. The mechanism is generally reliable, and as long as the oil level is maintained and regularly changed, the unit should give a long and reliable service. Output shafts are mounted on their own bearings which are held in place by circlips, and the oil seals for the shafts can wear and leak. Replacement is possible without removing the differential, but access is tight.

The differential hangs from the rear crossmember of the chassis on a pair of substantial rubber mounts, and is held in place by two rubber-mounted tie bars – one on each side – which are bolted to the side of the chassis. Like any other rubber item, the rubber mounts on the diff and tie bars can perish and should be checked, and renewed if worn. The front of the tie bar mounts are bolted onto the chassis using captive nuts. These can work loose and, if left, will result in stripped threads and elongated holes. While proper repairs will need welding, the author has seen examples of new L-section metal being bolted to the chassis to reinstate the mounts – any such repair is at best a temporary fix.

## JEFF BOUGHTON'S ELAN SERIES 3 SE SUPER SAFETY

Jeff Boughton has owned his 1967 Elan S3 SE SS since 2010. While he already owned an early Elan coupé, Jeff also wanted a convertible and the SS fitted the bill. The SS can be regarded as an interim model between the Series 3 and Series 4, and the export models are fitted with a number of safety-orientated features as specified by the US, including flush-fitting rocker switches, wheel spinners with the ears that bend inwards, and recessed door handles.

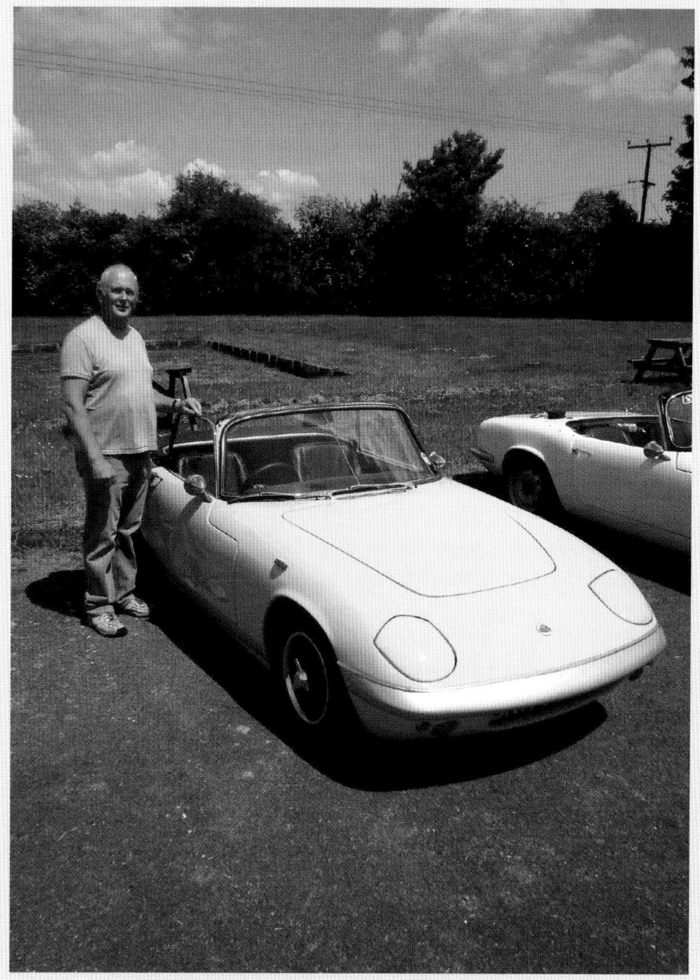

Jeff Boughton stands by his Elan Series 3 SS.

Jeff's Elan Series 3 sits by Brian Goodison's Series 2. The boot lid overlapping the rear panel was introduced with the Series 3.

Those that weren't exported generally retained the normal S3 features, and that includes Jeff's, which only has recessed internal door handles. And, of course, Jeff's car has the bright Lotus Yellow paint that makes it stand out from the crowd! While the Elan SS is a rare beast in the UK – as it was really built for the American market – interestingly, Jeff is aware of at least one more example that exists locally to him.

The car's engine had already been upgraded to Sprint specification by the previous owner, so it isn't lacking in performance, and in general the car has served him well over the past few years. The car is happy to cruise at around 80-85mph, and Jeff hasn't felt the need to venture beyond that in performance. Since buying the car, Jeff has, in that famous Lotus tradition, made a number of modifications to both improve the car and increase its usability. He has

Jeff found some interesting glass fibre bodges in his Elan when he was repairing some front end damage. The fixing point around the front turret had been very poorly repaired in the past.

fitted +2 front callipers and removed the servo, which has resulted in excellent brakes with plenty of feel and a reasonable pedal pressure. He also changed the diff ratio to 3.55:1, for slightly more relaxed motorway cruising. An electric fan lets the car cope happily with the heavy traffic experienced locally in the south east of England, while electric ignition makes the sparks reliable and strong. Finally, as he could not source any decent quality Rotoflex couplings a few years ago, Jeff fitted a set of a set of Sue

With a little bit of reading up and some guidance, Jeff effected a good repair on the body including refixing the important bobbin in place.

Miller's CV driveshafts, both for safety and reliability, and is very happy with the results. The car is a regular attendee at local car shows and Jeff is happy to venture further afield – he is a regular at the Club Lotus Spring Track Day at the Castle Combe race circuit for example.

A couple of years ago the car slipped off a trolley jack, which punched through the front undertray and wrecked the radiator. Jeff got local glass fibre expert Robin Alabaster to repair the nose, and he sourced and fitted a new radiator. While he was replacing the radiator, he noticed some loose glass fibre in the engine bay around one of the mounting points on the front turret. Rather than call Robin back in, Jeff decided to tackle the work himself. After digesting the sage advice given by Miles Wilkins in his seminal book *How to Restore Fibreglass Bodywork* (see Bibliography), Jeff set to the job and found that he was looking at the result of a previous repair. It had been very badly done, with the new glass fibre being slathered on top of existing paint and oily dirt! He stripped it all off and repaired the area properly, including doing the fiddly bits

While the gloss white household paint was an unwelcome discovery, it did at least seem to have prevented any significant corrosion in the chassis. After trying to remove it by hand, Jeff had the chassis professionally blasted, saving himself a lot of time and materials. ➤

The first major milestone of Jeff's restoration: the completed rolling chassis. The modern paint mimics the 'red oxide' finish of the original chassis, all parts are refurbished and rebushed, and it is looking superb. ➤

around the bobbin. A couple of coats of satin black paint around the repair completed the job.

However, as is often the case with old cars and Elans especially, while getting down and dirty in the engine bay he realised that there were some other problems. The worst was the presence of lots of peeling paint on the chassis – and it wasn't just any old paint, it was household gloss white. So, Jeff took the decision to give the car what it really deserved – a full body-off rolling chassis restoration. You see what can happen with just a bit of careless jack work!

With the aid of several of his local 'Lotus Lads,' the body was removed and the true extent of the paint was revealed. The whole chassis was coated in it, without any preparation – covering oil, dirt, and the original red oxide. While it was certainly not an original Lotus feature it did seem to have saved the chassis from any serious rust, so it had served some purpose after all. Jeff removed all the mechanical elements from the chassis and started to clean it up. This proved to be a job too far – the white paint was sticking tenaciously, and eventually Jeff sent the chassis off for blasting and painting. He reckons the cost was less than he would have spent on sandpaper and spray cans of paint, to say nothing of the time saved! The chassis was finished in two spray coats of the modern version of red lead, which was a close match to the original Lotus 'red oxide' primer in appearance. While the chassis was away, Jeff refurbished or replaced all the suspension components. When the chassis and running gear were re-united, Jeff realised that the engine looked a bit drab, so he stripped off all the ancillaries, degreased it, and repainted the block and head in the correct Lotus grey paint, while also giving the cam cover a new coat of original green paint. With the engine and gearbox back where they belonged, the 'Lotus Lads' were reassembled and the body dropped onto the immaculate chassis, where it was securely bolted back on.

Jeff then turned his attention to the wiring. The loom had been wrapped in insulation tape a long time ago, and which was now gently unravelling and looking very untidy, so had to be sorted. Removing the tacky and horrible tape revealed a sticky, oily mess of wires that all had to be cleaned with white spirit, cleaning cloths and cotton buds – a long and messy job. Jeff added some extra wiring, including a circuit for the electric fan and one for air horns, then rewrapped the loom in proper self-amalgamating loom tape. After all the hard work he has put in, the only bad thing about the restoration has been fending off his mates' questions of "When's it going to be finished then?" Of course, he doesn't want to tell them (or himself) that with an Elan the job is never finished, and he still has his coupé to go ...

To keep him going through the rebuild, Jeff likes to remember one of his best journeys in the car; picking it up from Anglesey, in North Wales, when he first bought it. Sprinting through Snowdonia in the Elan had his wife struggling to keep up in her Peugeot 206 GTI, while Jeff relished the wind-in-the-hair motoring that he couldn't get from his Elan coupé. His worst memory came when he ran over his big toe while trying to move the car in the garage – luckily the car was so light and no lasting damage was done. At the time of writing the car was almost ready to go back on the road, although the COVID-19 shutdown has prevented that first road test so far! Once the clampdown is lifted, Jeff is looking forward to rekindling his love affair with the car!

CHAPTER 5

# Elan and +2 Modifications

## INTRODUCTION

Lotus owners have a long and distinguished record of modifying and upgrading their cars. Today, while there is a growing trend for original cars, the modification culture is still thriving, with many companies supporting owners' quests to make their cars faster, more reliable, more comfortable, and longer lasting. Modifications and upgrades for the Elan and +2 are, in the main, easily reversible, but all will impact on the originality of the car to a greater or lesser extent. Note that it is the owner's responsibility to ensure that any modifications are safe and suitable for the use the vehicle is being put to.

## UPGRADES OR MODIFICATIONS

There is a lot to be said about the essential 'correctness' of the Elan and +2 design, which has Chapman's fingerprints all over it. It is light, cleverly engineered, and culminates in an excellent sports car with ample performance and exemplary handling and roadholding. Nevertheless, there are lots of modifications that have been designed and developed over the years, and any owner should be aware of them. The vexed question of whether to favour originality or upgrade, and the pros and cons of carrying out modifications, is really up to the owner to decide. Back in the day, modifications were often made out of necessity – for example, when original Lotus chassis were in short supply in the 1980s, often the only choice an owner had to keep their car on the road was to replace an original rusted-out chassis with a Spyder Cars spaceframe example, which had the benefit of being less rust-prone than the original. Some modifications are improvements to the original design – for example, the use of solid driveshafts, which were originally introduced and homologated for the Elan 26R racers, as the Rotoflexes couldn't take the pace with super-tuned engines. So, when supplies of good quality Rotoflexes started to become expensive, many owners switched to solid shafts.

Spyder Cars has been supplying a large number of well-engineered modifications since the 1980s, starting with its spaceframe chassis, and now ranging from electric headlamp lift kits through to complete chassis. It also provides the service of fitting its products to a customer's

In the Series 1 and 2 Elan, the boot lid is recessed into the deck. This means there are drain pipes running from the lid surround down to the boot floor. If these are blocked or disconnected then leaks will occur.

car. The company offers the products needed to build what is probably the ultimate modified Elan or +2: a Spyder chassis, which will enable a customer to build an Elan or +2 fitted with a Ford Zetec engine; a Ford five-speed gearbox; a Sierra differential; and wishbone rear suspension with CV driveshafts. While such an Elan or +2 is undoubtedly an impressive vehicle in its own right, it is interesting to consider whether such a car retains the essence of Colin Chapman and Ron Hickman's combined genius.

## BODYSHELL AND FITTINGS

### INTRODUCTION

There are a number of areas of the bodyshell that can benefit from various modifications, both to improve reliability and solve inherent problems.

### WATERPROOFING

In general, the Elan and +2 are pretty watertight, apart from the usual leaks from the convertible Elans. However, the Series 1 and 2 Elans had a recessed boot lid that sat in a well on the top of the rear deck. There are a pair of drain holes, which have pipes to drain water out of the well and through the boot floor. If these are blocked, or the tubes dislodged, water can leak into the boot. From the Series 3 onward the boot lid was extended into the rear panel, so water drains naturally from the well onto the rear panel.

On the +2, water in the boot is also a common problem. At first glance the +2 does not share the issue seen on the Series 1 and 2 Elans, with their inset boot lids; its boot lid extends over the rear face of the car, offering good drainage, so the usual thought on water ingress is that it must be getting in via the rear screen seal, petrol cap seal or radio aerial. However, the true design fault is lower down than these obvious entry points: water ingress is usually caused by the water penetrating the boot via the bumper mounting bolt holes, which are positioned on the top edge of the lip that the bumper sits on. While the lip is roughly horizontal, water will drain onto it from the boot lid drain channels, and leak into the boot through the bumper fixing holes. The holes can be sealed using silicone sealant around the bolts.

Rainwater often leaks into the +2 boot through the fixing bolt holes on the ledge that the rear bumper sits on.

Elans and +2s should have a little rubber sealing strip on the door opening.

Finally, perished seals under the rear light clusters can also allow water into the boot in both the Elan and the +2.

On the Elan and +2 there is a secondary door seal designed to stop rainwater getting into the interior by diverting it away from the main seal. This is a short length of L-shaped door seal positioned on the bodyshell, on the top front of the door, and is often missed out, which gives rise to leaks and draughts. It is fixed in position using an aluminium strip and pop-rivets.

## LOCAL BODY STRENGTHENING INTRODUCTION

While it doesn't improve the car's weight, it can be worthwhile to put some local strengthening on the rear of panels, or areas of the body that are prone to stress cracks. As most of these fixes will involve working behind panels, a tip is to use small pieces of mat or roving cloth – around 1-3cm$^2$ – to build up the section. While it seems like a good idea to cut a piece of glass fibre to the size required, gravity will dictate that it will proceed to peel off as you try to stipple it in position on the underside of a panel, resulting in an unsavoury mess of resin and mat on the ground. Small sections of mat should stay in place, and you can use them to build up a neat and strong repair. Lotus reinforced large panels using string or rolled up paper tubes bonded into the rear face of panels; this method can be used on larger panels for additional strength. You must make sure the area that you are bonding the reinforcement to is thoroughly cleaned, and that there is a good glass fibre surface free of contamination to give the reinforcement a good bond.

## ELAN AND +2 BODY STRENGTHENING

Wheelarches on the Elan and +2 are relatively thin and, while well designed with a decent lip to add strength, they are prone to cracks. These cracks usually start due to damage to the wing – like a vehicle clipping the wing in a car park, or some other impact knocking the wing – and can propagate up the body if left unrepaired. A strip of 1in (2.5cm) wide glass fibre tape can be bonded onto the inside edge of the arches to give them a bit more strength. You may be lucky and manage to persuade a single length of glass fibre tape to stay in place if you start at the top middle of the arch and work your way down to the bottom, but short lengths of the tape are easier to fix in place. If you do use short lengths, you will have to overlap the edges of each piece for the strengthening to work.

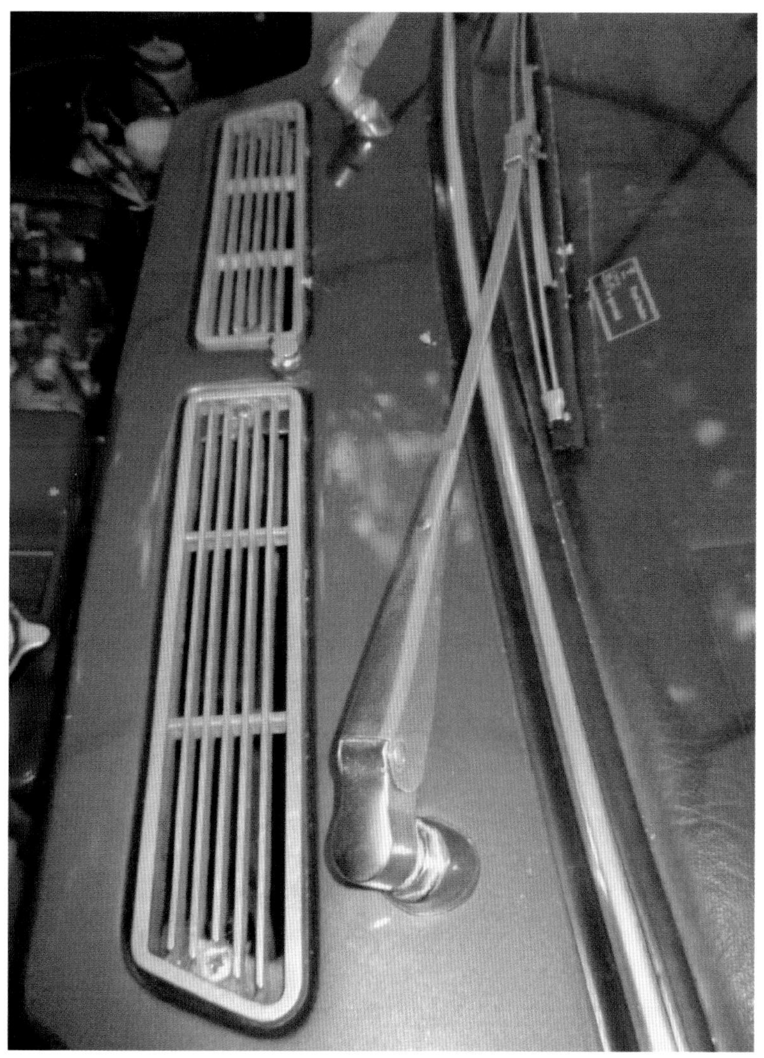

The area around the windscreen wiper spindles on the Elan and +2 can be usefully reinforced by laying mat around them under the panel.

The area in front of the windscreen, around the wiper spindles, is often the site of gel coat cracks – especially in the Elan. Reinforcing this area needs to be done carefully, making sure you do not make the skin too thick to accept the spindles. One or two sheets of mat placed on the undersurface of the panel should suffice. The top of the door skins on the Elan and +2 can flex and crack if the door is slammed by pushing it too hard. Taking a string or thin tube made from rolled up paper, and bonding it fore and aft across the whole length of the door skin, at the level where it is natural to push the door closed, will help to prevent cracking on the skin itself. The location holes for the locks and handles on the door are also high stress areas, so prone to cracks, and again can benefit from local reinforcement behind them. Note that any reinforcement around locks and handles must not be too thick to prevent the handles and locks being bolted back on. The boot lid hinges concentrate stress into a small area, and so are prone to developing cracks around the bolt holes, especially on the rear deck. Again, a little localised strengthening around the bolt holes will help to reduce the problem.

## +2 SPECIFIC BODY STRENGTHENING

On the +2, cracks are prone to occur on the rear edge of the headlamp pod hole, in the top surface of the flat nose panel ahead of the bonnet opening (see image on page 93). There is no local strengthening on the underside of the rear edge of the hole, and cracks can propagate from the top corners, running in line with the top edge of the hole. To prevent cracks appearing and propagating here, bond a couple of layers of mat or roving cloth on the underside of each corner, building up a consistent layer of reinforcement around the perimeter of the opening, going about 4-6cm down and across, and bonding to the vertical plate that carries the bobbins for the headlamp pod pivot bolts.

## +2 PEDAL BOX

The first +2s had a pedal box that was clamped through the glass fibre body onto a separate rectangular steel sandwich plate, which also incorporated brackets for the handbrake lever and steering column. This plate was replaced with a pair of brackets at chassis number 0367, which fitted on the rear and side of the box, and studs and washers covered the rest. On later +2s (from chassis 0928), the pedal box was narrower and retained the pair of brackets. Suppliers can provide an additional steel reinforcing sandwich plate to help strengthen the mounting.

A common modification that can be made to the pedal box is to cut an access hole in its top face. It is a tricky job

Early +2 pedal boxes were fitted with a mounting plate that helped to stiffen the box and its mounting. It is a useful upgrade to retrofit one for these same benefits.

Another useful modification to the +2 pedal box is cut a hole in the top and fit a closing plate. This gives easy access to the clevis pins that connect the pedals to the clutch and brake master cylinders.

to get at the clevis pins that connect the clutch and brake pedals to their respective master cylinders, and by cutting a hole in the top of the box, access can be improved. Make sure that there is a cover for the hole, which should be waterproof and securely fixed in place.

## FUEL TANK AND BREATHER SYSTEM

Both the Elan and +2 have mechanical fuel pumps, and issues can arise if the car has been left standing for a while. In the Elan, fuel can drain back into the tank, which is below the boot floor, while in the +2 the tank is mounted higher, but fuel can still evaporate from the carburettor's float bowl. In both cases, the engine will need to be cranked to run the fuel pump, which in turn will pump fuel to the carbs. The solution is to fit an electric fuel pump or manual booster pump. This is reasonably easy on the Elan, with its fuel tank and feed readily accessible from the boot; a manual or electric pump can be fitted under the boot floor. However, it is a bit more complicated with the +2, as its fuel tank is mounted between the boot and the passenger compartment, and access to the feed, sited above the differential, is limited. In this case, an electric pump is best fitted in the engine bay. If you do fit an electric pump, it is important to fit an electric cut-off valve to stop the pump in the event of a crash or other impact. The last thing you want is for fuel to be being pumped out if you are in an incident.

There has been a great deal written about the +2's fuel tank venting system. The UK system can occasionally make the car smell of petrol, so there are a number of adaptations of the closed-circuit Federal system that use a vent connected into the filler pipe to allow for vapour release when filling, and a one-way valve to allow air into the tank as fuel is used. Club Lotus have issued a bulletin on how to carry out the conversion. In a +2, fuel should not leak from the filler cap when cornering; if it does, then there is a fault somewhere. This could be an issue with the rubber elbow between the tank and the cap assembly, damage to the metal sealing rim of the fuel filler orifice, a faulty seal in the fuel cap itself, or simply that the wrong fuel cap is fitted. The design of fuel cap was produced for many British cars and motorcycles, the Norton Commando notably among them. In the relatively common motorcycle application, the cap has a built-in vent hole that will leak if fitted to the +2. In the Lotus application, the cap has two separate rubber seals: a flat main one mounted on a sprung plate, which seals against the rim of the filler and is visible when the cap is open; and a secondary circular item, which seals the inside

▲ This shot shows the +2 fuel tank out of the car. The yellow arrow shows the position of the filler inlet, halfway down the side of the tank, and the red arrows show the vents on each side of the top of the tank.

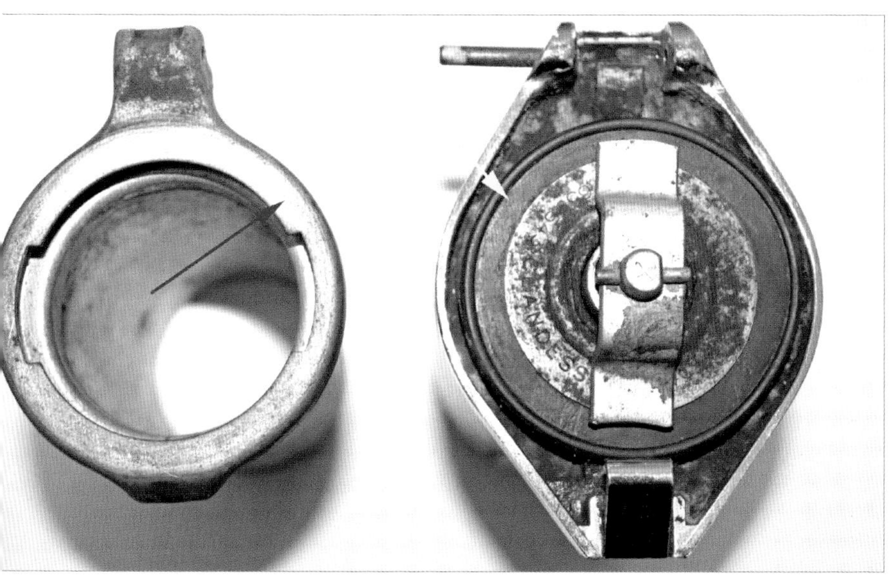

▲ The +2 fuel cap should not be vented, and there should not be a small hole in the filler cap plate. This picture shows the main seal on the cap (yellow arrow) which should seal onto the filler neck (red arrow)

▲ This picture shows where the second seal is positioned on the filler cap (red arrow), which seals against the filler cap plate, and the lock seal (yellow arrow), which is used on locking caps to seal the lock mechanism.

edge of the plate against the cap. In addition to these two, if your car has a locking fuel cap, there is a third seal in the form of an O-ring surrounding the locking mechanism in the centre of the cap.

The lotuselan.net forum also has a lot of information on the issue. One common fix is to fit a Mazda MX-5 fuel filler valve in the +2's fuel filler. This valve allows fuel to flow into the tank but blocks it running in the opposite direction, stopping fuel sloshing up the filler neck and out through the cap.

### SEATS

While Elan and early +2 seats are relatively comfortable and light, any of the original vinyl coverings, zig-zag springs, and foam padding used to upholster them will be getting tired and showing their age. A competent trimmer should be able to restore the seats back to standard without too many issues, and a useful upgrade can be made by replacing the vinyl with leather, to add a bit of luxury and tradition to the cockpit. Some owners have fitted Mazda MX-5 seats to their Elans and +2s, which are small enough to fit, provide a similar degree of comfort, and secondhand examples can be found for less than the cost of a re-trim.

Seat choices for the +2 and +2S are more numerous, and include Jaguar XJS items. Remember you need to retain the seat-back hinging if you want to use the rear seats, and so will need to source seats from a two- or three-door coupe.

## CHASSIS OR SUBFRAME

### INTRODUCTION

Firstly, it is important to understand that the steel backbone chassis used in the Elan and +2 is considered to be a subframe by the licensing authorities in the UK. This is a position originally negotiated by Lotus director Graham Arnold, and reinforced by Club Lotus director Alan Morgan. It is based on a number of arguments, including the facts that the subframe on its own is not drivable, the car relies on the body and subframe being bolted together to form the overall structure, and the subframe – if damaged in an accident or by corrosion – can be swapped for a new one in the same way that the original BMC Mini's front or rear subframes could be swapped. It is important to make this distinction, as changing a chassis can have implications for a car's identity in the UK. In the case of an Elan or +2, a change of 'subframe' does not change the car's 'official' identity, and the DVLA does not need to be notified.

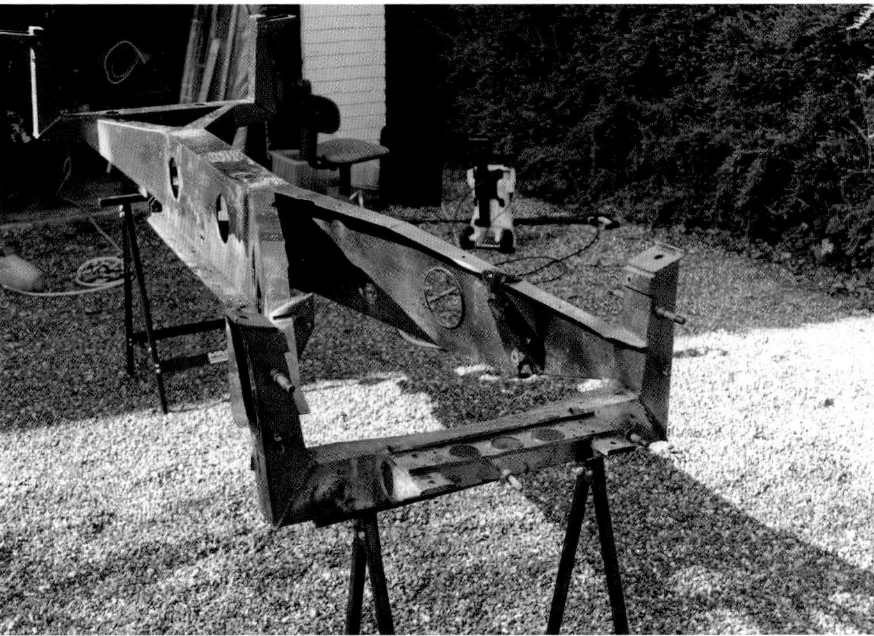

▲ The standard Elan and +2 chassis are made from folded sheet steel. The +2 has a longer central tunnel and wider rear turrets.

### REPLACEABLE ENGINE BAY CROSSMEMBER IN ELAN

The Elan has a fixed U-section crossmember under the engine. This is designed to be in tension to stop the lower chassis side bowing in when the engine is installed. It does a good job, but does make removing the sump almost impossible when the engine is in the car. The +2 has a removable crossmember, which makes life easier when doing work that requires the sump be removed. It is possible to replace the Elan's existing welded-on crossmember with a bolt-on item – either fabricated yourself or using a +2 unit. In order to do this you should cut off the existing member along the edge of the chassis, leaving the welded-on ends in place. Then grind or cut down the remaining channels on the remaining pieces, to leave a flat piece of steel welded to the bottom of the chassis. Drill the fixing holes for the replacement chassis in these plates, and use at least a 5⁄16in hi-tensile bolt at each end to fix the new crossmember onto the chassis.

## NEW CHASSIS OPTIONS

There are currently two options available for a new original-type chassis: an original Lotus replacement, or Spyder refurbished units. As the name suggests, the original Lotus items conform to the original design. During the '80s and '90s, Lotus had these replacements zinc-coated to give great corrosion resistance. However, it was found that the process could distort the chassis, so replacement units reverted to a painted or powder coat finish. In addition to its spaceframe unit, Spyder offers the option of a refurbished original Lotus chassis with a new front end grafted on. New turrets have a closing plate welded in to prevent water and road dirt accumulating in the base, and a circular crossmember incorporating a towing lug completes the modification.

The Spyder spaceframe chassis replaces the sheet metal design with a triangulated spaceframe, built from square section tubing. It is a neat and strong design, and due to its better corrosion resistance is often seen as a more viable option than the Lotus original. In addition, Spyder has been supplying chassis to owners since the early 1980s, during times when genuine Lotus items were often scarce or unobtainable, thus keeping many Elans on the road. Two major advantages of the Spyder chassis is that the crossmember under the engine is detachable on both the Elan and +2 units, and that the engine mounts are not fixed to the chassis – they bolt on to a plate on the side of the engine bay. These modifications make engine and gearbox removal and replacement a lot easier than in the Lotus item, where the bellhousing doesn't fit between the fixed engine mounts, so requiring the engine to be lowered in at a precise angle in order to fit between the mounts and the top brace rail, while persuading the gearbox end to go into the chassis tunnel.

Originally Spyder offered its spaceframe chassis as a straight swap with the Lotus item, using common suspension pick-up points. A further option on later Spyder units offered double wishbone rear suspension, with pick-up points for the new top wishbones fitted to the unit.

The Spyder chassis also has a sightly raised rear crossmember, which makes removing and refitting the

Spyder makes spaceframe chassis using mainly square section tubing. They are less prone to corrosion than the standard chassis.

differential easier than with the stock item. This does mean that additional spacers may be needed between the top face of the differential mounting lugs and the rubber mounts to position the differential at the correct height. Spyder also offers a chassis that has a cutaway in the front crossmember to give clearance for a Ford Zetec engine. On the Spyder chassis the front suspension wishbone spindles are removable – they are a tight push fit into fittings on the chassis. These need to be lubricated when inserted, otherwise they can seize in place. If they are seized – if, for example, a thread has stripped, or they have been bent – then replacement can be difficult. Use 'copper slip' or a similar anti-seize compound on them when fitting.

▲ In order to fit wider wheels to the Elan the wheelarches usually need to be modified. This 'Modsports' Elan was pictured at a 1980s Blackbushe drag racing meet – for road use, less extreme changes are needed! (Courtesy John Humfryes)

## RUNNING GEAR

### INTRODUCTION

One of the more controversial areas of Elan modification is the running gear. There is a school of thought that Chapman got it right from the off; that by changing the suspension and wheels you are unlikely to improve on what was there originally, and might even compromise the poise and balance of the standard car. On the other hand, there are homologated changes made to the driveshafts, wheels and springs of the Type 26R racing Elan, and these can be applied to road cars to their advantage – especially the use of solid driveshafts. Other modifications, such as wider wheels and tyres or the Spyder rear wishbone setup, are alternatives to the standard setup – not necessarily better, but more able to cope with the increased power of a highly-tuned Twin-cam or a larger, 200bhp modern engine. Does a +2 with a Zetec engine, Spyder chassis, Sierra differential, five-speed gearbox, and twin wishbone rear suspension still adhere to Chapman's original philosophy of the Elan and +2? This book is not going to state an opinion, but it will make owners aware of what is possible!

### SOLID DRIVESHAFTS

The rear driveshafts, with their flexible rubber Rotoflex couplings, were one of the first components to come under the scrutiny of modifiers. They were an inspired choice for the original road-going Elan: simple, light, effective, virtually maintenance-free, and cheap. However, for the racing Elan – the 26R – Lotus homologated 'solid' driveshafts. Why were they introduced? Mainly because the then-standard Rotoflex couplings wilted under the power of race-tuned Twin-cam engines, and could not cope with the additional stresses placed on them when the cars were being used to their maximum potential. Also, many drivers disliked the 'wind-up' inherent in the couplings, which robbed them of some feeling of what the rear wheels were up to. The original homologated items comprised a splined sliding shaft to allow for the relative movement between the rear hub and the differential output shafts as the suspension moved, and a Hooke's-type universal joint on each end. A second type appeared some years ago with constant-velocity joints at either end, joined by a splined shaft to allow for the changes in driveshaft length.

Today, if you inspect the boot floor of many Elans and +2s, you will find evidence of Rotoflex failure in the shape of glass fibre repairs to the rear bulkhead and boot floor – in the author's experience, around 25 per cent of the cars he has looked at over the years have evidence of damage

Seen here is the original type of solid driveshaft. As homologated for the 26R racers, they use a pair of Hooke's universal joints at each end and a sliding spine to take up changes in length.

The second type replaces the Hooke's joints with constant-velocity joints, and retains the sliding spline.

to the boot area, probably caused by Rotoflex failure. As the cars got older, and the need to regularly inspect and replace the Rotoflexes was ignored, failures became more common. A catastrophic failure of a Rotoflex could result in a driveshaft penetrating the rear of the cabin as it flailed around, which poses risks to the driver and passenger's safety, or the locking up of a rear wheel. Lotus introduced a modification to the driveshafts, differential shafts and inner hub drives, in the form of a peg on the diff and hub shafts, and a socket on each end of the driveshaft to retain the driveshaft in position should a Rotoflex fail. The modified parts were introduced at about the time of Sprint and +2S 130, when the more powerful engine increased the number of failures. Regarding the Rotoflexes, while there are good quality replacements currently available, they are not cheap, and a set of four will approach the cost of a set of solid units.

The advantages of fitting solid driveshafts include: less maintenance; a lower chance of failure (and likely a less catastrophic result if the shaft does fail); a more direct feel to the drive-train; no 'wind-up' effect when accelerating; and, apart from periodic greasing, they are very much a 'fit and forget' item. The downside is the loss of some (some will say too much) flexibility in the drive-train, and a loss of originality. Currently, there are two types of constant-velocity joint driveshafts available: the Sue Miller design (now supplied though Kelvedon), and the Australian Elantrikbits. Tony Thompson Racing supplies 26R-type universal joint driveshafts for Elans and +2s, and Spyder still supplies its hybrid Rotoflex and universal joint types.

Paddy Byers' Series 1 Elan has slightly modified front arches to allow the fitment of wider tyres. ➤

In contrast, Brian Goodison's Series 2 Elan has wheelarches that retain their original profile. ➤

Dave Groves' Elan Sprint shows the profiles of the Series 3 and 4 wheelarches, which were slightly flared and flattened when compared to the Series 1 and 2 to give more clearance. ➤

## WIDER WHEELS AND TYRES

Wider tyres and wheels – if the width is greater than 175mm – will probably require thinner rear springs and the associated perches to give sufficient clearance. In addition, you will probably need to relieve the front and rear wheelarches to prevent the tyres rubbing at full suspension travel, especially on a Series 1 or 2 Elan.

## SUSPENSION UPGRADES

There are a number of upgrades that a keen owner can do to the car's suspension. At the front, the easiest and probably most popular upgrade is the replacement of the standard spring and damper units with higher specification ones with adjustable damping and spring height.

Adjustable replacement damper inserts for the rear suspension are also readily available. Changing the diameter of the rear springs is possible, but means some alteration to the fixed bottom spring perch on the standard rear upright. Narrower rear springs are usually fitted to provide adequate clearance if the owner is going to fit significantly wider wheels and tyres.

Replacing the metalastic bushes normally fitted to the inboard ends of the front wishbones and rear A-frames with modern polyurethane bushes is a popular, relatively cheap modification. When originally introduced, polybushes tended to be hard and more suited to racing applications, but today softer varieties are readily available.

Spyder Cars provides a number of front and rear suspension upgrades, including new front uprights that use the standard Ford four- or five-stud pattern hub, and replaces the brass bottom trunnion with a ball joint. This is

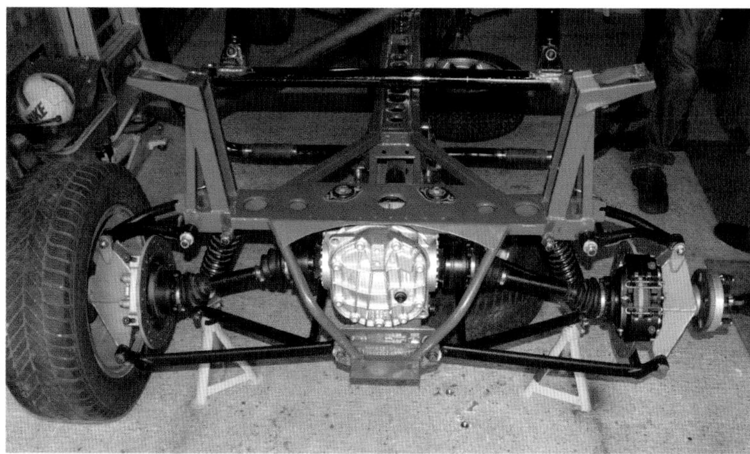

An option with the Spyder chassis is double wishbone rear suspension. This chassis is also set up to accommodate a Ford Sierra differential.

The Spyder chassis has additional pick-up points for the top wishbone and the top mount of the shock absorber. The original turrets are retained.

On the Spyder chassis, the original lower A-frame design is modified to carry the lower mount of the shock absorber.

intended to be fitted to Spyder chassis-equipped cars and used in conjunction with Spyder's own double wishbone rear suspension system. The system was designed to update the original and replace Lotus' proprietary strut with its Lotocone top mount.

### ADJUSTABLE SUSPENSION

As standard, the Elan and +2 suspension geometry was fixed with no facility for adjustment. However, the 26R front suspension top wishbone was rose jointed to enable adjustment of the front wheel camber. This is a simple retrofit to the Elan, and versions are available for the +2.

At the rear, some people advocate inserting a screw mechanism into the front arm of the lower A-frame, to enable the rear wheels' toe-in to be adjusted.

### BRAKES

New standard front callipers are available, and putting +2 callipers onto the Elan is easy and gives slightly increased braking power. Braided hoses from the chassis to the callipers is a worthwhile modification, as it will help to protect the lines from rubbing.

Stainless steel pistons are available for front and rear callipers. If you are rebuilding the brakes then this is an option that will avoid the rusting problems that the standard chrome plated pistons can suffer from.

The handbrake mechanism can be improved by fitting adjustable operating rods. These are available from most specialists (see Chapter 6), and enable the owner to ensure the handbrake mechanism operates evenly on both sides.

## THE TWIN-CAM ENGINE MODIFICATIONS

### INTRODUCTION

As outlined in Chapter 1, the Elan and +2 were offered with their Twin-cam engines in three stages of tune. To summarise, the original standard engine in the Elan was fitted with Lotus 'B' specification camshafts, and gave 105bhp at 5500rpm and 108lb/ft of torque at 4500rpm. The SE specification unit provided in the SE Elan, +2, and +2S gave 115bhp at 6000rpm and 108lb/ft of torque at 4500rpm, which was achieved with Lotus 'C' Specification camshafts. The final iteration of the standard engine was the Sprint or Big Valve spec unit. This produced 125bhp at 6500rpm and 113lb/ft of torque at 5500rpm, and was achieved with Lotus 'D' specification camshafts – which are identified by having two rings engraved on the cam chain sprocket boss, along with a slightly larger inlet valve and re-profiled ports. The +2 came with the SE specification as standard, and the +2S 130 was fitted with the Sprint specification unit.

There are lots of options for modifying the Twin-cam. However, one thing to bear in mind is the level of tune you want, and this should be ascertained by the use you want to put the car to.

In general, the Twin-cam can give up to about 140bhp reliably – ie, slightly tweaked to above Sprint specification – and still produce the power in a usable way, with adequate torque and, importantly, reliability for fast road use. Any more than this can result in less tractability, and can be a bit peaky for day-to-day use. You pay your money and take your choice!

The Sprint engine is the final incarnation of the Lotus Twin-cam. It is only distinguishable from the other versions by the 'Big Valve' cam cover.

## ELECTRONIC IGNITION

There are many aftermarket electronic ignition systems available, ranging from bolt-in kits that simply replace the points, up to complete replacement distributors, with electronically-controlled advance curve as well as pointless triggering. The main advantage of electronic systems is that they are fit and forget – no more worn points, necessitating fiddling around with the relatively inaccessible distributor to adjust them. To the author this modification is a no brainer; however, some people prefer to keep the roadside 'fixability' of mechanical points, rather than the unfixable electronic black box.

## FUEL-INJECTION

It is possible to fit new throttle bodies incorporating electronic fuel-injection to the Twin-cam. Whether using a proprietary kit, or a set of motorcycle fuel-injection units, such a conversion will also need a suitable electronic control unit to control the injection system. Throttle bodies designed to look like Weber carburettors are currently available.

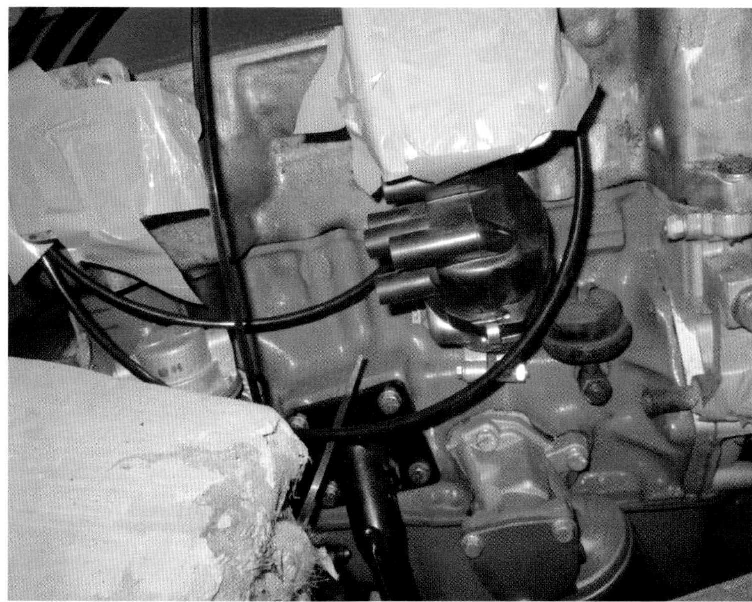

▲ The Twin-cam's distributor is somewhat buried under the carbs – here it is before the carbs have been fitted, and even then access is limited.

## ENGINE TUNING

In general, any Twin-cam fitted with the later (6-bolt) crankshaft and standard connecting rods can be safely tuned to produce around 140bhp, but you should replace all highly-stressed components – such as main bearing cap and conrod bolts, main and big end bearing shells, and pistons – with new standard-specification components from reputable suppliers. Connecting rods should be the later standard 125E type. All the engine components should be properly balanced and the engine 'blueprinted' – that is, assembled so that everything is to the tighter end of all clearance specifications. Even so, with the standard crank and rods the engine should not exceed 6500rpm, but you may get away with the occasional foray up to 7000rpm for short periods. To reliably achieve higher power and revs, you should switch to a racing specification crankshaft and con rods, as well as replacing the standard main bearing caps with stronger units, and replacing the standard cast pistons with stronger forged versions.

## ALTERNATIVE BLOCKS

The use of a 1600cc 711 crossflow block from a crossflow engine is a popular choice of today's engine builders, especially as supplies of original pre-crossflow blocks are becoming rare. The block is often referred to a 'Tall Block', with the crankshaft centre to block top being about 7⁄16in, or 4mm, taller than a crossflow L-block, and the unit has a slightly longer stroke at 77.6mm to the standard Twin-cam's 72.75mm. So, with standard Lotus 83.5mm bore, the capacity of the engine is raised from 1558cc to 1699.75cc. The taller block calls for a modified front timing cover; firms now supply them with the extra 4mm added, or distance pieces to fit between the standard case and the head are also available. The larger engine tends to result in slightly more torque and potentially a bit more power, but, in general, the conversion keeps the character of the standard Twin-cam. It is also pretty much impossible to see that the conversion has been done, with the main giveaway being if a spacer piece has been used between the timing cover and the head, which is visible on the front of the engine. The only downside is that there is slightly reduced clearance for the top of the engine and the bonnet, but in most cars this is not an issue.

### SHORTENED JACKSHAFT

The Twin-cam jackshaft is the original Ford camshaft, and runs the length of the block on the carburettor side, supported by three circular shell bearings. In the Twin-cam it is used to drive the oil pump and distributor from a screw gear at the front, and one camshaft lobe is used to drive the fuel pump. A common mod in racing or highly-tuned engines is to use a shortened camshaft – basically cutting off the rear half of the shaft behind the central bearing. This cuts down on inertia and reduces rotational friction, giving a small boost to power output. This is probably unnoticeable on the road, but does have bragging rights! One point to remember if you do decide to cut down the jackshaft is to rotate the rear bearing shell in the block, to cut off the oil feed to the bearing. If you don't, your engine will not have any oil pressure, as the jackshaft bearing oil is fed from the main in-block oil gallery.

### CARTRIDGE WATER PUMPS

The Twin-cam's water pump is sited in the timing cover on the front of the engine, and is driven from the fan belt that also powers the generator. The pulley that drives the pump also carries the car's cooling fan, and can be easily overtightened, putting stress on the pump bearing and seal. In addition, the pump bearing can also be stressed if the fan was damaged or put out of balance. It is a known weakpoint of the engine in the Elan and can be tricky to replace if the bearing or seal fails, as to get at it the head should really come off. Changing the bearing or seal means gaining access to the front half of the timing case. While it is possible to remove the front half of the case with the head in place, it is difficult to reseal the case-to-head joint and is very fiddly, so Lotus advise removing the head to get at the pump.

A number of suppliers have designed and developed replacement front timing covers that incorporate bolt-on water pumps, which can be removed and refurbished without having to disturb the timing case, and so are easily repairable without having to remove the cylinder head.

▲ The Twin-cam's only real weakness is the water pump. Mounted in the front timing cover, it can run its bearings if the fan belt is too tight, and will need the head taken off to replace.

### ENGINE SWAPS

Fitting an alternative engine is popular, and the most common choice is a Ford Zetec unit. This retains both the Ford heritage and the layout of the inlet and exhaust ports found on the Twin-cam. The unit is slightly larger than the Twin-cam, and on a standard chassis will require some surgery to the front crossmember to allow room for the front pulley. Spyder can provide a chassis designed specifically for the conversion.

## GEARBOX, DIFFERENTIAL AND FINAL DRIVE

The Lotus five-speed box used Austin Maxi internals, and was originally designed for the Elite/Éclat range. When the box was used in the Elan and +2, it shared the same centre section as that used on the Elite and Éclat, containing the gears and shafts, but was fitted with a different bellhousing and tail casting. To fit an Elite/Éclat specification box into an

The Ford Zetec unit is a popular, modern and powerful alternative for the Twin-cam. This unit is being fitted into a Spyder chassis, which has a cut-out in the front crossmember to give clearance for the crank pulley.

This is a fuel-injected Ford Zetec unit in a standard +2, albeit fitted with an early Spyder chassis. Note the cut out on the top of the pedal box, which gives access to the clevis pins that attach the master cylinders to the pedals – a useful modification.

Elan will need the Elan/+2-specific bellhousing and end tail casting. While secondhand Elite/Éclat boxes come onto the market fairly often, the Elan/+2 castings are rare. Otherwise, the fitment of a Lotus five-speed box is straightforward, and only needs a revised gearbox mount to fit.

The most common alternative five-speed gearbox to the Lotus unit is the Ford T9 unit, as used in the UK market Ford Sierra. The installation of a Sierra box does require some changes, including a modified bellhousing and tail piece to fit the Elan and +2. Voigts is the main suppliers of the conversion, and can supply kits of parts which include its own design of bellhousing.

Sprints and +2S 130s had a steel L-section reinforcing strip bolted across the top of the differential to prevent the casing and mounts flexing. This is a useful modification that is easily retrofitted to earlier cars, and the part is readily available.

## COOLING SYSTEM UPGRADES

Apart from replacing the rubber hoses with silicone versions, there are two common modifications that can be made to the cooling system: fitting an electric fan and an alloy radiator.

While Lotus fitted electric fans to the later Elan and all models of the +2, the fan was simply mounted in front of the radiator on a set of rudimentary arms. A ducted fan – such as those made by Kenlowe, which fits close to the outer face of the radiator and is significantly more aerodynamic – offers a significant improvement. The standard fan is operated by an 'Otter' switch, which was a press-fit into a grommet in the radiator, and early Kenlowe installations controlled the fan using a capillary tube slotted under a hose. Both these can leak, and a better and nicely integrated switch is produced by companies such as Revotech, which is inserted in-line in the top hose and has variable temperature control.

The Sprint and +2S 130 were fitted with a differential brace to enable them to cope with the extra power. It is a simple L-shaped section of steel that bolts to the top of the differential, and is a worthwhile modification on any Elan or +2. ➤

In the past alloy radiators were seen as an expensive racing fitment, but prices have now come down in the mainstream modification market. The main advantage of an alloy radiator is the lighter weight than the traditional fitment, but they can also offer increased cooling capacity so can be a useful addition to a tuned engine.

On the +2 with its air blend heater, there is no way to turn the water supply to the heater box off. This means that in hot weather you may get warm air leaking into the cabin. Some owners advocate fitting an in-line water valve into one of the heater lines to manually cut off the water flow to the heater box, which can result in a cooler interior on hot days.

An in-line switch such as this Revotech item is a neat and leakproof way to switch an electric fan.

## ELECTRICAL UPGRADES

### INTRODUCTION

Both the Elan and +2 were designed in the 1960s, when vehicular electrical systems were relatively simple. Lotus was forced to use standard proprietary items from manufacturers such as Lucas, Wipac and Smiths, as custom-made items like wiper, heater and window motors, voltage regulators, and switch gear would have been very expensive to produce in-house, due to the relatively small numbers of cars Lotus made. So, Lotus had to make do with what was available and priced at an acceptable level. This meant that while the electrical system did its job, it was not as resilient or reliable as it could have been, and that there is scope – especially with the availability of more modern components – to make significant improvements to the original system.

### FUSEBOXES

The Elan and +2 are fitted with two fuses, while the +2S had a more impressive 12. This means that, with the exception of the +2S, each fuse is doing several jobs. As such, an individual fuse is probably too highly rated for some components it is supposed to protect, and if one blows you will lose more than one circuit. Modern cars have multiple fuses, and most individual circuits are protected by a single fuse. This not only makes the system more resilient to failure, but also helps with fault finding. Finally, the glass cylinder fuses used in the standard car can be hard to source in an emergency – most modern garages do not stock them any more. So it makes a lot of sense to replace the existing fuse box(es) with a modern unit using readily available fuses. In the case of the Elan and pre-'S' +2, it is also worth setting up individual fused circuits for components.

### RELAYS

It is a worthwhile modification to fit relays to many of the circuits on the Elan and +2. By doing so, you will cut down the current that is passed through the switch and the wiring behind the dash. This has two benefits: firstly, the lower current used to switch a relay will place less strain on the switches and the wiring, and secondly, you will be able to wire in a new power line to the relay which – if sized correctly for the current – will supply maximum voltage with minimal losses to the component(s) being supplied. Relays are relatively easy to fit – you retain the original wiring that supplied power to the component, and use it to switch the relay. Run a direct (preferably fused) new power line to the relay from a live source; the solenoid is a good supply point in the engine bay. Then, for the power feed from the relay, you can use the existing wiring to the component if it is good condition and the correct size for the load, or if there is any doubt replace it with new wiring. It is well worth using the correct original wiring colours, documenting what has been done, and labelling the relays for your convenience and any future owner's benefit.

## HEADLAMP SYSTEM INTRODUCTION

While the standard headlamp system is surprisingly reliable, despite its relative complexity, there are a number of upgrades and modifications that can increase the reliability, and generally enhance the overall operation of the system.

## FAIL-SAFE HEADLAMP CONVERSION

Later cars were fitted with a fail-safe headlamp lifting system. In this system, the headlamp pods are by default held up by springs. In the original system the pods were held down by the springs and lifted by the vacuum, so their default position was down. A failure in the original system, such as a pipe becoming detached or a leak in the crossmember, would result in the headlamps going down – not good on a dark night! The fail-safe system linked both pods and used a single vacuum chamber to pull the pods down, so not only was it safer, it used fewer components as well.

## SOLENOID-OPERATED HEADLAMPS

The last +2s replaced the vacuum switch on the dash with an electrically-operated solenoid to work the vacuum mechanism. This can be retrofitted to earlier cars, and is a useful conversion as it cut down the amount of vacuum hose needed – the solenoid-operated vacuum switch can be fitted in the engine bay, close to the reservoir and the headlamp lifters. At the time of writing, reliable dash vacuum switches were hard to find.

## ELECTRICALLY-OPERATED HEADLAMPS

Spyder offers an electric headlamp conversion for the Elan and +2. This utilises proprietary electric motors and

The later +2 had a relay-operated vacuum switch to operate the lights. This reduced the amount of vacuum hose needed, and meant the vacuum switch in the dash could be replaced with a simple electrical switch.

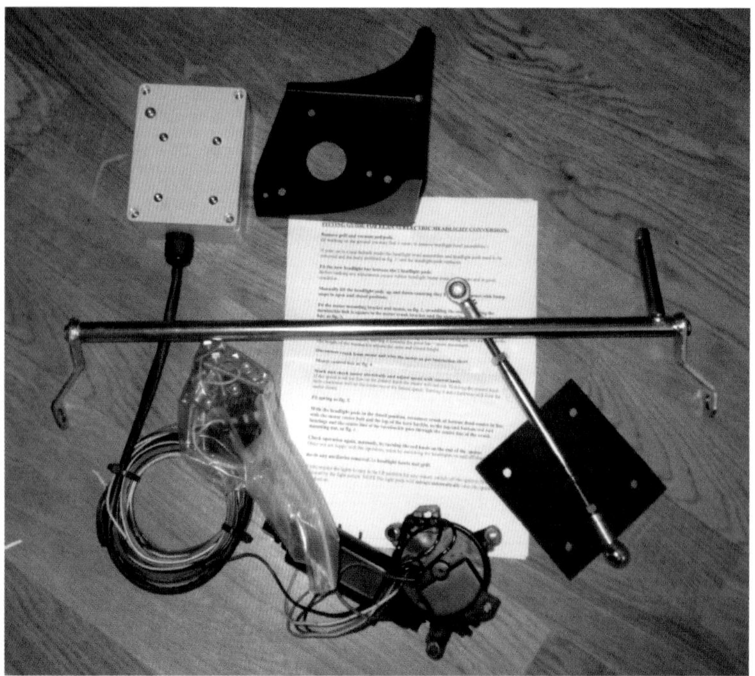

Spyder produces a kit that converts the headlamp lift mechanism from vacuum to electric operation. It is a good kit and, if your vacuum actuators need to be replaced, makes financial sense.

a custom-built linkage to raise and lower the lights, and is a straight bolt-on conversion. Many owners have made their own conversion, usually using Mazda MX-5 Mark 1 headlamp lift motors and their own custom-built brackets.

## +2 BATTERY COMPARTMENT

In the +2, the battery was mounted in the front right-hand side of the boot. In later cars, with the transverse exhaust rear box, the battery area moulded into the boot floor is only about 6.25in (16cm) deep and 10in (25.4cm) wide and – with the boot floor being the limiting factor – has a height of about 9in (23cm). These dimensions limit the number of batteries that will fit. It is relatively easy to increase the size of the tray, by cutting out the rear edge of the tray, extending the cut to around 4-8cm into the boot floor. Turn the cut-out piece upside down and back to front, and bond it back into the boot floor by chamfering the sides and laying strips of mat onto the join. Then, lay a layer of mat or woven cloth over the top to seal it all in place. Now the original boot floor section forms an extension to the battery tray area, giving extra room for a bigger battery, which widens the choice of batteries that you can use.

## ALTERNATOR CONVERSION

The Elan and the +2 both benefit from an alternator conversion – the latter especially, with its greater electrical demands. Lotus fitted them as standard to the +2 from the start of the +2S model in 1969, but do not appear to have fitted them to the Elan, although some of the last Sprints may have had them fitted. It is an excellent upgrade, and is easily reversible as well as increasing the usability of the car. There are two options: replace the existing dynamo with a lookalike alternator, which retains the authentic appearance and brackets of dynamo cars but is relatively expensive, or simply replace the dynamo with a modern alternator. Fitting a modern alternator requires the correct bracketry. A favourite bodge, done by the impecunious converter, is to cut the original dynamo bracket in half, re-drill each half so it can be bolted onto the block with the brackets repositioned to fit an alternator, and to reuse the dynamo strap. A modern alternator will require a new lower bracket that bolts to the block in place of the dynamo lower bracket, to give proper support to the unit, and a new adjuster 'strap' bracket for the top mount. If you use the dynamo adjuster strap then it will fit on the wrong (front) side of the alternator top bracket, and the adjuster bolt may foul the belt in some of its range. The proper alternator strap will fit on the rear face of the alternator mounting lug. In addition, there is a reinforcing strip available that bolts onto the back face of the timing cover using three of the casing bolts. It is important to fit this plate as, if you don't use it, fitment of a modern-style alternator may crack the timing cover. The Ford alternator bottom bracket is easy to find new or secondhand, while the alternator top strap and reinforcing strip are available from most Lotus spares stockists. With an alternator, it is useful to fit a voltmeter to monitor battery condition rather than rely on the standard ammeter, which simply provides the current state of the charging system.

An alternator is a simple conversion from the original dynamo, and provides a significant boost to the power output. Note the alternator-specific adjustment bracket bolted to the timing cover.

This is one of the Shapecraft Elans, registered AUT 173B, in action. It is being driven by R J Crossfield at Mallory Park in May, 1965. ➤

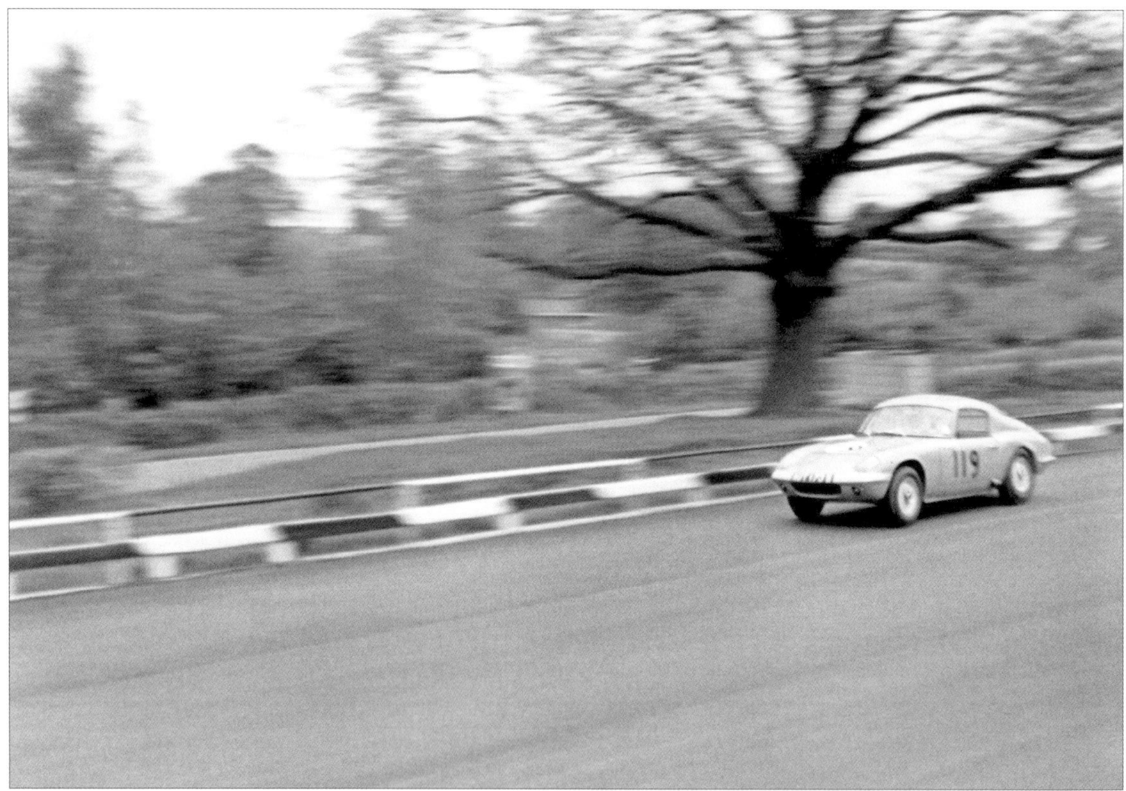


And this is the Shapecraft Elan AUT 173B today, pictured racing at the 77th Goodwood Members Meet in 2019, driven by Mark Midgley and M Corfield. ➤

# MODIFIED ELANS AND +2S

## INTRODUCTION

There have been a number of companies that have, over the years, modified Elans and +2s and made them available to the public, usually in very small numbers. This section takes a quick look at the most common and well known.

## THE SHAPECRAFT FASTBACKS

The Shapecraft Elans came about as a result of a liaison between small Lotus dealer Surbiton Motors Ltd (run by Barry Wood) and Shapecraft, a small fabricating firm that usually worked in alloy and stainless steel. Both companies were based in Surbiton, and Wood was a keen club racer. In early 1963 Wood bought an Elan S1, and decided to have a fastback-style hardtop added to the car. He approached Shapecraft to produce an alloy fastback 'add-on' to the Elan, along with an aerodynamic nose. Shapecraft produced a lightweight alloy top, which was then bonded to the car to form a coherently-designed and attractive car. This was the first of around 10 Shapecraft Elans, and was raced by Wood in the latter half of the 1963 season, where it was entered as 'Shapecraft Lotus Elan.'

The second conversion was carried out at the end of 1963, and was displayed at the Racing Car Show at London's Earls Court early in 1964. This car was bought by actor Peter Sellers and given to Britt Ekland as an engagement present.

The fastback improved the Elan's aerodynamics and – despite the extra weight – performance, with a claimed top speed of over 120mph (192km/h) with no deterioration in acceleration times. The conversion was popular with racers both then and now, and the design is accepted for historic racing classes.

## ELAN ESTATE – THE ELANBULANCE

Hexagon of Highgate was a Lotus dealer in the 1960s and 1970s that was based in Highgate, North London. In 1972 it launched its Elan Estate, which, to quote Hexagon's brochure, was aimed at "professional photographers, surveyors, golfers and others who periodically need to accommodate awkward or bulky equipment which will not fit conveniently into a basic sports car."

The conversion was a thoroughly engineered exercise, with the rear half of the body being cut off and a new double-skinned section – incorporating the extended roof, side windows and rear wings – was bonded on to the internal wheelarches and floor. Additional mouldings were then added to form the interior. The double-skinned roof had a foam polyurethane filling to strengthen the structure and cut down noise, while the tailgate was formed from three separate mouldings, and had built-in steel strengthening. Refinements included a rear wiper and gas struts to hold the tailgate up, while the tailgate window was bonded in place.

The car was aimed at the market filled by the MGB and Reliant Scimitar GTE. However, the load bay was compromised by the intrusion of the rear strut towers, as well as the lower part of the rear opening having to fit between the standard rear lights, making it a narrow and awkward shape. Demand for the car was small and only two cars were completed.

Hexagon was so pleased with the Elanbulance that it featured on the cover of the company brochure. However, only one or two were made.

## THE CONVERTIBLE +2S – HEXAGON AND CHRISTOPHER NEIL

Lotus never offered the +2 as a convertible, but at least two dealers offered conversions: Hexagon and Christopher Neil. Hexagon offered its take on the convertible +2 at the same time it offered its 'Elanbulance.' The Hexagon example had steel reinforcement in the windscreen frame, but the hood – while looking good when up, and, with extra side windows, gave better visibility than the standard car – was a rather untidy design when down. Unfortunately, the hood did not fold down flush, and sat high on the rear of the cabin. Only two cars were made.

Christopher Neil's conversion, named the 'C N Cabriolet,' was a much neater job. More extensive modifications were made to the bodyshell to allow the hood to sit much lower than the Hexagon example, giving the car much cleaner lines when down, and, like the Hexagon, mimicking the original lines when up. It is not known how many cars were converted by Christopher Neil, but it is certainly more than the two produced by Hexagon.

Hexagon also produced a convertible +2. With the hood up, the car followed the lines of the original, and the rear quarter windows improved visibility.

With the roof down the Hexagon convertible was not quite so elegant, as the hood sat quite higher than the rear deck. Only two were made, and here they both are at the Club Lotus Castle Combe trackday in 2018.

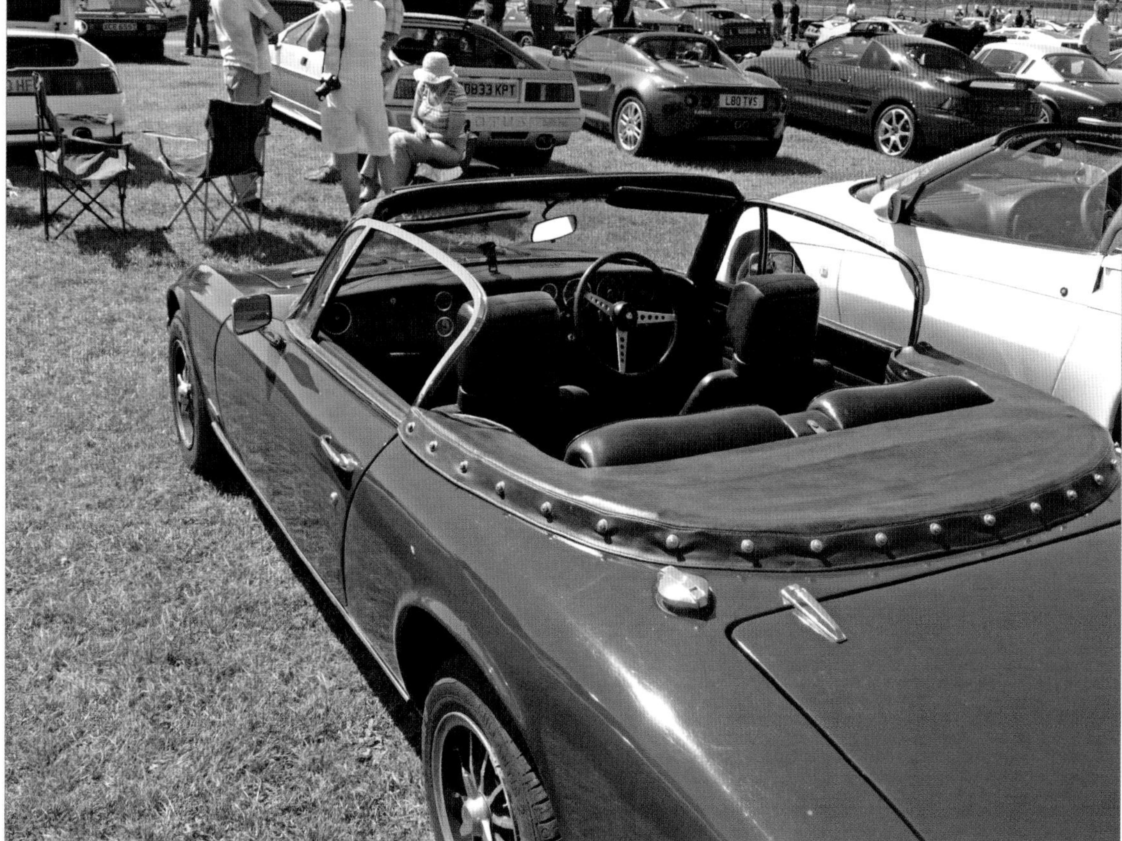


Lotus dealer Christopher Neil produced a very neat +2 convertible. In this conversion, the hood retracted into a well behind the rear seats, giving a very smooth and neat appearance.

## DAVE GROVES' 1972 ELAN SPRINT

Dave Groves bought his 1972 Elan Sprint coupé in November 1982 to upgrade from an MGB GT. He wanted a car that was a bit more modern and had more performance than the MG, and the Elan fitted the bill. However, in his first real drive in it – bringing it home to the South East, after buying it in Yorkshire – he thought he had made a major mistake. As he headed off down the A1, he struggled to get comfortable. The seat wouldn't go back any further, and so he had a bad 200-mile run home thinking that he had just spent £4000 on a car that he didn't fit into. Now Dave is slightly taller than your average build, but not a monster, and he'd never had this problem before. As it turned out, the previous owner was quite a bit shorter than Dave, and had moved the seat to its forward fitting position, as Dave discovered when he got the car home. Two bolts later, and Dave had the seat repositioned in its rear setting, and the car fitted him like a glove. Reading the manual has its benefits!

Once the seat had been moved, Dave was more than satisfied with the Sprint. With its Pistachio Green over white paintwork the car stood out from the crowd, and the original black trim was in good condition, making the interior a nice place to be. As a coupé, the car was snug and warm in winter – although Dave is planning to fit a Webasto fabric sunroof for the few sunny days in the UK, which can make the interior a bit warm. The handling and performance were a revelation when compared the MG – in fact, there was no comparison! Dave describes the handling as "unbelievable" when compared to the MG, while the Sprint's sparkling performance emphasised how antiquated the MG's really was. Dave, ever the blunt Yorkshireman, finds the Sprint's acceleration "bloody quick," and the brakes "bloody good."

The car served Dave well and he ran it as his second car. This didn't mean short local trips – he often used it to travel up north, on 400-mile round trips from his base in the South East, to visit friends and relations around York. At the start of returning from one such trip he learned about another Elan foible – the QD bonnet. He pulled into a petrol station to refuel and give the car a quick check over; it was a bit of a blustery day, and when Dave pulled the bonnet catch, he was somewhat surprised when the wind caught the bonnet as it popped up, and whisked it away like a kite ... Luckily the garage was in a rural area, and the bonnet, after its brief taste of freedom, descended into a soft landing in a field. With the bonnet retrieved, luckily with no damage, Dave continued his rapid journey home

A proud Dave Groves stands by his newly refreshed Elan Sprint. The Pistachio Green over white paintwork was one of Lotus' very 1970s paint schemes.

➤ Dave Groves' Sprint engine bay has a few non-standard features, such as the chrome number plate lights in use to illuminate the bay, a tubular exhaust manifold, and an alternator.

➤ The interior of Dave Groves' Sprint is mostly standard, although he has fitted a neat auxiliary switch panel on the centre console to operate running lights, spotlights and a rear fog light.

contemplating another lesson learnt. Dave continued to use the car like this for many years, until around the year 2000, when he took it off the road for a general spruce up. The engine was getting a bit tired, and there were a few minor issues that needed sorting.

16 years later, as other commitments were addressed, Dave eventually got round to starting the spruce up! The engine was rebuilt – there were no major issues, just a light hone for the bores, new rings, new bearings, and a chemical clean of the block followed by a new coat of grey paint. The head was in pretty good condition and only needed the valves lapping in and the valve clearances done. The original interior turned out to be hard wearing and still in good condition, so needed just a bit of cleaning to make it good as new. The car hasn't been painted since Dave bought it, and as far as Dave knows the paint is original. It is still looking good, and just needed a decent polish and wax to bring it up to a good standard. Mind you, Dave is still learning: when he returned the car to the road after the refresh, he was surprised that the headlamps would just slam down when he turned off the engine. He was sure they didn't do that before, and suspected that the non-return valve was jammed open. The funny thing was, when he checked the brass vacuum take-off fitting in the head, where he thought the non-return valve was, it was just a bare tube. So, he contacted the author, who in turn checked one of his spare heads and found the fitting was, like Dave's, just a bare tube. Somewhat puzzled, the parts list was consulted and that's when Dave found that the valve was an in-line item in the tube from the head to the T-piece. Dave had missed this when he replaced the vacuum tube during the spruce up, as he was using a photo of an original Sprint engine bay, without realising that he had mistaken the non-return valve for a simple tube joining two short lengths of the flexible hose, which he had removed when he refreshed the vacuum pipework by fitting a new one-piece length of tube. Of course, he found his original valve in his tin of discarded bits in the garage after he had ordered a replacement.

⮝ Dave Groves has fitted a pair of spotlights behind the grille for better lighting, and as insurance should the headlights fail.

⮝ Just as visible is the left-hand side LED running light that Dave Groves has installed on the Sprint. Despite the bright green paintwork, Dave feels a lot safer with the lights on when on the road.

➤ Dave Groves' Sprint has knock-on Minilite alloy wheels, which complement the look of the car while remaining in period.

During his ownership of the Sprint, Dave has made some subtle modifications. Small but bright LED daytime running lights were fitted just below the front bumper to help make the diminutive car a bit more noticeable, while a high-level brake light and bright LED rear bulbs were fitted to increase visibility at the rear (despite the bright Pistachio Green paint, other drivers seem to have difficulty seeing the car). Sharing the grille space are a pair of spotlights, in case of headlamp lift failure at night. Fitting hazard warning lights will help to keep the car safe during one of the 'Loads Of Trouble, Usually Serious' moments that Lotus owners know so well. An alternator ensures the battery is fully charged, even in winter and slow moving traffic, and electronic ignition means ignition problems are a thing of the past. A manual override switch for the electric fan was, Dave felt, a useful addition for use in slow moving traffic, and a new fuse box with eight fuses added some sophistication to the electrical system. A high-intensity fog light was faired into the rear panel, the radio aerial was repositioned on the roof, and a discreet switch panel was fitted just in front of the gearlever to operate the new electrics. Mechanically speaking, Dave also fitted a set of Mick Miller CV driveshafts, which complemented the Minilite alloys, and the brakes were given Goodridge steel braided flexible pipes and silicon brake fluid, with a low fluid warning light wired into the handbrake light. The final modification was to convert the chassis front lower crossmember to be removable, as seen on the +2, which aids engine installation and removal – not that Dave is planning any more major maintenance.

Talking about engine removal, it was Dave's engine that he and the author struggled to replace while writing this book. Dave and the author had a wonderful morning trying to persuade the engine and gearbox to go in together, with a singular lack of success! Putting the gearbox in first then adding the engine proved to be a much easier, less stressful and quicker experience.

Now that it's back on the road, Dave is revelling in the performance and handling of the revitalised car, and his only regret is that he didn't get it back on the road sooner!

CHAPTER 6

# Other Sources and Bibliography

## INTRODUCTION

There is a massive range of resources available for Elan and +2 owners, ranging from paper manuals, parts lists and books, through advertising literature and press briefings, and onwards to forums and websites available on the internet.

This chapter identifies the various pieces of Lotus literature available in the form of parts lists and workshop manuals, looks at the books that have been published about the Elan and +2 over the years, gives details of suppliers of parts, and provides directions to the many and varied web resources available to the Elan and +2 enthusiast.

The Elan is a sleek, small high-performance car, with looks that complement its performance. It is well supported in terms of spares and expertise.

# FURTHER READING

## INTRODUCTION

There are a large number of books and manuals on the Lotus Elan and +2. The most important manuals are the Lotus-produced workshop manuals and parts lists; these are still available new from Lotus spares stockists, with specific versions of each for the Elan and the +2.

## ELAN AND +2 SPECIFIC BOOKS

The author's previous book on the Elan and +2 covers the design and development and history of the cars, as well as covering the later M100. *Lotus Elan – The Complete Story* by Matthew Vale, The Crowood Press, ISBN 978-1-847975-10-2.

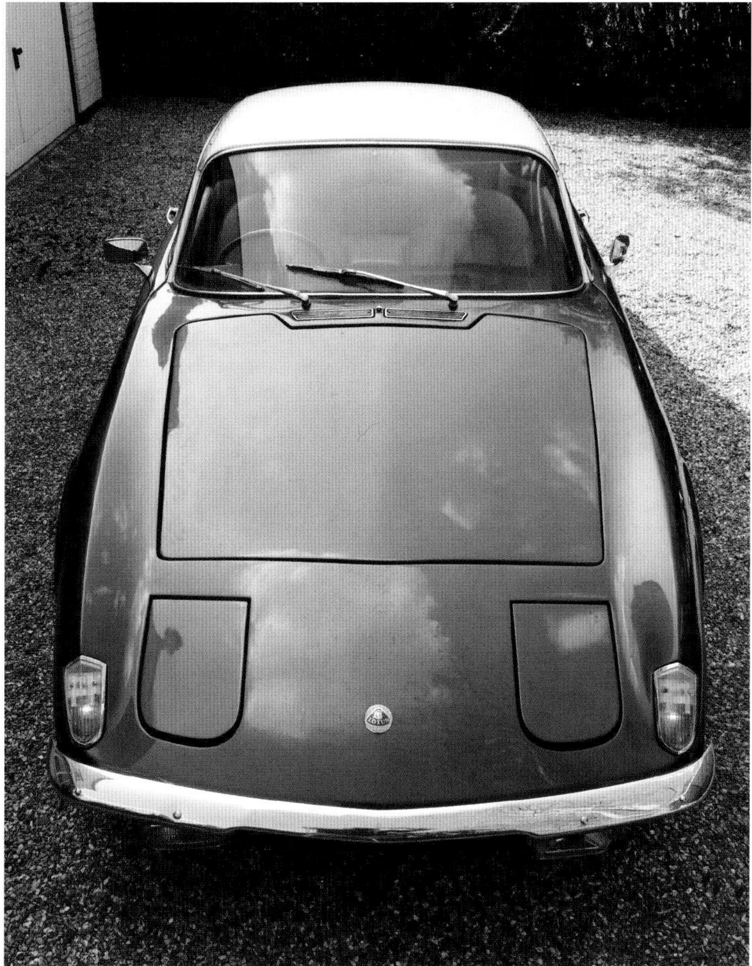

⅄ The Elan's larger cousin, the +2, has very a different look to the Elan, but is still an outstanding GT car in its own right. The +2 shares most mechanical components with the Elan.

The author also wrote the *Elan and +2 Essential Buyers Guide*, published by Veloce, ISBN 978-1-787112-86-5, which provides prospective owners all the information they need to make an informed decision when buying an Elan or +2.

Paul Robinshaw and Gordon Lund, a pair of Elan enthusiasts, have produced several useful books on the Elan and +2. *The Original Lotus Elan 1962-1973* by Paul Robinshaw and Chris Ross was originally published by MRP in 1989, and now reissued by Brooklands Books with an ISBN of 978-1-783180-00-4. This is generally considered to be the originality bible of the Elan, and covers the origins of many parts used in the Elan, details of significant specification changes and change points, as well as an explanation of the homologation specifications for the Type 26R.

This book was expanded to also cover the +2 and reissued as *Authentic Lotus Elan and Plus 2 1962-1974* in 1995, with an original ISBN-10 of 0-947981-95-0; while it covers the +2 along with the Elan, it has not been re-issued at the time of writing.

Gordon Lund's book *Lotus Elan Restoration Guide* was published by Brooklands Books in 2002, ISBN 978-1-855209-46-6. The author has run and carried out body-off restorations of a +2 and an Elan Sprint, and has produced an excellent guide to the restoration process for the Elan, much of which is relevant to the +2. There is lots of useful information in the book that has obviously been learnt from experience. The book was updated with a second edition in late 2012, with additional information and a description of an Elan +2 estate conversion.

Brooklands Books is also famous for its collections of contemporary road tests, and the Elan and +2 are featured in *Lotus Elan Gold Portfolio 1962-74* by R M Clarke, ISBN-10 1-855205-51-3. This gives a great range of original road tests of the Elan and +2, as well as some later articles from the classic car press on the buying and running the cars. Earlier collections of Elan and +2 road tests were produced, but the *Gold Portfolio* collects most of these into a single volume.

▲ The Elan is still popular on the track, especially in its Type 26R or GTS guise. Here, an original Shapecraft Elan dices with a 26R at Goodwood in 2019.

Brooklands also has a reprint of the 'Autobooks' *Lotus Elan Owners Workshop Manual*, ISBN 978-1-855200-22-7, which covers the Elan and +2. A good aftermarket workshop manual.

Brian Buckland's *The Rebuilding of a Lotus Elan – Addendum Engineering Workshop Manual*, Elanman Ltd, ISBN 978-0-955284-90-8, is a large loose-leaf book, and describes how to restore, rebuild and maintain an Elan. The author has distilled some 39 years of experience of working on the Elan into this book, and it gives invaluable advice and guidance on how to do just about anything on the Elan, and is relevant to the +2 as well. The book has recently been revised and reissued, and is available from theelanman.com.

Kevin Whittle, a stalwart of the Historic Lotus Register, has produced what is probably the only book written with the +2 as its subject – *Lotus Elan Plus 2*. Privately published, the book covers the history of the +2 as well as his restoration of a BDA engined car. It is available from his website, whittlebooks.com.

*Lotus Elan – Coupe, Convertible, Plus 2* by Ian Ward, Osprey AutoHistory, ISBN-10 0-850455-50-2. The author takes his experiences of running an Elan and weaves his Elan story with the production history of the range.

*Lotus Elan – Super Profile* by Graham Arnold, Haynes Publishing Group, ISBN-10 0-854293-30-2. The good value Haynes Super Profile series gives a useful overview of the Elan and +2, along with buying guide and reprinted road tests. The author is the former Lotus Marketing director.

*Lotus Elan – The Complete Story*, by Mike Taylor, The Crowood Press, ISBN-10 1-855233-49-4. This book gives a good technical background to he Elan and has interviews with some of the personalities behind the Elan.

*The Lotus Elan and Plus 2 Buyers Guide 1962-1975* by Graham Arnold, published by Club Lotus with no ISBN. Published in 1981, this booklet was produced by Graham Arnold for Club Lotus, and gives a concise guide to buying the Elan and +2.

➤ The early Elan interior was surprisingly comfortable for a 1960s British sports car. This is Brian Goodison's Series 2.

## BOOKS THAT REFERENCE THE ELAN AND +2

The following books provide additional information and details on Lotus, the company's story, and its other cars, and most also reference the Elan and +2. While some of the books are out of print, secondhand copies are usually available through online sources such as Amazon or eBay.

*Lotus File Seven, Elite, Elan, Europa (Classic and Sportscar File)* by Mark Hughes, Temple Press, ISBN-10 0-600552-07-1. Along with the Seven and the Elite, this book has a number of informative articles on the Elan and +2, as well as some nice pictures of the cars.

*Colin Chapman – Inside the Innovator* by Karl Ludvigsen, Haynes Publishing Group, ISBN 978-1-844254-13-2. A comprehensive account of Colin Chapman's engineering achievements, based around themed chapters looking at specific topics, such as suspension, downforce, structures, etc.

*Colin Chapman's Lotus – The Early Years, Elite and Origins of the Elan* by Robin Read, Haynes Publishing Group, ISBN-10 8-854297-03-0. This book looks at the early days of Lotus, just hitting the introduction of the Elan, and provides a useful background to the Elan's ancestry.

*Colin Chapman Lotus Engineering – Theories, Designs and Applications* by Hugh Haskell, Osprey Automotive, ISBN-10 1-855328-72-0. This book takes a look at Colin Chapman's engineering skills, and describes how he and his team brought many innovative ideas into reality. Has some coverage of the thinking behind the Elan and +2.

*Colin Chapman – The Man and His Cars* by Gerard 'Jabby' Crombac, Haynes Publishing Group, ISBN-10 1-859608-44-2. This is the authorised biography of Chapman, written by a long-term Lotus owner and fan who was also a noted Formula 1 journalist and a good friend of Chapman. It gives a comprehensive picture of Chapman and the evolution of his company up to his death in 1982.

*Colin Chapman – Wayward Genius* by Mike Lawrence, Brooklands Books, ISBN 978-1-855209-50-3 (original ISBN-10 1-859832-78-4). Originally published by Breedon Books, this biography of Chapman covers his achievements in a 'warts and all' fashion, and makes for an interesting read. It gives alternative interpretations of many of the legends that have grown around Chapman.

*Illustrated Lotus Buyer's Guide* by Graham Arnold, Motorbooks International, ISBN 0-87938-217-1. Written by the former Lotus marketing director, this book covers buying Lotus road cars ranging from the 6 and Seven through to the Esprit, and has a reasonable section on the original Elan and +2.

*Lotus Elan* by Duncan Wherrett, Osprey, ISBN-10 1-855323-77-X. This book is a mainly photographic record of the Elan, from the S1 through to the Sprint, the +2, the 26R racer, and the M100. The book is nicely produced on high-quality paper, with excellent pictures throughout.

*Lotus Elan and Europa – A Collectors Guide* by John Bolster, Motor Racing Publications, ISBN-10 0-900549-48-3. This is a good overview of the Elan (and Europa), with a reasonable amount of detail on the Elan and +2, along with lots of useful illustrations.

*Lotus – The Elan, Cortina and Europa* by Richard Newton and Raymond Psulkowski, Tab Books Inc, ISBN-10 0-830621-06-7. This is a good book with detailed coverage of the Elan, Europa, Lotus Cortina and the Twin-cam engine.

*Lotus – The Elite, Elan, Europa* by Chris Harvey, Haynes Publishing Group, ISBN-10 0-902280-85-6. In this well-illustrated volume, author Chris Harvey traces the design and development of the Elite, Elan and Europa along with anecdotes, contemporary road test experiences and competition history.

*Lotus – The Complete Story* by Chris Harvey, Haynes Publishing Group, ISBN-10 0-854292-98-5. A history of Lotus from its inception to the early 1980s. While primarily a company history, it includes some details on the Elan.

*Lotus – The Early Years* by Peter Ross, Coterie Press, ISBN 1-902351-12-6. This book tells the story of Lotus up to about 1954 – referred to as the 'amateur years' before Chapman started working full-time at Lotus, and when he relied on a group of gifted part-timers to design and produce the early cars.

*Lotus Racing Cars – Club Racers to World Champions 1948-1968* by John Tipler, Sutton Publishing Ltd, ISBN-10 0-750923-89-X. In the main, this book covers the Lotus racers, but does have a short section on the Elan 26R.

*Lotus 2+2s – Elan, Elite, Eclat, Excel and Evora* by Matt and Mike Younger, Amberley Publishing, ISBN 978-1-445682-53-2. This book has a chapter on the +2 as Lotus' first 'four-seat' coupé, and gives a brief history and overview of the car.

*Practical Classics and Car Restorer on Lotus (Including Elan) Restoration* by various authors, Kelsey Publishing, ISBN-10 1-873098-26-X. This is a collection of articles from *Practical Classics* magazine, and includes a series of articles on the restoration of an Elan, the rebuilding of a Twin-cam engine by Miles Wilkins, and articles on glass fibre repair.

*The Story of Lotus 1961-1971 – Growth of a Legend* by Doug Nye, Motor Racing Publications, ISBN-10 0-900549-15-7. This book mainly covers the Lotus racing history from 1961 to 1971.

The Elan's interior did not change much throughout the life of the car. This is a Sprint, which retained many of the features seen on the Series 1 and 2 interiors.

The +2S had a much more luxurious interior than the Elan; it featured six minor instruments in a walnut-veneered dash, which was liberally sprinkled with switches for the many electrical gizmos.

Lotus never offered a convertible +2, but both Hexagon and Christopher Neil offered conversions for existing cars. This is the Christopher Neil conversion. Visible is the +2's luxurious interior.

Finally, *Absolute Lotus* magazine, published by Performance Publishing (see performancepublishing.co.uk) is the only current bi-monthly magazine that exclusively addresses the Lotus marque. Published every two months, each issue provides a range of articles on Lotus cars, ranging from early endeavours on road and track to the modern day range. As Lotus' most popular range, the Elan and +2 feature in most issues, alongside other classic road and race cars.

## OTHER USEFUL BOOKS

Miles Wilkins, a noted Lotus expert with a great deal of experience of repairing and restoring Lotus Elites, Elans, +2s and Europas, has produced a number of books on Lotus, and is an acknowledged expert on both the Twin-cam engine and glass fibre repairs.

*Lotus Twin-cam Engine* by Miles Wilkins, originally published by Osprey in 1988, and re-issued by Brooklands Books in 2012, ISBN 978-1-855209-68-8. The book gives comprehensive details on the development, dismantling, rebuilding of – and associated data on – the Elan and +2 Twin-cam engine, and is a must have for any Lotus enthusiast.

*How to Restore Fibreglass Bodywork (Osprey Restoration Guide 3)* by Miles Wilkins, published by Osprey Publishing Limited in 1984, ISBN-10 0-850455-56-1, is still the definitive volume on glass fibre repair techniques applicable to Lotus. This is complemented by *How to Restore Paintwork (Osprey Restoration Guide 4)*, by Miles Wilkins, ISBN-10 0-85045-557-X, again published by Osprey in 1984, which provides invaluable information on preparing and painting glass fibre cars.

Staying with the glass fibre theme, *The Glassfibre Handbook* by R H Warring, published by Special Interest Model Books, ISBN 978-0-85242-820-7, is another useful and informative book on the theory and practice of glass fibre work.

*Tuning Twin-cam Fords* by David Vizard, Motor Racing Publications, ISBN 978-0-851130-07-1. Back in the 1970s this was probably the definitive guide to hotting up your

Twin-cam, and is still full of good advice today.

*Tuning Stromberg CD Carburetters – For Motor Sport & High Performance*, by Martyn B Watkins, Speed and Sports Publications, ISBN-10 0-851130-06-2, is a small A3-sized book published in 1969, and gives a great little guide to setting up and tuning the Stromberg CD carbs fitted to the Elan and +2.

*Stromberg CD Carburettors Owners Workshop Manual*, by Don Peers, Haynes Publishing, ISBN-10 0-856963-00-3. This is an in-depth manual for all the Stromberg CD carburettors. As with all Haynes manuals, it is well illustrated and informative.

*How To Build & Power Tune Weber and Dellorto DCOE, DCO/SP & DHLA Carburettors* by Des Hammill, Veloce Publishing, ISBN 978-1-903706-75-6. This is the go-to book for the Weber and Dellorto carbs fitted to the Elan and +2. With instructions on how to tune, test, strip, inspect and rebuild the carburettors, it covers all the bases if you want to master your twin-choke carbs.

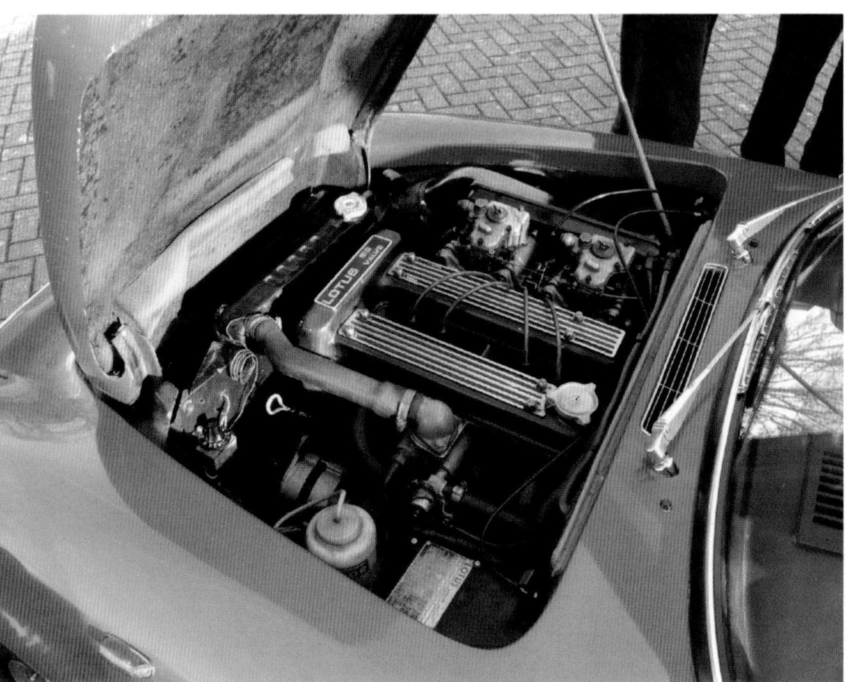


The Sprint, fitted with the Big Valve engine, was the ultimate Elan. A ribbed cam cover with 'Lotus Big Valve' on the front identifies the unit.

## WORKS BROCHURES AND LITERATURE

Throughout the life of the Elan and +2, Lotus issued brochures and flyers as well as producing press releases and press photos for the motoring press of the day. While the brochures are a useful record of the Elan and +2, and describe the models reasonably accurately, they should not be taken as definitive. Lotus prepared their brochures before the final production specifications were decided, and cars used in the brochures were often pre-production prototypes that could differ from production models. As such, brochures are not the best guide to originality.

The first Elan brochure was an extravagant, roughly A4 format, multi-page affair, with high-quality artwork and copious illustrations of the car – but, tellingly, no actual photographs. One interesting point is that there are two versions: the first for the Elan 1500, and a revised version for the Elan 1600 (ie, the actual production version with the 1558cc Twin-cam). The first version lists the engine capacity as 1498cc, and has 'Lotus Elan 1500' on the title page. The second version has the engine capacity as 1558cc, and the

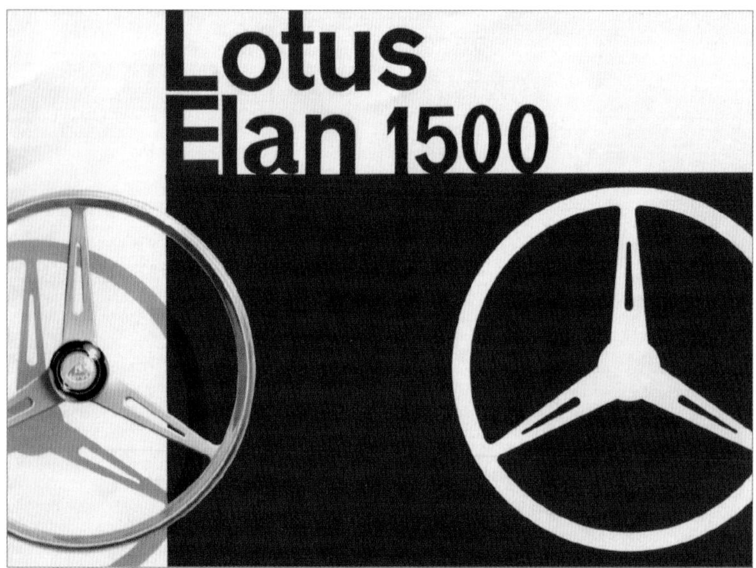


The first Elan brochure was titled 'Lotus Elan 1500.' This was quickly changed, by deleting the '1500,' when the production cars were produced with the 1558cc Twin-cam engine. (Courtesy Lotus Cars)

title merely says 'Lotus Elan.' After this extravagant brochure was produced, Lotus back-peddled on brochure production through the 1960s, with these becoming mainly single- or twin-sheet attempts, printed on relatively low-quality paper, until the launch of the more upmarket +2. This warranted a 12-page decent quality brochure, that incorporated some information on the development of the +2 as well as plenty of photos of an actual car, both in colour and black and white. Later +2 brochures reverted to mainly single-sheet folded examples like those produced for the Elan.

Brochures come up for sale on online auction sites reasonably regularly. There are also a number of dealers in the UK, most of which are on eBay, who buy and sell car-related brochures and photographs.

## EXPERT SUPPLIERS FOR SPARE PARTS

The following suppliers all stock various levels of Elan and +2 (and other Lotus model) spares, and have either been used by the author or have a good reputation.

Boss Motors produces new bodyshells and repair panels for the Elan and +2, as well as other Lotus cars. It is based in the UK at Chalk Lane, Snetterton, Norwich, Norfolk. Tel: +44 (0)1953 887471.

Dave Bean Engineering Inc has been running for many years, and is a great source for hard-to-find parts. It is based in the USA, at 636 E Saint Charles Street, Star Route 3, San Andreas, CA 95249. Tel: (209) 754 5802, fax: (209) 754 5177, web: davebean.com.

⋏ Taken from the first Elan brochure, this picture shows the clean and crisp lines of the original Elan. This also shows the – now very rare – beige interior. (Courtesy Lotus Cars)

Elantrikbits is an Australia-based engineering company that engineers and supplies specialist Elan parts, including CV driveshafts, 4- to 6-bolt crank seal conversions, gated baffle sumps, and various other products aimed at making the Elan better. Web: elantrikbits.com.

Kelvedon Lotus Ltd (KelSport) is a Lotus historic parts dealer, supplying mainly racing parts for the 26R, and also carries out servicing. It is based in the UK, at North Gate Mill, North Gate, Pinchbeck, Lincolnshire PE11 3SQ. Tel: +44 (0)1775 725457 and +44 (0)1775 711082, web: kelvedonlotus.co.uk.

Mick Miller Classic Lotus supplies many parts for the Elan and +2. The proprietor, Sue Miller, is an expert in Elan and +2 parts, commissions the manufacture of scarce or hard to find parts, and makes sure that all the parts supplied are of the highest quality. It is based in the UK, at Carlton Cross, Main Road, Lelsale, Suffolk, IP17 2NL. Tel: +44 (0)1728 603307, web: mickmillerlotus.com.

Paul Matty Sportscars is a long established Lotus dealer with a good range of Elan and +2 parts, and also sells used Elans and +2s. It is based in the UK, at 12 Old Birmingham Road, Bromsgrove, Worcs, B60 1DE. Tel: +44 (0)1527 835656, web: paulmattysportscars.co.uk.

RD Enterprises, established over 40 years ago, supplies parts for all classic Lotus, including the Europa. It is based in the USA, at 290 Raub Road, Quakertown, PA 18951, USA, Tel: (01) 215-538-9323, fax: 215-538-0158, web: rdent.com.

SJ Sportscars is the stockist of a wide range of Elan and +2 parts, and commissions the manufacture of hard to find or scarce parts. It is based in the UK, at Lotus House, Marsh End, Lords Meadow Industrial Estate, Crediton, Devon EX17 1DN, Tel: +44 (0)1363 777790, web: sjsportscars.com.

Spyder Cars supplies replacement chassis and modified front and rear suspension components for the Elan and +2. It also builds complete cars, including carrying out engine conversions and revised rear suspension. It is based in the UK at 136 Station Road, Industrial Estate, Whittlesey Peterborough, Cambs, PE7 2EY. Tel: +44 (0)1733 203986, web: spydercars.co.uk.

Tony Thompson Racing has many years experience in restoring and preparing Lotus Elans for racing. It provides a wide range of 26R parts, as well as for the road Elan and +2, including chassis and solid driveshafts. It is based in the UK, at Units 4 & 5, Kings Road, Melton Mowbray, LE13 1QF. Tel: +44 (0)1664 566777, web: tonythompsonracing.co.uk.

Alan Voigts Gearboxes has designed a five-speed conversion for the Elan, which uses the core Ford Sierra Type 9 box with new alloy bellhousing and tail piece. It is based in the north east of the UK, in Wallesey near Liverpool, at 4 Toronto Street, Wallesey, Merseyside, CH44 6PR. Tel: +44 (0)151 630 3575, web: alanvoigtsgearboxes.co.uk.

Glass fibre suppliers are fairly common, and are usually sited on the coast as their main business is supplying boat builders. The author has used CFS, based in Redruth, Cornwall, for many years and has always experienced excellent service from the company. It can ship glass fibre resins, mat and tools worldwide. It is based in the UK, at CFS Works, United Downs Industrial Park, Redruth, Cornwall, TR16 5HY. Tel: +44 (0)1209 821028, web: cfsnet.co.uk

Racing Elans are common in the historic racing world. This GTS was owned by the late Peter Shaw, who campaigned the car very successfully.

Option 1 is an experienced glass fibre specialist that understands Lotus and the problems inherent in the use of glass fibre. By all accounts it produces excellent results, although the author has not personally used it. It is based in the UK, at Unit 5, Shaw Lane Industrial Estate, Stoke Prior, Bromsgrove, Worcestershire, B60 4DT. Tel: +44 (0)1527 557111, web: option1sportscars.co.uk/contact/.

## EXPERT SUPPLIERS FOR TWIN-CAM PARTS

The following suppliers provide spares specifically for the Lotus Twin-cam engines:

Burton Power is a supplier of quality parts for the Lotus Twin-cam, among other engines. Burton produces an excellent catalogue that covers the Lotus Twin-cam unit, and also has useful notes on engine specifications, as well as rebuilding techniques, such as camshaft fitting and formulae for calculating various engine-related values. It is based in the UK, at 617-631 Eastern Ave, Ilford, Essex, IG2 6PN. Tel: +44 (0)20 8518 9136, web: burtonpower.com.

The final +2 was a sophisticated grand tourer that was a match for more expensive rivals. This is Jon Bradbury's 1973 +2S 130/5 in its striking Roman Purple metallic paint with metal flake silver roof.

The +2 is an attractive car from any angle. This is Melody and Henry Kozlowski's very early car from 1968 – the 60th produced.

QED Motor Sports Ltd is an engine specialist, and has been developing, manufacturing and tuning engines – including the Lotus Twin-cam – for over 40 years. It has a wide range of quality products and spare parts for the Twin-cam, which include new cylinder heads, blocks and timing covers, as well as various consumables and standard or uprated internal parts. It is based in the UK at 4 Soar Road, Quorn, Leics, LE12 8BN. Tel: +44 (0)1509 416317, web: qedmotorsport.co.uk.

## OTHER SPARES SOURCES

Online auction sites, such as eBay, are excellent sources for used parts and some new spares. However, with the increasing number of counterfeit parts being produced, buyers should treat any apparent bargains with caution, and satisfy themselves that the parts are genuine. The best way to ensure new spares and consumables are properly engineered and genuine is to buy from established dealers.

## WEB RESOURCES FOR ELAN AND +2 OWNERS

Probably the best web resource for the Elan and +2 is the lotuselan.net forum. This friendly forum is open to all and free to access, although donations are welcome. The forum covers all aspects of Elan and +2 ownership, with friendly and informed discussion threads on technical queries, spares availability, and 'what did you do with your Elan today?' It includes sections for cars and parts for sale, and these are often offered to the site members before they go out to the other advertising media. It is an invaluable resource to the Elan owner and enthusiast, and is highly recommended.

The website for the Elan Sprint is lotuselansprint.net. This site is run by Tim Wilkes, and is a mine of information on the Sprint, as well as recording details of surviving cars.

For information on existing Elans and +2s, the Lotus Elan Registry, at elanregistry.org, records details of many existing cars, giving the chassis number and brief ownership details.

As the name suggests, thelotusforums.com supports a number of forums about all Lotus cars, including a classic Elan thread.

The Lotus Drivers Guide website, lotusdriversguide.com, has been created to collect information on all Lotus cars including the Elan and +2. It is a useful source of information on books, brochures, history, etc.

The Golden Gate Lotus Club website, gglotus.org, has a huge amount of Lotus-related information, with lots on the Elan and +2. It also gives details of this US-based Lotus club's activities.

Lotus Talk, lotustalk.com, is a US-based forum covering most of the current and historic Lotus cars.

## UK CLUBS FOR ELAN AND +2 OWNERS

Club Lotus is (to quote the club) "the world's first and biggest club for all Lotus enthusiasts." It supports many local areas in the UK, has a good quality quarterly magazine, and organises and runs national and local events throughout the year. It also has a specific Elan and +2 section, which publishes Elan-specific articles in the club magazine. Contact details: Club Lotus, 58, Malthouse Court, Dereham, Norfolk, NR20 4UA, United Kingdom. Tel: +44 (0)1362 694459 / 691144, email (membership enquiries): annemarie@clublotus.co.uk, web: clublotus.co.uk.

The Lotus Drivers Club was set up in the UK in 1976, and was originally based in the West Midlands. It has now grown to have branches across the UK. It supports many events across the UK and has a magazine, *Chicane*, which is published every four months. Contact Details: Lotus Drivers Club, PO Box 9292, Alcester, Warwickshire, B50 4LD. Email: admin@lotusdriversclub.org.uk, web: lotusdriversclub.org.uk.

The Historic Lotus Register (HLR) keeps records of most Lotus cars other than the 'production' road cars, which usually have their own supporters club. So, in this context, it supports the Elan Type 26R race cars. HLR Car records are held by individual registrars who specialise in their model. HLR also publishes a quarterly high quality magazine, which has lots of articles on the historic Lotus

John Humfryes has owned his 1968 Elan S4 for many years. It is painted in Ferrari Giallo Fly Yellow, and was a Mike Spence car that was tuned to BRM spec from new.

⋀ The Elan Series 1 offers the Elan experience in undiluted form. This is Paddy Byers' lovely example.

⋀ The +2 is an attractive and practical car. Owned by the author, the car has been extensively rebuilt to +2S 130 specification.

⋀ The only special edition Elan or +2 produced was the John Player Special. Essentially a top-spec +2S 130, with gold metalflake roof and sill trims and black paint, it celebrated Lotus' Grand Prix wins of 1973. (Courtesy David Beresford)

scene. The HLR can be contacted through its website, historiclotusregister.co.uk.

The Lotus Enthusiasts Club, SELOC, was formed in 2002 and is mainly aimed at owners of more modern Lotus, but has useful forums and benefits that can still be used by Elan and +2 owners. Its website is seloc.org.

## USA CLUBS FOR ELAN AND +2 OWNERS

The Golden Gate Lotus Club was formed in 1973 and covers all Lotus cars, owners and enthusiasts. It is based on the West Coast, and can be contacted through its website, gglotus.org.

The Lotus Owners of New York (LOONY) is based on the East Coast, and is an active club that runs various all-day and breakfast meets throughout the year. It can be contacted via their website at lotusowners.com.

## GLENN MOULE'S 1966 ELAN COUPÉ

Glenn Moule is a professional car restorer, working on many exotics ranging from Lamborghinis and Ferraris to E-Type Jaguars, but for his personal car he chose the Lotus Elan. Glenn bought his 1966 Elan coupé from the USA in 2019. Wanting a 'busman's holiday,' it was a complete car in need of total restoration – it's not as if he spends much of his time restoring cars ...

When he got the car home and started to dismantle it, he realised that he had a vehicle on his hands that was largely complete and, more importantly, not mucked about with – it was pretty much standard. There were some significant issues: paintwork was poor, interior trim was complete but tatty, and the chassis suffered from substantial rust – one front turret was so badly corroded that in the 'before' pictures you'll see a length of 2x4 wood being used to stop it collapsing inwards! So, while the car was too far gone to be in the 'survivor' category, it was very original. So original, in fact, that after he had removed the bodyshell, Glenn realised that the chassis was the same unit supplied by the factory – evidenced by the chassis number stamped on it. The chassis also had '3.7' painted in yellow on the top of the rear crossmember – this, he surmised, was done at the factory to indicate that the chassis had a 3.7 differential fitted. This was an option on the newly introduced Elan coupé, and inspection showed that Glenn's was fitted with just such a differential. Glenn was taken with the overall originality of the car, and decided to repair and refurbish what he could to keep as much of the car to factory specification as possible. As part of this policy, Glenn decided to retain the original chassis despite having already procured a replacement. He had the original repaired by a pair of artisans in North Hampshire – John Humfryes and Bob Stainthorp, both skilled metal workers with significant experience of working on Lotus cars. While John and Bob worked their magic on the chassis, Glenn set to on the rest of the car.

Rebuilding the engine was pretty straightforward. While it had been rebored in the past, the bores only needed a hone and the pistons got new rings. The mains and big ends were in good condition, with only slight wear on the main and big end bearing shells, and the journals were fine, as were the jackshaft bearings. So, there was no need to regrind the crank, and Glenn just fitted new shells all

▲ This is Glenn's starting point for his early Elan coupé restoration. While the chassis was rotten, he managed to have it repaired so he could reuse it.

▲ Another view of Glenn's rolling chassis. The front turrets were rotten, and a piece of wood is keeping it in roughly the right position!

◄ The bodyshell was in reasonable condition, but in need of paint and some minor repairs. All in all, it is a great base for a restoration.

◄ The interior of Glenn's Elan coupé is in need of bit of work – the dash veneer is lifting, there is evidence of mice taking up residence, and there are some extra dials and switches fitted.

round, after thoroughly cleaning and repainting the block. He also fitted a new dip stick tube and water pump to the timing case, along with new chain and sprockets. The head was the original – evidenced by the engine number stamped on it – and just needed new guides, valves and springs, and Glenn gave it the lightest skim he could. It appeared that the head had been fitted with Sprint-specification inlet valves at some time, and standard camshafts. New cam bearings and sprockets finished the head refurbish.

Oddly, the gearbox threw up some very heavily worn selector forks but otherwise was in good condition, and apart from the selectors only needed bearings, seals and gaskets.

The suspension components were all crack tested and totally refurbished. Its a quick sentence but hides a huge amount of effort, as every suspension component was rusty and tatty, and needed considerable work to bring back to 'as new' standard, and every bush had to be renewed.

While stripping the interior of the car to get the shell ready for the paint shop, Glenn made a couple of discoveries that helped to confirm the originality of the car. In the left-hand side footwell, he found a inspection tag from the Lotus factory. Along with an original Lotus wiring loom tag also discovered, these rare survivors from the Lotus factory endorse his decision to keep the car as original as possible.

When the chassis returned from John and Bob – with two new front turrets, repaired gearbox mounts, reconstructed differential torque bar mounts, repaired and strengthened engine mounts, and various other repairs completed – Glenn had it painted in satin red 2K RAL 3009, a two-pack paint that will give a great deal of protection to the unit while retaining the look of the original Red Oxide paint finish. Then, while the body was at the painters, the great reassembly commenced.

One interesting feature on Glenn's coupé is the use of Series 1 and 2 boot lid hinges, with the recess that located the hardtop on the open cars. This was probably Lotus using up old stock before moving to the newer part.

Unfortunately, the COVID-19 shutdown resulted in Glenn's plans being disrupted and, at the time of writing, the bodyshell was still at the painters and the final reassembly had been delayed. However, at the end of the process Glenn should have a very original and immaculate Elan coupé, which will be a credit to his meticulous handiwork.

# Lotus Europa & Lotus Elan
## The Essential Buyer's Guides

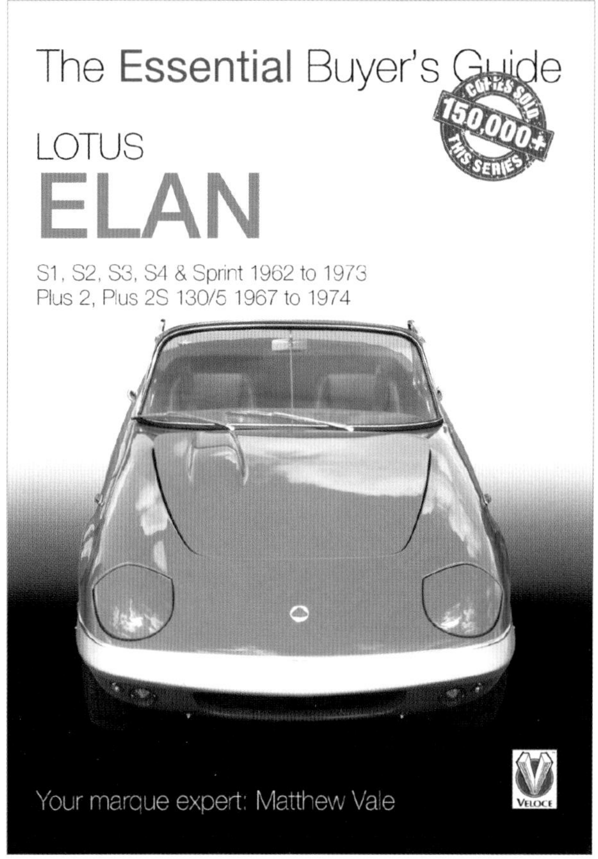


If you are interested in buying a Lotus Europa, Elan or Plus 2, these books will give you the background information and technical details to ensure you purchase the car you want. Written by an author with experience of restoring classic Lotuses, the books will give you the knowledge you need to identify and assess any potential purchase.

Lotus Europa ISBN: 978-1-787112-87-2
Paperback • 19.5x13.9cm • 64 pages • 90 pictures

Lotus Elan ISBN: 978-1-787112-86-5
Paperback • 19.5x13.9cm • 64 pages • 103 pictures

For more information and price details, visit our website at www.veloce.co.uk • email: info@veloce.co.uk • Tel: +44(0)1305 260068

# Lotus Europa
## Colin Chapman's mid-engined masterpiece

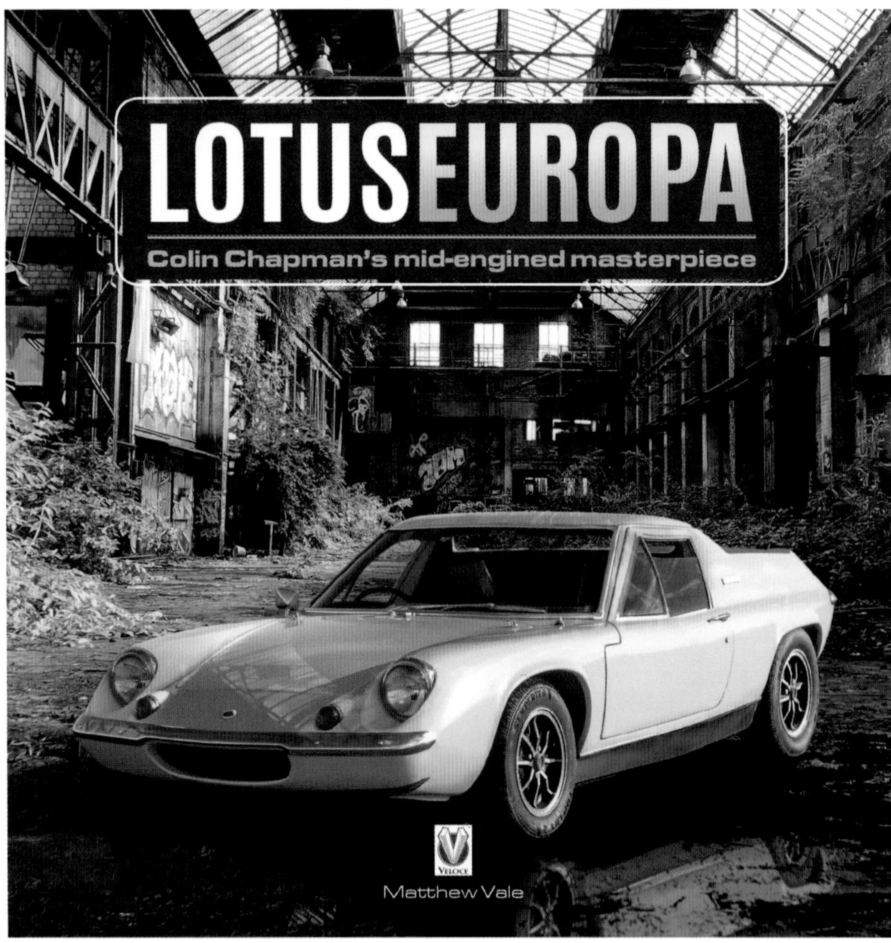

Explores the design development and production of the Lotus Europa, Lotus's first mid-engined road car. It covers the Renault-powered Series 1 and 2 cars, the Lotus Twin Cam-engined versions, and the Type 47 racing models.

ISBN: 978-1-787112-84-1
Hardback • 25x25cm • 160 pages • 175 colour and b&w pictures

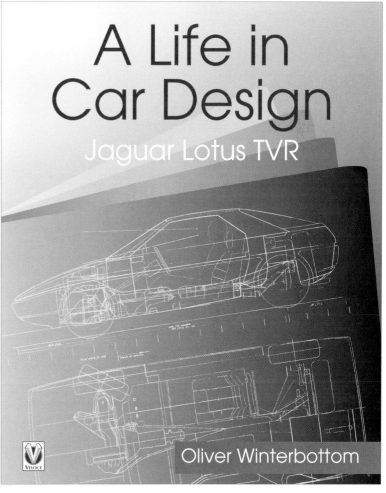

# Driven
## An elegy to cars, roads and motorsport

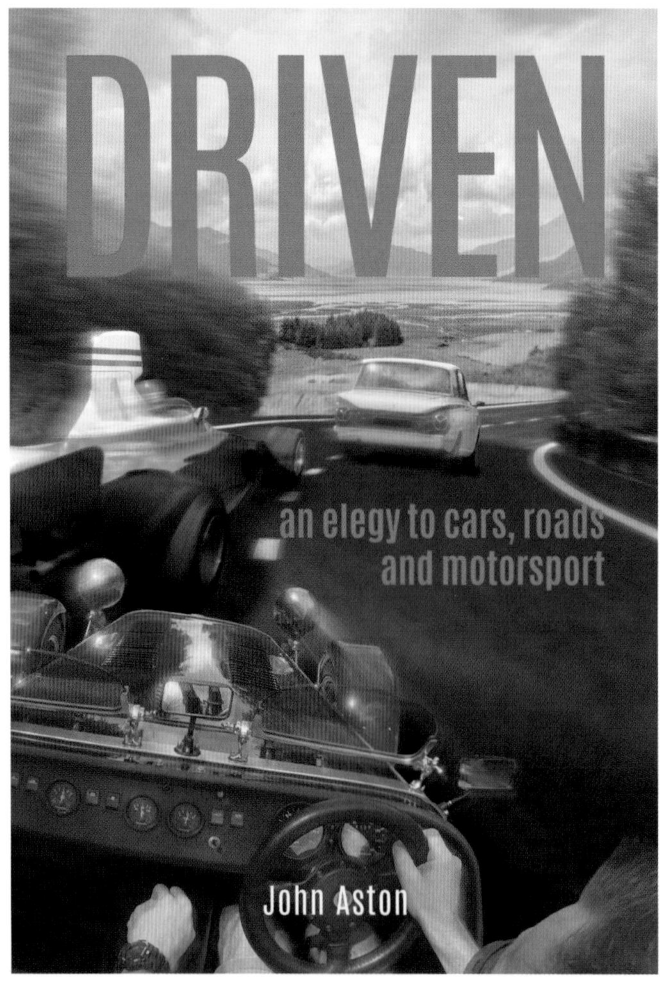


John Aston's anecdotes, wit, strong opinion and acute observations recount insightful and affectionate portraits of the many facets of motor sport, its people and its places. DRIVEN takes you on a journey from Lake District vintage car trials to drag racing at Santa Pod, NASCAR racing in North Carolina and international events at Silverstone.

ISBN: 978-1-787114-39-5
Paperback • 21x14.8cm • 272 pages

# Index

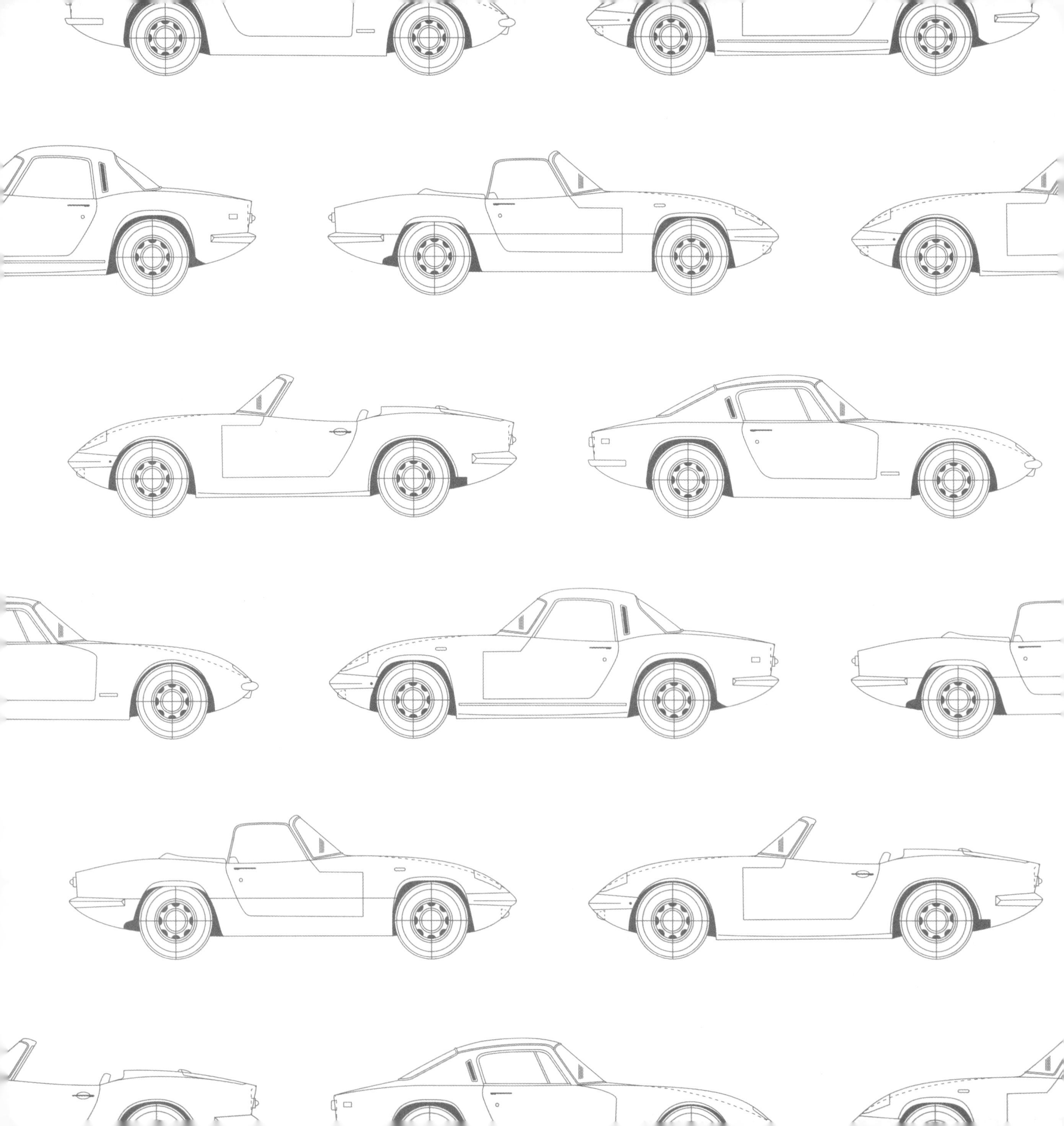